The Shrigley
ABDUCTION

For our families

The Shrigley
ABDUCTION
A Tale of Anguish, Deceit and Violation of the Domestic Hearth

ABBY ASHBY AND AUDREY JONES

SUTTON PUBLISHING

This book was first published in 2003 by
Sutton Publishing Limited · Phoenix Mill
Thrupp · Stroud · Gloucestershire · GL5 2BU

Paperback edition first published in 2005

British Library Cataloguing in Publication Data
A catalogue record for this book is available from the British Library

ISBN 0 7509 3297 X

Typeset in 10/12pt Photina.
Typesetting and origination by
Sutton Publishing Limited.
Printed and bound in Great Britain by
J.H. Haynes & Co. Ltd, Sparkford.

Contents

If this were played upon a stage now, I could condemn it as an improbable fiction.

William Shakespeare,
Twelfth Night, Act III, sc. iv

Preface

In 1997 we joined an adult education course offered by Keele University, at Tabley House, Knutsford. It was entitled 'The Buck Stops Here', and required students to research and present to the group their own chosen aspect of Georgian history. In order to conceal the somewhat delayed onset of our research, we cast around for a local scandal, hoping that it might at least entertain, if not inform. A friend suggested a tale dredged up from her schooldays, the abduction in 1826 of Ellen Turner, a fifteen-year-old heiress of the Shrigley Estates. Consequently, we presented a dramatised account of this extraordinary story. Amazingly, none of the Cheshire ladies and gentlemen in our history group had ever heard of it – they thought it was a spoof!

Encouraged by their response, and at the insistence of our tutor, Lesley Edwards, we decided to pursue this 'tale of real life', which, in May 1826, *John Bull* declared: 'far surpasses everything we have ever met with in imaginary history'. During the writing of this 'tale' we found ourselves, like the ladies of his day, under the spell of this charismatic Lothario, Edward Gibbon Wakefield, his magnetism as potent now as it was then.

Researching this book has proved an unexpected pleasure, not least because of the many people we have met along the way who have afforded us such interest, kindness and encouragement. Notable among these is Priscilla Mitchell MBE, the remarkable 95-year-old direct descendant of Edward Gibbon Wakefield's brother Daniel. Named after their grandmother, Priscilla Wakefield, and a great-great-great-niece of Elizabeth Fry, she has inherited the philanthropic zeal of her forebears; in her own words, 'Quakers are restless people'. In memory of Edward Gibbon Wakefield and his brothers, she has built twelve almshouses, and endowed university scholarships for students from New Zealand, Australia and Canada.

THE SHRIGLEY ABDUCTION

In the year of the 150th anniversary of Edward Gibbon Wakefield's arrival in New Zealand, it is, perhaps, appropriate that the story of this pivotal episode in his life should be told.

Abby Ashby and Audrey Jones
Altrincham, 2003

Acknowledgements

We owe much to Mrs Priscilla Mitchell MBE, who not only welcomed us into her home, but generously allowed us unrestricted access to her collection of family letters and documents, permission to quote from them, continuing to offer us help and encouragement throughout this project. We must also thank Molly Spink, resident of Shrigley, and local historian, who first told us about the abduction of Ellen Turner and without whose inspiration the book would never have been conceived. Throughout the writing of this book we have been most grateful to Lesley and John Edwards for their unstinting support and suggestions; and to the members of the Tabley group for their help and endorsement.

We would also like to thank the following (with apologies to any we have inadvertently omitted): Alexander Turnbull Picture Library (Tim Corballis); Blackburn Library; British Library; Canterbury Museum (Christine Whybrew); Chester Record Office; Chetham's Library (Dr M. Powell); Ewart Library, Dumfries (Graham Roberts); Gretna Hall; Higher Mill Museum Trust; John Rylands Library; Kendal Library and Record Office; Lancashire City Museums (Dr Andrew White); Lancaster Castle (Christine Goodier); Lancashire County Museums (Ian Gibson); Lancashire Record Office; Liverpool Record Office; University of Liverpool (Dr Chris Lewis and Rachel Kemsley); Lord Newton; Lyme Hall (Nick Ralls); Macclesfield Library; Manchester Central Library; Manchester Law Library (Jane Riley); The Met Office (Bill Giles and Ian MacGregor); National Library of Wales; National Portrait Gallery; National Trust (James Rothwell); Public Record Office, Kew; Public Record Office, Norwich Castle Museum; Barbara Riding; St Oswald's Church, Winnick (Canon Lewis); Mr and Mrs Stewart; Timperley Library; Sir Humphry Wakefield Bt, of Chillingham Castle; Wellington City Council (Melissa Brown); *Westmorland Gazette*; and in particular,

Tim Lovell-Smith, of the Alexander Turnbull Library in New Zealand, for all his help and advice. And of course, the Internet, without which the far-reaching research for this subject would not have been possible.

We are indebted to our agent, Chelsey Fox and her partner Charlotte Howard, for having faith in two novice authors; to Christopher Feeney of Sutton Publishing, who commissioned our book, for his optimism and expertise; and Alison Miles for her help and guidance.

Finally, the book could not have been written without the help and support of our families; in particular Audrey's husband John, and Abby's partner John O'Connor, whose genius on the computer and help with the illustrations have been invaluable.

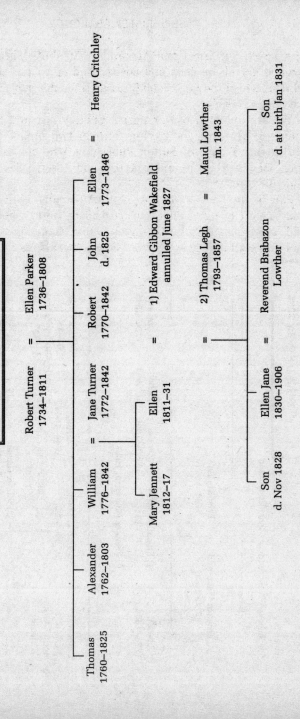

TURNER FAMILY TREE

Robert Turner = Ellen Parker
1734–1811   1736–1808

Thomas   Alexander   William   Jane Turner   Robert   John   Ellen   =   Henry Critchley
1760–1825   1762–1803   1776–1842   1772–1842   1770–1842   d. 1825   1773–1846

                                 Mary Jennett = Jane Turner   = 1) Edward Gibbon Wakefield
                                 1812–17   annulled June 1827

                                            Ellen
                                            1811–31

                                                                    = 2) Thomas Legh   =   Maud Lowther
                                                                          1793–1857   m. 1843

                           Son   Ellen Jane   =   Reverend Brabazon   Son
                           d. Nov 1828   1830–1906   Lowther   – d. at birth Jan 1831

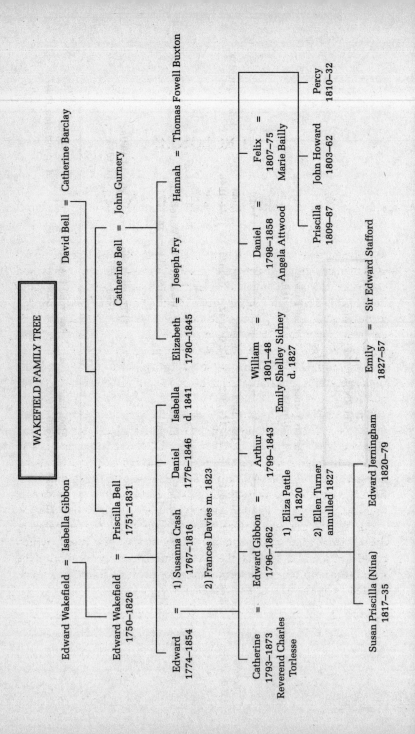

WAKEFIELD FAMILY TREE

David Bell = Catherine Barclay

Edward Wakefield = Isabella Gibbon

Edward Wakefield = Priscilla Bell
1750–1826   1751–1831

Catherine Bell = John Gurney

Elizabeth = Joseph Fry
1780–1845

Hannah = Thomas Fowell Buxton

Edward = 1) Susanna Crash   Daniel   Isabella
1774–1854   1767–1816   1776–1846 d. 1841
          2) Frances Davies m. 1823

Catherine = Edward Gibbon = 1) Eliza Pattle   Arthur   William = Emily Shelley Sidney
Reverend Charles 1796–1862   d. 1820   1799–1843   1801–48   d. 1827
Torlesse   2) Ellen Turner
                               annulled 1827

Daniel = Angela Attwood   Felix = Marie Bailly
1798–1858   1807–75

Priscilla   John Howard   Percy
1809–87   1803–62   1810–32

Susan Priscilla (Nina)   Edward Jerningham   Emily = Sir Edward Stafford
1817–35   1820–79   1827–57

Prologue

Friday 23 March 1827

'All Lancaster was in motion',[1] the rain that had persisted all month failing to deter the crowds thronging the streets and courts of the small town. For several days the inns and lodging houses had been full of 'persons of distinction' who had travelled great distances to attend the Spring Assizes. Beneath the commanding towers and battlements of the castle, carriages vied with each other on the narrow cobbled streets, the striking of hooves and the clanking and grinding of iron-clad wheels underpinning the strident cries of postillions as they jockeyed for position.

By the stroke of seven, there was great anxiety and excitement among the huge concourse of people flooding the terraces and courtyards of the castle. At this hour all those lucky enough to possess tickets were to be admitted to the trial of two brothers, Edward Gibbon and William Wakefield, and their stepmother, Frances, for a crime denounced by the *Sunday Times* as 'a tale of anguish, deceit and violation of the domestic hearth'.[2]

At twenty minutes before eight the doors of the court were opened, and almost immediately 'every spot of the court, which could command a view of the proceedings, was occupied with the greatest avidity, for on no former occasion was the interest so much excited as by the trial of the Wakefields'.[3]

1

... when Wisdom wakes
Suspicion sleeps ...

At six o'clock on the morning of Tuesday 7 March 1826, James Brown, a post-boy at the Legs O' Man, Prescot, waited in the porch of the inn for the carriage he could hear approaching from the direction of Warrington. It appeared quite suddenly out of the early morning mist, a dark green barouche, its door already opening as it drew to a halt. Instantly, a 'man of fashion' jumped down, followed more sedately by an older companion. The younger of the two men, introducing himself as Captain Wilson, lost no time in delivering clear instructions to the post-boy. The horses were to be changed without delay as he and his servant had to reach Liverpool within the hour.

Thus, by half past seven, Brown had brought the carriage to the outskirts of the city, where he stopped outside the Blue Bell Inn. There Captain Wilson left the carriage, pausing only to press something into the hand of his servant, saying, 'Thank you for the ride Thevenot, you have given me a great lift'.[1] After watching the Captain walk quickly down the street, and disappear from sight, Thevenot ordered Brown to drive him to Breck House, a Ladies' Seminary on the West Derby Road.

Some fifteen minutes later they came upon the school, where Thevenot asked to see the mistress on an urgent matter which concerned one of her pupils. He was duly received by Miss Elizabeth Daulby, to whom he handed a letter, which he had retrieved from his waistcoat. Written at half past twelve that very morning, at Shrigley Hall near Macclesfield, it read:

1

Madam,

I write to you by the desire of Mrs Turner, of Shrigley, who has been seized with a sudden and dangerous attack of paralysis. Mr Turner is unfortunately away from home, but has been sent for, and Mrs Turner wishes to see her daughter immediately. A steady servant will take this letter and my carriage to you to fetch Miss Turner; and I beg that no time be lost in her departure, as, though I do not think Mrs Turner is in immediate danger, it is possible she may soon become incapable of recognising anyone. Mrs Turner particularly wishes that her daughter may not be informed of the extent of the danger, as without this precaution, Miss Turner might be very anxious on the journey; and this house is so crowded, and in such confusion and alarm, that Mrs Turner does not wish anyone to accompany her daughter. The servant is instructed not to let the boys drive too fast, as Miss T. is rather fearful in a carriage.

I am, madam,
Your obedient servant
John Ainsworth M.D.

The best thing to say to Miss T. is, that Mrs T. wishes to have her daughter home rather sooner, for the approaching removal to the new house; and the servant is instructed to give no other reason in case Miss Turner should ask any questions. Mrs Turner is very anxious that her daughter should not be frightened, and trusts to your judgement to prevent it; she also desires me to add that her sister, or niece, or myself, should they continue unable, will not fail to write to you by post.[2]

Clearly shocked by this news, Miss Daulby enquired when Mrs Turner had been taken ill; whereupon Thevenot, in 'an accent rather foreign', informed her dramatically that it had happened 'the night before last at supper when the knife and fork had suddenly dropped from Mrs Turner's hand'.[3] Without further delay, Miss Daulby sent for the fifteen-year-old Ellen Turner. While they awaited her arrival, Miss Daulby continued to question the man, enquiring whether Ellen would recognise him as one of her father's servants.

Thevenot responded that unfortunately she would not, as he had only recently joined Mr Turner's household, having previously been in the employ of Thomas Legh of Lyme Hall, a close neighbour of the Turners.

When Ellen arrived, Miss Daulby explained that as her mother was unwell, she was needed at home 'rather sooner, for the approaching removal to the new house',[4] and that the servant who stood before her would take her straight home to Shrigley. While Ellen hastily made preparations to leave, Miss Daulby sought further assurances from Thevenot regarding the impending journey, asking whether she would be travelling alone. 'Only as far as Manchester', was Thevenot's reply; there they would take up her mother's physician, Dr Hull, who resided there. Her concerns apparently addressed, Miss Daulby furnished the elderly Thevenot with a brandy, for he had confessed that he had been on the road all night and was suffering from a bad headache. When Ellen returned, Elizabeth Daulby escorted them both to the waiting carriage. However, the moment Ellen set eyes on the green barouche she exclaimed, 'This is not my Papa's carriage';[5] whereupon Thevenot's immediate response was that, indeed, it belonged to the doctor. Without demur, Elizabeth Daulby handed her young charge up into the carriage, which was to take her on the journey – a journey that would reach far beyond the bounds of Shrigley.

Despite the dramatic nature of her departure from school that fateful morning, Ellen appeared generally unperturbed, no doubt due in some degree to past experience of her mother's somewhat dramatic approach to the exigencies of her health. An only child, following the death of her younger sister, she had probably grown to know her mother well, particularly in view of her father's regular absences connected with the family calico-printing business in Blackburn. William Turner's success had enabled him in 1818 to purchase the Shrigley Estates, close to the silk manufacturing town of Macclesfield. When Ellen was seven years old they had moved into the old Shrigley Hall where they had lived until a new house was completed on the site. At Shrigley, she had enjoyed a comfortable and privileged childhood: her father, a Radical and a philanthropist with political ambitions, shared with his wife an enlightened and progressive view of education, and was evidently determined that Ellen, heir to his considerable fortune, should be well prepared for her future in every respect.

Consequently, at the age of nine, while most girls of her age were educated at home by a governess, the young Ellen had been sent as a boarding pupil to the Ladies' Seminary in Liverpool. The academy was a well-known and highly respectable school run by the formidable Margaret Daulby and the daughters of Daniel Daulby, a notable artist and connoisseur, and brother-in-law of the accomplished and influential William Roscoe, an attorney well known in Liverpool for his support of the city and its arts. The sisters were consequently renowned as much for their social connections as for their academy. For William Turner, astute not only in matters of commerce, this was to be a long-term investment. His daughter was tutored in history, reading, writing, French, Italian, drawing and music: the required accomplishments of a young lady of means, designed to prepare Ellen for a marriage equal to her father's expectations – 'girls for the drawing room and boys for life' was the pedagogical maxim of the day. Her father, no doubt, would have considered his money well spent when assured by Elizabeth Daulby of Ellen's cleverness and capacity for learning and that she displayed 'great quickness and sagacity, and an excellent hand'. Her nature she described as 'easy and confiding, remarkably so, distinguished among her companions, and of a good temper and disposition'.[6] She was, it appeared, the model pupil, the model daughter, a girl who would, in all probability, become the model wife.

Despite Mrs Turner's explicit instructions, James Brown set the horses at a lively pace into the relentless drizzle. Behind him Thevenot sat huddled on the dickey, leaving Ellen alone inside the carriage which, although comfortable enough, had seen better days, the interlining of oiled linen torn in several places. Brown drove the carriage back to the Legs O' Man, where the young schoolgirl briefly alighted while the horses were changed. Soon they were on their way again with a new post-boy at the reins, travelling in the direction of Warrington.

Within the hour they had reached the outskirts of the town, and by eleven o'clock were entering the courtyard of the Nag's Head. Ellen, who had remained in the carriage while new horses were ordered, noticed Thevenot in close conversation with a tall, rather presentable young man who had been waiting at the door of the inn. As the horses wheeled about, setting off on the last stage of the journey to Manchester, she watched the young gentleman turn abruptly on his heels and disappear into the inn, calling for the innkeeper, Jane Hughes. Inside, having hastily penned a letter to a Captain Wilson, he instructed the woman to 'Go immediately to where we dined yesterday; she must be made to expect her father; she is to wait for her father; she has just left this place at eleven o'clock'. He handed the letter to Mrs Hughes entreating her to keep it safe 'in case the Captain should return'. Thevenot, bolstered by 'the success of his own grave and unsuspicious deportment' at the Ladies' Seminary, 'had made the capital blunder of leaving Liverpool without Captain Wilson'.[7]

Once through the narrow, twisting streets of Warrington, the barouche reached the 'galloping road', where could be found 'scarcely a hill steep or continuous enough to check the speed of wheels' – soon they would be in Manchester. It was Tuesday, when manufacturers from the adjacent countryside and neighbouring towns would attend the markets for the sale of cotton and other goods. Now their carriage joined the mêlée of motley horse-drawn vehicles jostling along the wet road.

Reaching Piccadilly in the heart of the city, the carriage finally drew to a halt outside the door of the Albion Hotel. Within moments, Robert Wilson, the landlord, had opened the door of the barouche and was inviting Ellen to step down, ushering her inside, calling for the waiter, James Holgrave, and instructing him to take particular care of her. Escorted by Thevenot, she was taken upstairs and shown into a fine parlour, where Holgrave asked if they would take refreshment. Thevenot declined, assuring the waiter, 'You need not trouble to attend on my young mistress, I will attend to her myself.'[8] When Ellen turned to him, demanding to know why she had been brought to this place, Thevenot invited her to sit down and make herself comfortable, saying, 'The gentleman will be here directly. Your Papa would wish you to wait.'[9] Whereupon Ellen took a seat by the window which looked out on to Piccadilly. Facing her was the Infirmary, a plain brick building railed off from the street with plain iron palissading; a pond in front stretched its whole length.

5

Ellen drew Thevenot's attention to the time. She was concerned for her mother, and anxious for her father's arrival. Since he was so long in coming, she suggested to Thevenot that she should wait for him at her Uncle Robert's house which was only a few hundred yards away; indeed, she urged, her Uncle Henry too lived close by. Thevenot, knowing that he must detain Ellen, hastened to reassure her, 'Don't go, your father will be here directly'. There was the sound of footsteps on the stairs. Opening the door, he found Captain Wilson on the threshold. Ellen, turning from the window, was confronted with a man 'of some fashion of appearance and of some address'.[10] In brown wool frock coat, white linen shirt and black silk stock, he presented a slim and elegant figure. Short, fair, curly hair and cropped whiskers framed a face which indicated openness and charm, an invitation to trust – but it was not her Papa.

She made as if to leave the room, but paused as he requested that 'she would not go', professing himself to have been 'commissioned by her Papa to take her to him'.[11] Ellen countered that she could not understand why her father had not come; to which the Captain replied that she 'might be sure that it was no slight circumstance that prevented her Papa from fetching her himself'.[12] The entrance of Holgrave, carrying a glass of Madeira 'for the gentleman', broke the tension. Returning to her chair by the window, Ellen was joined by the Captain who once again assured her that the carriage would be ready in a moment, and promptly engaged her in conversation. She brightened perceptibly when asked about the journey; despite the rain she had enjoyed their progress through the noisy, colourful, even dangerous streets of Manchester, the contrast with the sedate and isolated countryside of the Shrigley estate both fascinating and exciting her. She appreciated the life of the town, and still more the sight of her favourite shops and the elegant squares to which she was no stranger. Captain Wilson found her lively responses both engaging and reassuring, as it prevented her 'from asking questions for which he could have no answer'.[13] Together they admired the 'curious clock' of the Infirmary.

Within ten minutes, the carriage was ready. In the hall Ellen held the Captain's arm as he talked to the waiter, enquiring whether 'if he came back in six weeks he could have a bedroom and sitting room adjoining upstairs', and asking Holgrave if he knew Robert

Turner, to which the waiter replied he 'couldn't tell'; he 'didn't know that gentleman by name'.[14] Ellen then joined Captain Wilson in wishing the landlord, Robert Wilson, 'Good day', before they made their way through 'a crowd of idle gazers', which the Captain's hurried arrival 'had collected around the inn'.[15] Beside the door of the barouche stood a young man whom Ellen thought she recognised, until Captain Wilson introduced him as his younger brother, who handed her into the carriage before joining Thevenot up on the box. Seating himself beside her, the Captain turned his attention at once to the raised blinds. Knowing that Ellen 'had often been at Manchester and that she knew perfectly well that the horses' heads were turned in an opposite direction to the road to Shrigley', he feared that 'such an appearance of concealment might excite her curiosity', so lowering them he asked if she had forgotten anything, before 'desiring the boys to drive on'.[16]

2

Even a Child is Known by His Doings

The slender young gentleman close beside Ellen Turner in the carriage had no claim to military status. He was in fact Edward Gibbon Wakefield, a thirty-year-old widower and father of two children, born into a family of prominent Quakers, on 20 March 1796, thirty-six years into the reign of George III. Only two months earlier, George's son, the gay and reckless Prince of Wales, had celebrated the birth of his daughter Charlotte while the triumphant Bonaparte revelled in his Italian victories, and Britain, alone in Europe, stood firm against the Frenchman and his imperial ambitions.

Eldest son of Edward Wakefield and Susanna Crash, Edward Gibbon had been named after both his father and grandfather, and his great-grandmother, Isabella Gibbon, a distant relation of the historian. His grandfather had inherited a fortune, which he had lost when his business failed. He was a weak man, 'his only claim to remembrance lay in his good looks',[1] and, according to his wife Priscilla Bell, had a fit of hysterics when anything disagreeable happened. On one occasion, when their house was on fire, Mrs Wakefield, with her usual energy, had organised her maids and other helpers who, forming a chain, had hauled buckets of water to the men trying to subdue the flames. Mr Wakefield, however, had retreated to a distant part of the house where he was found weeping and wringing his hands. The grandfather does not seem to have possessed that charm of manner so conspicuous in his sons and grandsons: his mother-in-law remarked that she did not 'doubt his affection for his wife, but wishes that he could express it with a greater degree of politeness'.[2]

In contrast, his wife Priscilla Bell, descended from the Barclays who had founded the banking business, was a remarkable woman, a noted author of children's books whose 'whole life was devoted to benevolence'.[3] Two years after her grandson's birth she not only established the first savings bank for the poor but published one of the earliest feminist books, *Reflection on the Present Condition of the Female Sex, with Suggestions for Its Improvement*. Her sister Catherine was the mother of Elizabeth Fry the prison reformer, and mother-in-law of Thomas Fowell-Buxton, a committed campaigner for the abolition of slavery.

While inheriting his mother's Quaker strengths and philanthropic and educational interests, Edward Gibbon Wakefield's father, eldest son of Edward Wakefield and Priscilla Bell, had also, unfortunately, inherited his father's irresponsible attitude to life and weakness of character. He was described as

> a warm hearted, loveable man; an enthusiast with regard to everything that concerned public welfare; and an ardent philanthropist – all of which must have been indirectly stimulating and inspiring to his children. But on the other hand, his extravagance and improvidence, his erratic ways and easy indulgence to their faults, must have had a pernicious effect on them especially in the case of a high spirited lad such as Edward Gibbon.[4]

Edward Wakefield maintained a life-long interest in the social conditions of the poor and disadvantaged. In 1801 his mother recorded: 'Prisons and workhouses are his game. May he be inspired to enlarge the sphere of human happiness and virtue!'[5] An acknowledged authority on agricultural reform and a skilled statistician, he was best known for his account of Ireland in the early nineteenth century, *Ireland, Statistical and Political*, published in 1812 and acknowledged in the *Edinburgh Review* as the most complete work on Ireland since Arthur Young's tour. In the same year, he was to become acquainted with the leading Radical, Francis Place, champion of the working class in their battle for improved conditions. Evidently, Francis Place and Edward Wakefield were brought together by their shared passion to improve the lot of those less fortunate:

When we first became friends, Mr Wakefield's circumstances were by no means prosperous, he was, however, an active, zealous advocate for anything likely, in his opinion to be useful to mankind, and especially to the working people of Great Britain and Ireland and was anxious to promote education amongst the poor, and I found in him an excellent co-operator for many useful purposes.[6]

In 1814 Edward Wakefield sat on a committee with Francis Place and the economist James Mill, whom he had introduced to Place, to consider a plan for the establishment of a London asylum 'for the care and cure of the insane'. By 1815, Edward Wakefield was sufficiently intimate with Francis Place to request of him a loan of £100. As their friendship grew Mill and Place came to be both concerned for and interested in the welfare of Edward Wakefield's family, but, ironically, it was the conduct of both father and sons which eventually ended the intimacy between Wakefield and Place.

Edward Wakefield had married Susanna Crash, daughter of a farmer at Felstead, Essex, on 3 October 1791, the bride and bridegroom both seventeen years of age. Susanna was an acknowledged beauty with masses of golden hair; dressed in scarlet and indulging in her favourite pastime of hunting, she was said to cut a most attractive and engaging figure. She was, her adoring husband proclaimed, 'the most beautiful woman I have known – a soft angelic beauty and a model for a sculptor'.[7] Unfortunately, her attributes did not compensate for her husband's shortcomings; moreover, although her outward charms impressed many, she was not, it would seem, a woman of great intellect. Her mother-in-law regarded her as a young woman of 'prudence and natural good sense',[8] with quite simple tastes and interests who did not appear to exercise any real influence on the characters of her nine children. Consequently, Edward Gibbon's childhood was spent in a 'curiously unsettled and unstable atmosphere'.[9] Nowhere is this illustrated more clearly than in the diary of his grandmother, a diary which graphically chronicled the progress of both her own errant son and his increasingly problematical eldest boy. Priscilla was to find herself inescapably embroiled in the problems of her son's family, despite concerns of her own. In the year of Edward Gibbon's birth she wrote, 'The consideration of money matters depress me, as I am certain our expenses exceed the limited sum'.[10] Sixteen months later she is still worrying that her husband 'is engrossed by his new concern' and 'wishes he may not assume an increase of expenditure until all the encumbrances are discharged'. She is, however, cheered by the arrival of the Blue coach from Ipswich, noting with pleasure, 'Little Edward [Gibbon] is left with me'.[11]

Soon after Edward Gibbon's birth his parents had moved to Romford in Essex, where his father began farming. When this venture failed, he took on another large farm at Burnham Wyck, where he stayed for some time. It may well have been here that Edward Gibbon developed his love of animals, particularly dogs and horses.

In March 1798 Priscilla visited her son and daughter-in-law at their farm in Romford, where she wrote that she had 'found Susanna and her infant well, and they had named the child Daniel', adding with misgiving, 'Saw an instance of Susanna's injudicious mode of education that made me tremble for the effects it may one day produce in the minds of her children'.[12] When Edward and Susanna's third son Arthur was born in 1799, Priscilla had noted: 'Edward's plans as usual too wild for the promotion of a sober uniform system of life. I wish he had fewer occupations and was more inclined to turn his mind to parental duties and the regular objects of the chief of a family.' But Priscilla was pleased to observe an encouraging sign: 'Susanna's natural good sense co-operating with her own endeavours, has produced a general improvement in her manners and, when not under the influence of an irritable temper is a sensible woman of the best principles.'[13] Although often 'oppressed with anxiety' on their account,[14] Priscilla pursued a busy and interesting life of her own, recording an encounter with a 'Mr J Constable, a pleasing modest young man who had a natural genius for painting'. She also met the young Joseph Lancaster, whose system of education for the poor, based on the use of class monitors, attracted widespread support, including that of George III. Priscilla visited his school in Borough Road, London, where the senior class of boys used her book *Mental Improvements*, and was impressed by what she saw. Her son Edward, though regarding Lancaster as an inherently unpleasant character, conceded: 'I am inclined to think that he will be as great an instrument in enlightening the human mind . . . as Luther.'

Edward Gibbon and his siblings were to grow up against the background of war with France, although their father had doubted that it would ever really occur: 'Poor miserable degraded England, unhappy country – we are so poor we cannot go to war, if we would.' However, he did not underestimate the desire of Napoleon's supporters for a war: 'Bonapartists want war. Parisian Bonapartists – the whiskered savages *demi-solde*, who prowl about coffee houses and pub walks in frock coats hiding their ragged and dirty shirts by black velvet stocks and proving their courage by the enormity of their spears and bludgeons.'[15] The approaching turmoil was announced by a stark entry in his grandmother's diary for 18 November 1799: 'Bonaparte has effected a revolution in France.'[16] Meanwhile Priscilla's fondness for her eldest grandson grew, 'Susanna brought her dear children to London'. Evidently this was so they could receive the smallpox vaccination recently developed by Jenner. Shortly afterwards she wrote: 'Walked to see my sweet Edward [Gibbon], who gives me great pleasure by the sweetness of his temper and behaviour.'[17] When Edward Gibbon's favourite brother William was born in 1801 Priscilla had fresh cause for concern for their father. As Napoleon's ambitions grew, she wrote, 'The dread of invasion causes general alarm and preparation. My Edward is a Lieutenant Colonel of Volunteers. Sincerely I do pray that he may never be called upon to expose his own life or destroy that of others.'[18]

Susanna's poor health meant that Priscilla found herself in sole charge of Edward Gibbon and his sister Catherine, sometimes known as Kitty. Her young grandson, who had afforded her so much pleasure, was now evidently beginning to give her cause for concern, and making increasing demands upon her time. Her diary records: 'I fear my reading and writing must be sacrificed for the next three months at least, but I hope to render in that time some essential benefit to my dear little boy, whose extreme habits of liberty at home increase the difficulty of ordinary restraint.'[19] To add to her concerns, by 1806 Susanna's health had deteriorated further, she was 'worse, fatigue almost unsupportable',[20] and consequently the whole family moved to live with Priscilla in Tottenham. On 8 January she 'accompanied the children to London to see the funeral of Lord Nelson by water', a day which she described as 'not altogether to my taste'.[21]

Inevitably Priscilla began to act *in loco parentis*, putting the ten-year-old Edward Gibbon and his brothers Daniel and William to study at Mr Haigh's school near her home in Tottenham. Unfortunately, it was not long before she was summoned 'to Haigh's, on account of a great delinquency of dear Edward [Gibbon]', something, she recorded, 'which almost rendered me incapable of application'. She observed, 'How much our happiness is entwined in the good account of those we value'.[22] For the next few days she continued to worry about young Edward Gibbon; entries in her diary were to prove particularly prophetic:

February 5th – My mind is painfully engaged with the perverseness of dear little Edward [Gibbon] – his obstinacy if he inclines to evil terrifies me – turned to good it would be a noble firmness.

February 8th – 'My thoughts much occupied with my little Edward [Gibbon], whom I dearly love, but whose inflexible, pertinacious temper makes me fear for his own happiness and that of those connected with him.

February 14th – My dear little Edward [Gibbon] still in disgrace. My heart yearns to forgive him – he has some fine qualities, but he is a character that requires delicate handling.[23]

The problem was temporarily resolved when Edward Gibbon left Tottenham, and his grandmother's protection, 'for the dangers and temptation of Westminster School'. His time there does not seem to have suited him – as one might expect of such a resolutely free spirit. Older and wiser, he was to write, 'I don't meddle with Greek and am nervous about Latin! So much for Westminster!'[24] In the same year, and despite Priscilla's preoccupation with her wayward grandson, this redoubtable woman found the time to complete two volumes of her *Conversation on Chemistry by a Lady*, and one of her many children's books, *Zoological Anecdotes – a funny collection of stories without order*. In 1796, the year of her grandson's birth, Priscilla had published another book for children entitled *Juvenile Anecdotes – Founded on Facts*. The story entitled *The Boys and the Butterfly* might well have served as an admonishment to her errant grandson:

. . . a temptation presents itself and you cannot resist it. The true business of life is to learn to subdue our inclinations, and pursue the path of rectitude, though we are solicited by ill-example and our own love of pleasure, to depart from it. You have both acted improperly, and yielded to the first impulse of pleasure that tempted you to neglect your duty, and you have gained nothing but fatigue and disappointment. But you may improve this circumstance to your advantage, by remembering, whenever you meet with temptation to do wrong, the painted butterfly that led you on a wild-goose chase.[25]

By October 1809, Priscilla is yet steadfastly prevailing upon her wayward son Edward to return to his family. She wrote to him at the house he had taken in Duke Street, Westminster, after his return from Ireland where he had been researching his book *Ireland, Statistical and Political.*

I never was so long without hearing from you since you left us. I believe it is a full five weeks since I received your last . . . I assure you that you are the prominent object of my thoughts and my solitude. I am very naturally [pleased] that you are settled in some comfort . . . and . . . still more am relieved to hear that you have determined to return for a time at least to visit your wife and children if anything can allure you back surely eight lovely promising children should have that power, how can you reconcile turning your back upon them who have never offended you but have the strongest claims upon your care and protection, if you stay much longer you will fancy that you cannot come back. By banishing yourself from children you so dearly love, you'll deprive yourself of one of the greatest delights in life . . . Your correspondence with your children mark you for an affectionate and judicious friend, your letters reflect the highest honour on your heart and your understanding. Why then do you not come to behold the good effects of your advice – Edward [Gibbon] in particular requires the eye and the company of a father, to choose friends for him, to form his character and to shelter him from the dangers to which a lad of his age is exposed. – Hitherto there has been an apology for your absences but now except finishing your tour for your book, I know of no motive to detain you. . . .[26]

A fortnight later she wrote to her son again, 'I hope to hear you have determined to set your face homewards that your wife may remember she has a husband and your children that they have a father', adding the postscript, 'Pray renew your correspondence with your boys'. Employing all her literary powers Priscilla painted an irresistible picture of his eighteen-month-old son in the hope that it would bring him back to his family:

> Felix has been with us more than a week. I wish I could send you his picture. I think it would draw you home. He is just so high and so full that he looks almost square, he has fine complexion and blooming colour, neck, throat, and shoulders really beautiful, a tongue the most engaging you can imagine, the picture of every man he sees is Papa.

And with undisguised guile she added, 'Susan is very thin, but I do not doubt that the prospects of your happy return will enliven her countenance and revive her good looks'.[27]

Meanwhile Priscilla nursed the hope that her grandson Edward Gibbon had settled into his new school. But for 1 July 1810, Priscilla's diary records, 'Anxiety from a new quarter. All is not pleasant at Westminster.'[28] Five days later his father and mother visited him at school, and Priscilla was relieved to hear that 'Edward Gibbon has got his remove and all is well'.[29] However, her joy was to be shortlived, for on 21 September she noted that Edward Gibbon was 'returned from an attempt to go to school'; his 'perverseness frustrates his father's views for him'. The next two days were spent in a vain attempt to counsel the obdurate student; Priscilla wrote, 'He continues obstinate and will not be persuaded to return to school'.[30] Later it transpired that the young Edward Gibbon had been engaged in not only a long-running battle with the class bully, but also a feud with a fellow student, William Erskine, later to become Lord Mar, one of Wellington's generals, who committed suicide two years before the Battle of Waterloo. Priscilla's description of her fourteen-year-old grandson as 'inflexible' proved to be correct, for once again his father gave way. Edward Gibbon was sent to the Royal High School in Edinburgh, where, his grandmother conceded, he would at least be instructed in religion and morality as well as Latin and Greek. She was further comforted by her belief that education in Scotland was in advance of that in England.

Consequently, Edward Gibbon went to live with a friend of his father in Edinburgh, James Gray, a cleric, writer and distinguished Greek scholar. The handsome young Wakefield, with his open and cheerful personality, his sense of fun and love of practical jokes, was soon to become a great favourite; but his tomfoolery was not appreciated by the more sedate members of the family, and eventually his father was asked to find him alternative accommodation. However, the family retained much affection for him, and continued to befriend and correspond with him. His two years in the Royal High School were spent in the Rector's class. His intelligence was never in doubt, but his love of fun and freedom evidently resulted in a total lack of application to his studies. On one occasion, he passed himself off as a blind man, his performance so clever as to deceive even his friends, many of whom were tricked into making considerable charitable donations. Policemen, too, were frequently the butt of his humour.

In 1812, at the age of sixteen and having concluded his troubled education, Edward Gibbon returned to live with his constant and forgiving grandmother. At the age of sixty-one Priscilla had begun to learn Italian, 'If I can increase my amusement without hurting anybody it is surely allowable and reasonable'.[31] Predictably, with the return of her grandson she was soon to be preoccupied once again with his welfare, reporting that 'he is discontented for want of profitable employment', but 'he has a most independent mind'.

For the next two years the family desperately tried to find him gainful employment: a situation with the East India Company never materialised; later a legal career was chosen, perhaps on the advice of his uncle Daniel, the barrister. In due course, on 5 October 1813, he was admitted as a member of Gray's Inn. After only a few months, however, it became clear that he was singularly unsuited for the legal profession. Eventually, he was secured a position with the Honourable William Hill, British envoy to the court of Turin, where he was to spend the winter of 1814. His relieved father confided in Francis Place that 'he had been at his wit's end to know what to do about his tiresome son'; he remarked, 'Edward's going abroad is an amazing relief to me, for although he has many good points he was quite out of management'.[32] However, his father's relief in one direction was shortlived in another, for his son was so engaged in the life of the court of Turin that he found little time to correspond:

> I cannot say how much I lament the manner in which he conducts himself towards us for an intimate constant and unreserved communication between such near connections is certainly one of the greatest sweetness in life – How different and contrary to the manner in which Arthur behaves – he is making strong friends everywhere and is I think sure to do.[33]

During the next few years, under the watchful eye of his mentor William Hill, Edward Gibbon was to hold various minor posts in the diplomatic service, one of which was that of King's Messenger and entailed his travelling on the Continent in the aftermath of Waterloo. This clearly concerned his grandmother, who in July 1815 reported, with evident relief, 'Edward [Gibbon] most unexpectedly arrived in London with despatches . . . greatly improved in body and mind, his aspect and manners pleased me, but what most delighted me was his noble independent spirit'.[34] Somewhat less enthusiastically, Francis Place, himself the father of fifteen children, wrote to James Mill:

> Wakefield's son returned from Turin, soon after you left London, much improved in appearance, and somewhat softened, though not much, in manners; this has been produced by the contrasts his journeys have presented him; and the visible superiority of the English over all the nations of the Continent has made him like them better than he did; his conduct has, however, been very ambiguous, and his tales have contradicted one another, so that his father, who has more of feeling than of solid judgement in his composition, has been distressed beyond anything you will be able to imagine. I have not allowed him to trifle, but have plainly and fully told him of his follies, and, as I think, with some effect. He has left Mr Hill, but not with disgrace.[35]

And later,

> I can tell you very little respecting Edward [Gibbon] Wakefield; his conduct is wholly inexplicable. He despises his father's advice,

he laughs at his opinions; he talks largely of being on his own hands, and independent of his father. I hope, and expect too that he will obtain some employment at the Foreign Office, he is best adapted for that line, and it is well adapted to him. I wish his father could make up his mind to see only a common man in him.[36]

Clearly, the astute Francis Place did not agree with his friend Edward's perception of his wayward son, believing that the youth was less uncommon than his father fondly supposed. Edward Gibbon was soon to leave for Paris, having obtained a minor appointment with the Foreign Office. His grandmother could not help but once again grow anxious on his account, for Paris was 'a city torn by contending factions'. The day after her grandson left London, news came of the abdication of Napoleon; about whom Priscilla had wisely observed, 'There is a great distinction between a great man and a good. Bonaparte is great but not good . . . he has superior talents, but is void of virtue and religion, he seems to forget that men must give an account of their actions in another life.'[37] She need not have worried; it was clear from Edward Gibbon's letter that he enjoyed his stay, and was delighted to be part of the celebrations that heralded the restoration of the monarchy in France.

During this period, his mother's health continued to deteriorate. On the very day Edward Gibbon left for Paris his father had taken Susanna to London to seek medical advice. Indeed, Place and Mill were concerned that Edward Wakefield had refused to recognise just how ill his wife had become. It seemed clear to them that her health had completely broken down and she was deeply depressed. Her life with Edward had been far from easy; she had borne him nine children, of whom the eldest son was distinctly troublesome and two of his siblings, William and Felix, difficult. Her problems had been compounded by financial worries and the long absences of her husband. She was to return from London 'a great invalid',[38] her 22-year-old daughter Catherine leaving her grandmother's house to nurse her.

By December Edward Gibbon Wakefield was once more with the fatherly Mr Hill, Francis Place writing to Mill,

Edward [Gibbon] is with Mr Hill in London. Wakefield is in raptures with him, ridiculously so. Edward [Gibbon], is however, provided for, and that too in the line in which he is most likely to continue; and Wakefield, who expected him home without a shilling, and without employment, has much to rejoice at. It is a rascally employment, but the world does not treat it as disreputable, and Edward [Gibbon] cannot be spoiled by it. His manners are far more agreeable than they were; his knowledge of diplomacy has shown him the necessity of this.

Later in the letter Place observed,

Mr Hill will not allow him to be away from himself for an hour even, and endeavours to detach him from his family, telling him his father has eight other children and can spare him: he laughs at him for writing to any of them, and hints that he will be good for little until he divests himself of all affection and feeling for any of them. Mr Hill is right; to become an accomplished man in his employment, one must stifle humanity and destroy all the kinder emotions of the heart.[39]

Despite Hill's advice, Edward Gibbon never ceased to keep close contact with not only his father, whom he clearly loved, but also his brothers, sister Catherine and grandmother, who continued to fret about her favourite grandson. She had come to believe that he now enjoyed 'a respectable and luxurious situation, but one unfavourable to principles and morals'.[40] For his part, he was undoubtedly relishing this time in Paris, forming relationships that were to have far-reaching effects upon him. Following the death of his mother at forty-two, he returned to England on 10 February 1816. She had exercised little influence over her son's life, but he would always remember her with tenderness, and perhaps not some little guilt. His father, too, would surely have more than shared that guilt, although his thoughts, seven years later, suggest a reluctance to acknowledge his own failings, and a thinly disguised attempt to place himself in a better light:

I often think of her death; it was a fate of charity and love, her last breath lisping blessings on me and her children, no one is more aware of her failings than I am but she had many admirable points about her, her probity, truth . . . the severity of her long illness created a gentleness in her . . . I sat up with her many nights and hardly left her for months together.[41]

By the spring of 1816, Edward Gibbon was staying with the Hon William Hill in Princes Street, Hanover Square, London; living opposite was the widow of a wealthy East India merchant, Thomas Pattle, and her beautiful daughter Eliza, a sixteen-year-old heiress and ward of court, protected not only by her mother but also her two elderly uncles. Eliza was a delicate, dark-haired, dark-eyed beauty; a portrait of her painted by William Gynn in 1812 hints at the Eastern ancestry on her mother's side.

It would appear that Edward Gibbon and Eliza were never formally introduced; it is probable that he first encountered her while out walking, subsequently signalling to her from his window. Later the two contrived to meet for just half an hour each morning when Eliza's guardians relaxed their vigilance – 'love laughs at guardians as well as locksmiths'.[42] Within a very short time the couple had fallen in love. On 9 August, Francis Place made a startling announcement: 'He is to be married tomorrow.'[43] In fact, the marriage of the two young lovers, following a daring elopement, had already taken place in Edinburgh, on 27 July.

3

Says He, 'I am a Handsome Man, but I am a Gay Deceiver'

It was late afternoon on Tuesday 7 March 1826, when the green carriage drew away from the crowd of curious onlookers. Inside, the fifteen-year-old schoolgirl, beside her a disarmingly handsome stranger; and above, the young man and elderly servant. As the conveyance gathered speed, swinging around the corner of Oldham Street, Captain Wilson revealed his true identity. Circumstances had required that he assume the alias Captain Wilson, but in fact he was Edward Gibbon Wakefield, a friend and business associate of her father; the young man seated outside was his younger brother William. Venturing to ask whether she knew why she had been sent for from school, Ellen replied that Miss Daulby had told her that her mother was ill. Immediately, Edward Gibbon confessed 'it was not the case',[1] that he had 'reasons for deceiving Miss Daulby'. Mrs Turner was, he believed, 'quite well', and Ellen 'should have a full explanation by and by'. Ellen accepted this revelation, apparently unperturbed. She was, Edward Gibbon would discover, a young lady of maturity and a complexity well beyond the expectations of her fifteen years. As he would later testify,

> She seemed gratified to learn that her mother was not ill and neither expressed nor showed the slightest anxiety to know more. I then exerted every power of my mind to amuse and please her; – my great object was to draw her out, to see what sort of a mind she had, to learn what had been her education, and what were her opinions, manners and habits . . .
>
> I soon discovered . . . that she has a vivid imagination and a

judgement beyond her years. Why then it may be asked were not her suspicions excited? Because I answer, her imagination enabled her to discover at once the subjects that interested her, and by turning that discovery to account to make myself an object of interest to her, and her judgement enabled her to see and feel the great pains I took to treat her with the delicate and respectful yet tender kindness that her extraordinary situation demanded.

Arduous though the ascent to the moors above Manchester might be for others, time seemed to fly for the two protagonists:

A state of high excitement caused my spirits to overflow. She was almost equally elated. We talked and laughed incessantly. Never in my life did I say so much in the same time. All subjects came under discussion, the gravest and the most ridiculous – the most important and the most trifling. Her quickness, imagination and good sense astonished and delighted me. Instead of having to bring my conversation down to the capacity of an ordinary schoolgirl, I found that I could talk on at random, and that she understood every word I said. She too was gratified to discover that I enjoyed her display of a natural wit and a keen sense of the ridiculous with which she is gifted. Marriages it is said, are made in heaven – ours was made by the first two hours of our conversation.[2]

By the time they arrived at the Blue Bell Inn, the vehicle's steady ascent had long since exchanged the fine buildings of Manchester for the dark grey reaches of Saddleworth Moor. At the inn, the horses were changed, Thomas Fairman taking the reins, Richard Steele, postillion, riding the wheel. From within the carriage the sound of merry exchanges and peals of laughter reached them before they were snatched away on gusts of air, or drowned by a sudden protesting clatter of coach wheels. Horses and men joined forces, pushing through the mist and menacing darkness of the rising Pennines. Meanwhile Edward Gibbon was reaching his own heights, the success of his venture thus far, coupled with the astonishing amiability of his young companion, bearing him recklessly onwards.

At Marsden, the party stopped again to water the horses. As Steele and Fairman clambered stiffly up a nearby hillock, the sound of laughter caught up with them. Returning to the barouche, Steele was asked, 'What have you got there Richard, have you got some players?' He replied, 'No, I suppose it has been a wedding.'[3] Resuming their journey, almost gaily, the barouche borne forward by its team of men and horses began its glad descent towards Huddersfield. Inside the carriage, the courting of Ellen gathered momentum:

> No one can imagine the pains that I took to know my future wife and finding her as I did all that is delightful how I strove to interest her and make her pleased with me. That I succeeded there can be no doubt, for when, having made up my mind to propose marriage to her, I asked her if she knew where she was going, she said, 'No, but I suppose you do and I do not wish to be told – I rather enjoy the uncertainty'. I informed her that she was going into Yorkshire and that she would probably meet her father at Huddersfield. 'Very well,' she replied.
>
> As we proceeded we talked incessantly and often alluded to the strangeness of our situation. I gradually assumed towards her a manner, which I cannot readily describe. It was not studied, it was perfectly natural. I behaved to her as I would to a beloved sister whom I had just joined after separation from childhood, whom my whole soul was bent upon pleasing, with careful reserve and yet with the most affectionate frankness, with intimacy and without familiarity and with the greatest the most marked and thoughtful kindness but with no more kindness than any man of feeling would display towards a helpless woman, accidentally placed under his sole protection.[4]

Already, during the first few hours of their acquaintance, it appeared that this 'gay, witty, elegant, yet audacious cavalier'[5] had begun to enthrall Ellen. Perhaps it was hardly surprising that a spirited young schoolgirl should revel in such an unexpectedly romantic episode.

The darkness, as they approached Huddersfield, could barely have concealed the foreboding implicit in Edward Gibbon's gentle warning to Ellen: 'I mentioned the possibility of our not meeting her father there, and of her having to travel on with me till the following day.'

He was evidently both relieved and encouraged that she seemed 'agreeably disappointed at hearing that she might not see him so soon and that she might continue to travel with [him] till the next day'.[6] At half past seven in the evening the barouche drew up outside the George Inn where the landlord, Mr Wigney, helped Ellen down from the carriage. There, Edward Gibbon, asking for 'four horses out immediately',[7] was interrupted by Thevenot who informed him that a spring needed to be repaired before the carriage could go further. His brother William joined them as they were taken upstairs by Mr Wigney and shown into the sitting room. There they were attended by the waiter Charles Croft, who presently arrived with refreshment. As a man might his wife, or a brother his sister, Edward Gibbon made the tea and served Ellen with bread and butter, the two brothers making every effort to put Ellen at her ease. Later, Edward Gibbon recalled, 'We ate, drank, talked, laughed and almost played as if we had been a party of pleasure'.[8] Shortly afterwards when Croft entered to remove the tea things, and Mary Brock, the chambermaid, arrived to attend to 'Miss Turner', the Wakefield brothers seized the opportunity to leave, on the pretence of enquiring whether Ellen's father had yet arrived. Upon their return, Ellen's response to Edward Gibbon's news that her father had failed to come, and that 'there were no letters so [they] must therefore proceed to Halifax',[9] served to bolster his growing confidence:

> It was then dark, she expected to travel with me all night, and she knew neither to what place she was going nor with what object so strange a journey had been undertaken. But she *did* continue the journey, not merely with every mark of delight at our incessant conversation, but at the hurry and excitement of the whole adventure.[10]

The carriage repaired, Ellen came down the stairs on Edward Gibbon's arm to where William Langstaff, the George's post-boy, was waiting to drive them on to Halifax. As darkness closed in behind the barouche, snatches of merriment could still be heard – the journey from Huddersfield to Halifax seemed literally to fly by.

Left with William in the carriage, Ellen watched Thevenot carry his luggage into the bar of the White Lion. Moments later he returned and was soon deep in conversation with Edward Gibbon. Despite William's attentions, Ellen could not fail to be aware of the two men, illuminated as they were by the gaslight. Edward Gibbon's instructions to Thevenot carried clearly to her on the night air:

At Halifax my Servant on whom fright and fatigue had brought a fit of the Gout remained behind – openly and so that she must have heard me but in French [which I did not then know that she perfectly understood] I gave him orders to return to London. He asked me whether he should engage 'Family rooms' for me at the Brunswick Hotel: I said 'Yes but do not tell anybody that I am married and go to bed and stay in bed well or ill till you see me three days hence.' This I suspect did partially open her eyes to my ultimate object, for soon afterwards, as I was talking to my brother in French about her and the time when we might reach Scotland, she desired us not to tell secrets in French unless we wished her to understand them.[11]

Edward Gibbon returned, declaring himself 'much surprised to find neither [Ellen's] Papa nor letters waiting', explaining that it was therefore necessary to continue until they reached Kendal where they would 'be sure to find him'.[12] Consequently they set off for Keighley; there, when Henry Mason the new post-boy climbed down to water the horses, he could hear Ellen 'laughing in the carriage with the gentlemen'.[13] They were evidently still in high spirits.

Ann Bradley, who kept the Devonshire Arms at Skipton, saw their carriage and four arriving at ten o'clock. By the light of her lantern, she observed two gentlemen and a lady seated within. Fresh horses were ordered to take them on to Settle, and while they waited a serving-maid brought two glasses of water and some gingerbread, placing them on Ellen's lap. Ann Bradley offered the travellers her lantern and, believing that 'it was a runaway match', said that she would 'be glad to see them on their return'. As they departed she went inside, where, from the bar, she could still hear Ellen 'laughing in the carriage with the gentlemen'.[14]

It was a new day, Wednesday 8 March, when they arrived in Settle. It had been almost twelve hours since they had left the Albion Hotel in Manchester, and eighteen since Ellen's hasty departure from her school in Liverpool. At half past one in the morning, Mr Hartley, innkeeper of the Golden Lion, arranged for their horses to be changed. The road to Kirby Lonsdale was a continuous succession of thickly wooded hill and dale.

> We continued to travel through the night occupied as before with incessant conversation. Her spirits never flagged for a moment. Everything almost was converted into an excuse for laughing. The all but dangerous rapidity with which the Yorkshire post-boys drive through the darkness; the significant requests from more than one landlady on the road that we would honour them with our company on our return, my struggles after two sleepless nights with an almost overpowering drowsiness, various petty accidents; and the probability ascertained during the night that the carriage would break into pieces before daylight – all furnished us with reasons or rather excuses for being so merry that anyone who could have heard and seen us must have been satisfied with the perfect good will of both parties to lose no time in reaching Gretna Green.[15]

By four o' clock in the morning, as they approached the Rose and Crown in Kirby Lonsdale, the light rain of the previous evening had given way to mist and the promise of a warm day. Sarah Colman, quickly roused to attend to the passengers, had stumbled as she hastened to meet them, her mishap provoking yet more merriment from the occupants of the carriage; Ellen, in particular, laughing 'so loud as to make you believe there were two ladies'.[16] She exchanged a few words with Sarah before they left, 'What a beautiful morning it has turned out! – We are quite favoured with the morning.'[17] By breakfast, they would be in Kendal. Thus far, their journey had consumed the energy of three dozen horses, while Edward Gibbon's wooing had continued, tireless and unabated, feeding upon its own success, its instigator seemingly incapable of contemplating failure.

> I of course continued to direct the whole of my attention to improving her partiality to me, not merely by cheering and encouraging her joyous good humour but also by entering into all her feelings and by bestowing upon her such personal

attentions and caresses as without being indelicate or calculated to alarm her modesty, were an unequivocal declaration of my wishes and intentions. And I undoubtedly succeeded, for before we reached Kendall [sic] she treated me with all the affectionate confidence and gratifying intimacy, that a cherished friend and admitted lover could have expected from her.[18]

Reaching the outskirts of Kendal, Ellen asked how long they would be staying as she had an acquaintance there. Probably somewhat unnerved by that unwelcome information, Edward Gibbon replied that it would depend on her Papa, with whom he had led her to believe she would at last be reunited. On the dawn skyline stood the ruins of a castle, perched on a small hill in the middle of the valley, about half a mile from the town. Crossing the River Kent they arrived in Kendal, a neat and orderly town enclosed by barren mountains and craggy outcrops. Through the still-deserted streets their coach bounced over the cobbles, past Two Tan Yards, to an old and rambling hostelry, the King's Arms, where they were safely delivered at half past five in the morning; in the words of Edward Garratt, the Yorkshire post-boy – 'past perils safely surmounted'.[19]

Edward Gibbon, William and Ellen breakfasted in the warm and comfortable sitting room of the old-fashioned inn, Ellen afterwards withdrawing to a bedroom to be tended by chambermaid Hannah Simpson. Soon she returned to the sitting room, where Garratt entered to receive his payment, observing that 'The lady and gentlemen were there' and 'were talking together . . . walking backwards and forwards, alongside one another . . .'. Ellen 'was walking about very nimbly indeed, and looked very pleasant'.[20] She sat down, and Edward Gibbon and William moved to the other end of the room, to catch the light from the window to read a letter which the post-boy had brought. Sensing that Ellen was anxious for news of her father, Edward Gibbon, without revealing any details of the letter, told her that he would shortly explain why her Papa was not in Kendal to meet them.

At Kendal after breakfast I was about to undeceive her to explain the stratagem I had used in order to know her and make myself known to her and to attempt by a common course of supplication and argument to persuade her to marry me. The

Devil reminded me that besides the means of persuasion furnished by our already established intimacy I had a very powerful argument to use:- *She had passed one whole night with me!* And I could have urged that for her own sake she would do well to marry me without delay. True it was that I had treated her with the utmost delicacy and her conscience would have been clear though she had not married me. But then there was an ill-natured world, which knowing how much I *had* done, would never give me credit for any degree of forbearance. . . . The argument was indeed at least to a gentlewoman the wondrously powerful; but I felt an invincible objection to using it. A romantic fit, for which no stranger will give me either blame or credit came upon me, and under its influence I dreaded to appear a brute in the eyes of this sweet girl, who already so much inclined to take me, and whom had I used that ungenerous argument I should have married by a means that promised to insure for me her dislike instead of the tender love I then felt certain of inspiring her with.[21]

Despite an acquaintance of a mere eighteen hours to afford him insight into her character and intellect, so powerful was the impression Ellen seems to have wrought in him that he was entirely captivated, as by no other woman since the death of his beloved Eliza six years earlier. There is much to suggest that his 'romantic fit' heralded a change of course in this hitherto irresponsible adventurer. Edward Gibbon had often acted rashly, even unscrupulously, when he felt the occasion warranted, as the continual flaunting of the perceived restrictions of his schooldays and early manhood amply attested. His daring elopement with Eliza, a ward of court, typified his wanton disregard for authority and convention.

Edward Gibbon, it appears, had begun to believe that this young woman 'should not in her heart object to marry him', perhaps no longer regarding her as merely a means of securing a sound financial and political future, an entrée to public life. This escapade, undertaken in his usual casual and confident manner, had, it would seem, assumed a greater significance: the figure of Ellen no longer a means to an end, but an end in itself:

My head ached for some means of inducing and excusing her approval of an immediate marriage without destroying her good opinion of me. At last the device struck me which I afterwards used with success, and I declare that the pretext was employed not as the surest and readiest mode of persuading her, but as the only one which would enable me to marry her without in the very act of marriage risking the loss of her good opinion.[22]

His younger brother, William, was a shadowy figure in the corner of the carriage as Edward Gibbon tendered the first probing sentences of his carefully constructed plan. He had long since confirmed his prowess with words; Charles Allom, his secretary, was to write in later years, 'Edward Gibbon Wakefield was a master in the art of persuading, he seldom failed if he could get his victim into conversation.'[23] Allom's use of the word 'victim' suggests that Ellen was certainly not the last to succumb to Edward Gibbon's most potent skill. It would seem that throughout his life the written or spoken word proved the key to his success. Was she, he asked, aware of the failure of Ryle and Daintry's Bank at Macclesfield, and that its collapse had almost ruined her father? Her unexpectedly calm acknowledgement of this information both surprised and encouraged him, prompting him to add that it was fortunate that his uncle, a banker who lived in Kendal, 'a noble and generous minded man', had lent her Papa the considerable sum of £60,000, 'which had relieved him for a time'. Unfortunately, he added, her father's affairs had been reduced to an even worse condition by the subsequent failure of the Blackburn Bank, and he now found himself 'plunged into irretrievable difficulties and ruin'.[24] When Edward Gibbon asked whether she knew of Ryle and Daintry's Bank in Macclesfield, and whether she was aware of her father's commercial concerns in Blackburn, she replied that not only did she know of the Macclesfield bank, but she was also well aware of her father's commercial concerns in Blackburn; furthermore, one of his brothers also lived there and was engaged in commerce. In the light of what he now knew of her, her response should not have surprised him, further questions revealing that Ellen was her father's 'son' – heir to his fortune, educated as a son would have been to inherit his father's world. Warming to his task, Edward Gibbon outlined the terms of the loan to her father which required the estate of Shrigley as security. This gave his uncle the power 'to turn her Papa out of doors'.[25] Edward Gibbon paused for a few moments, allowing Ellen to reflect on the full gravity of her father's situation. His growing respect for this young girl perhaps prompting an unaccustomed caution; unused to failure, this might prove a salutary experience, but the possibility served only to encourage him – a challenge, reawakening the Edward Gibbon of his youth. He watched as Ellen weighed the import of his words, but saw no alarm register – it was time to drive home his advantage.

For her part, swiftly calling to mind all she knew of recent events, Ellen could set it against Edward Gibbon's profoundly disturbing disclosure. She had indeed heard that 'something of a tremendous convulsion . . . had happened in the commercial world of that time, and of a singular coincidence and no importance at the time it happened, but had a good deal of influence over her mind'.[26] She recalled how, during the journey back to Miss Daulby's school in Liverpool in the middle of February, her father had talked about various failures in the country, and of a fellow pupil, Miss Greenway, who had been forced to leave the school because of her father's newly straitened circumstances. Ellen's own father, discovering he did not have sufficient money in his pocket to settle Miss Daulby's account, had quipped, 'and I think I shall fail too'.[27]

Seizing the moment, Edward Gibbon put it to Ellen that the only way Shrigley could be saved was if she were to marry. If her husband was a 'Man of Honor [sic] then her Papa would be perfectly safe',[28] the estate would become the property of both her and her husband, and his uncle would no longer have a claim upon it. This expedient for relieving her father's distress and that of all her family had come from her father's attorney, Mr Grimsditch. At the mention of this name Edward Gibbon was rewarded by a light of recognition and relief in the eyes of his young charge. She had met Mr Grimsditch on several occasions, and knew him to be both friend and confidant of her father. With perfect timing Edward Gibbon applied the *coup de grâce* – it was Mr Grimsditch who had proposed that he, Edward Gibbon Wakefield, should be that husband; and, Edward Gibbon assured her, he was more than willing to comply. All that remained was for her to decide whether to accept this proposal – or to allow her father to be turned out of doors. Ellen declared firmly that she must first see her Papa before she could answer on so momentous a matter; undaunted, Edward Gibbon merely replied, 'Well, well, Carlisle is not far off and you will have an opportunity of seeing him there'.[29]

Pausing to water the horses on the road before the ascent of Shap, Robert Dover, the post-boy who had driven them from Kendal, noted that Ellen 'appeared rather fatigued with her journey' and 'a little pale'. He could not hear what the lady and gentleman were saying, but could see their lips moving; 'they appeared as any couple, looking pleasant, as a gentleman and lady in a carriage'.[30] Beginning the climb, Edward Gibbon must have felt at the most hazardous point of his venture, the austere limestone and bleak moorland landscape seeming to offer no comfort. If he was to succeed in his plan he must now muster all the charm and fascination experience had taught him he possessed. Predictably, by the time they reached the height of Shap Fell and the approach to its small village, he had restored Ellen's spirits. Leaving the village to begin their descent into the Lowther Valley, Edward Gibbon dropped the carriage window, instructing James Anderson, the post-boy, 'to make the best of [his] way, to drive fast', giving him the impression they were a wedding party. James heard them 'laughing in the carriage, seemingly in very good spirits'.[31] With Penrith but four miles distant, Edward Gibbon told Ellen of the nearby Lowther Castle, set on rising ground in the centre of a beautiful park, which was reputed to be 'the equal of if not superior to Chatsworth',[32] the seat of the dukes of Devonshire. Soon their route took them close to an ancient Druid temple; a welcome distraction, it lay 'surrounded by mighty mountains whose rocky and fantastic summits frowned and formed a magnificent amphitheatre, highly calculated to produce feelings of awe'.[33]

In sight of Penrith, the hitherto poor and barren terrain gave way to a fertile and productive landscape. Arriving soon afterwards at the Crown Inn, Edward Gibbon and William alighted, leaving Ellen inside the carriage. They rewarded the post-boy generously with 'six shillings a piece', and by half past ten had resumed their journey, the green barouche now drawn by four fresh horses. As Edward Baxter, their latest post-boy, enthusiastically tackled the hilly road to Carlisle, Ellen might well have envied him his energy and verve, for she had now been in the carriage since eight o'clock the previous morning. At a lively pace, they approached the Bush Inn, Carlisle, usually the last stage before Gretna for 'better-class travellers' from England. William and Edward Gibbon left the carriage as the landlady Sarah Holmes and her waiter Thomas Atkinson moved forward to assist Ellen.

> Our waiter and myself, tried to hand the lady out, but the taller gentleman put his hand on the carriage door and said, 'No'. The blinds were down, I could see the lady well in the carriage, she looked very dispirited that's why I went to the carriage to ask if she wanted to alight.[34]

Assuming them to be a wedding party, the waiter asked the gentlemen if they wanted horses for Gretna. Before answering, Edward Gibbon turned to look at Ellen, who clearly heard his reply, 'Yes, to Gretna'.[35] For almost a quarter of an hour Ellen waited alone in the carriage before Edward Gibbon emerged from the inn to join her, to be followed a few minutes later by William.

Leaving Carlisle, William drew up the carriage window, announcing that he had something of importance to communicate to his brother: he had just seen Ellen's father and Mr Grimsditch, concealed in a small room at the back of the inn. Ellen was delighted, relieved to hear that her Papa was nearby, and most anxious that they should return to see him. But William, taking out a map, explained to her that as both Mr Turner and Mr Grimsditch felt in such danger, they planned to cross the border near Longtown. So severe had been the danger, and so fearful in fact had been the two men of being discovered, that Mr Grimsditch had taken William 'by the shoulders and turned him out of the room',[36] begging him not to stay, because the sheriff's men were in pursuit of them. He had told William that they had already failed twice in their attempts to cross the border that day. William then asked Ellen if she had noticed the group of men standing in the courtyard of the Bush Inn on their arrival. He now understood them to have been the sheriff's men. So meticulous had been their planning, so near to fruition the outcome, that William could not but press home his advantage – her Papa entreated her, he said, that if she had ever loved him, she would not hesitate to accept Mr Wakefield. Scarcely allowing Ellen time to consider, William produced a letter, ostensibly from Mr Grimsditch, in which the attorney prayed that she would show the same fortitude as had been displayed by her 'excellent parent' during his travails. After a moment's silence, she responded with a question, asking Edward Gibbon whether her marriage alone would save her Papa. When Edward Gibbon confirmed that to be the case, Ellen consented. Her abductor 'thanked her, kissed her, encircled her in my arms, and from that moment I treated her as my future wife'.[37] Later he was to record,

> She entered at once and I may say eagerly into what she thought a scheme for securing her father's fortune. There was no holding back, no hesitation, 'Yes she said with pleasure for Papa's sake'. She evidently exulted at the ideal of being useful to her parents and expressed so beautifully her admirable feelings towards them that I was very near clasping her in my arms and betraying all.[38]

He added that he had assured her that if she felt any repugnance towards him, or felt herself unable to love him and be happy living entirely with him henceforth, she was to tell him without hesitation and he would immediately return her to Shrigley where her father's affairs would have to be arranged in some other way.

It is clear that Ellen did consent, and, needless to say, this delighted Edward Gibbon. She would also, as a dutiful daughter, have been glad to assist in alleviating her father's predicament; everything we know about her upbringing would support this. At this juncture, Ellen believed that the two men in the carriage were her family's saviours; she was completely unaware that they were, in fact, her captors. Whether or not the simple words 'I consent' masked feelings and thoughts outside those qualifying that consent can only be surmised. Ellen's acceptance filled Edward Gibbon with 'emotions of tenderness'; he 'swore to himself to render her the happiest of women', later recalling,

> . . . this tenderness from me and the caresses to which it gave rise soon restored our cheerfulness. As we passed the mountains of Westmoreland we projected a visit to the lakes. Near Carlisle and the border, it was impossible to speak of anything but Waverley and Walter Scott, and the last hour of our journey to Gretna was passed telling stories of the hair breadth 'scapes

of runaway couples and in all but boisterous mirth at the anticipated surprise of her Cheshire friends on hearing of her marriage.[39]

They crossed the border unaware, although it marked the point of no return. Approaching Gretna, Edward Gibbon was surprised to discover that Ellen was well acquainted with the marriage service; often, she confided to him, she had whiled away the tedium of church services by silently rehearsing the words of the marriage ceremony from the pages of her prayer book. Edward Gibbon, charmed away from the object of his enterprise by Ellen's romantic notions, resolved to fulfil her young ideals, determining to take care 'that the ceremony should be much more formal and solemn than is either usual or necessary at Gretna'.[40]

4

A Bold Stroke for a Wife

Edward Gibbon Wakefield and Ellen Turner were following in the footsteps of countless couples who had made the journey north to wed since Hardwicke's Marriage Act of 1753. Under this Act, marriages were prohibited between persons under twenty-one years of age, unless parental permission had been granted, and the ceremony was conducted in a recognised place of worship. No wedding, unless performed by an Anglican clergyman in church, or in a Quaker meeting house, or in a synagogue, had any legal standing. The Act also insisted on the publication of banns – 'the triple calling of the banns' – to ensure that each of the parties was eligible to marry. Anyone involved in an illegal marriage was liable to heavy penalties, including transportation. Tampering with a marriage register constituted a capital offence.

However, Hardwicke's Marriage Act did not apply in Scotland, where fourteen-year-old boys, 'young Solomons of the North', might take themselves wives; and females who had completed their twelfth year were eligible to wed. There, persons were not considered capable of 'consenting until pupillarity expires, which in females is twelve and in males fourteen'.[1] Consequently, those ineligible to wed in England crossed the border to avail themselves of a 'runaway marriage' at Coldstream Bridge, Lamberton Toll and, most famously, in Gretna, the first village to be encountered in Scotland, situated on the north-eastern shore of the Solway Firth. This small parish was close to the main road leading north through Preston, Penrith and Carlisle, but before the construction of the turnpike road in 1777 couples frequently made the dangerous journey to Gretna by boat or by fording the Solway. 'Great pains are taken in England to guard against the rashness and folly of youth, so apt to be led away by the headlong passions, but if they choose to pass over a small stream they are left to do as they please.'[2]

Large fees were paid to the 'parsons' who conducted these clandestine marriages, some having been rewarded with as much as £100 for five minutes work: 'high wages for a common labourer to receive, for merely putting on a black coat'.[3] Among the many hundreds, who, for a variety of reasons, had made the journey across the border, were three Lord Chancellors: Lord Erskine, who married his housekeeper Mary Buck at Gretna in 1816; Lord Eldon, who in 1772 eloped with a Newcastle banker's daughter, letting her down from an upper storey window by a rope ladder; and Lord Brougham, who made for Coldstream to marry Mary Ann Spalding, 'a showy, long, well dressed, red and white widow, a beauty',[4] who had been left an income of £1,500 per annum and a house in Mayfair by her late husband. When the marriage took place on 1 April 1819, Mary Ann was already pregnant with Brougham's child.

The post-boy, William Graham, himself no stranger to the abetting of eloping couples, drove them straight to the entrance of Gretna Hall. In front of the house was a lawn, green and pleasant, with trees and evergreens and adjoining shady, secluded walks where lovers could saunter at will in the cool of the evening. This approach was guarded by two splendid solitary trees: one a magnificent spreading oak, the other a fine old English elm; their leafy canopies lending some of their majesty to the growing reputation of this romantic eighteenth-century mansion house. Edward Gibbon, heartened by what he saw, and mindful of his silent promise to Ellen that the ceremony 'should be much more formal and solemn than is either usual or necessary at Gretna',[5] leaned out of the coach window to ask Graham whether this was where the old parson lived. The post-boy replied that, indeed, 'this was a place where marriages were made', and that the parson would need to be sent for. The Wakefield brothers stepped down from the carriage, Edward Gibbon proffering his hand and gently drawing Ellen to his side. If she harboured any misgivings about their impending union she showed no sign, as the landlord John Linton greeted them cordially at the entrance to the mansion.

John Linton, reputedly the model for Sir Walter Scott's *Young Lochinvar*, became the landlord of Gretna Hall in 1825, immediately setting about the refurbishment of the former family mansion, fitting it out as a first-class hotel and posting house. It was renowned as the principal aristocratic and fashionable resort of runaways, an elegant establishment set in twelve acres of fine grounds, where one could get a fair relay of horses and 'peradventure good entertainment', the place 'altogether tastefully laid out'.[6] With an astute eye to the marriage trade, John Linton had set apart a special chamber for these ceremonies, since his clients were the richest of the visitors to Gretna. They were also the most likely to be pursued, and on many occasions there would be a furious knocking at the door even before the 'priest' had spoken the necessary words to unite the couple. Entry would be refused until the ceremony was completed, whereupon Linton would hustle the newly-weds through his private apartment and into a secret chamber. There they would hide while he, suavely but firmly, dealt with the pursuing party, insisting that the angry relatives were too late, that the young couple had been married and left. Today, however, there would be no such high drama; the local schoolchildren would be deprived of their customary entertainment.

Whenever the school bell rang, the curious schoolchildren rushed out to catch a glance of the steaming horses and the agitated bridal couple, and the display of youthful curiosity was changed to intense excitement when, as sometimes happened, a second carriage dashed up, conveying the angry father of the blushing bride, his grim-faced lawyers – and, if the case was sufficiently serious Bow Street officers. On these occasions the language used was picturesque to say the least, and when it did not suffice to turn the young couple from their matrimonial escapade, heavy horse-pistols were brandished by the limbs of the law. It was a glorious spectacle for the children.[7]

A servant led Edward Gibbon, William and Ellen into a small parlour while Linton hastened upstairs to arrange for a fire to be lit in the drawing-room; this attended to by his own daughter, Frances. Clearly, they were perceived as a promising party, an impression later to be reinforced by the post-boy, whose intelligence would be instrumental in setting the marriage fee. The Bush Inn, Carlisle, had an arrangement with the parson who conducted marriages at Gretna Hall, an arrangement that had existed for the past year, since John Linton had become involved in 'the marriage business'. Frances met the Wakefield party on the staircase, Edward Gibbon and Ellen, their arms entwined. Returning to the drawing room soon afterwards to put sticks on the fire, Frances found Edward Gibbon sitting on the sofa with his prospective young bride seated upon his knee. Later, when the two brothers left Ellen alone in the room, she was observed by Mr Linton to be in 'a happy and relaxed state of mind' – not, as one might expect, either anxious or depressed.

The appearance of David Lang, the blacksmith priest from Springfield, may well have detracted from a generally pleasing impression. Anxious as Edward Gibbon was to foster Ellen's growing pleasure in the forthcoming proceedings, he must have been somewhat disconcerted by both the manner and appearance of this rather vulgar old man. Lang was dressed in a dusty black coat and breeches; velvet waistcoat and white stock; and a hat, commonly known as the 'clerical cock', below which a ruddy, rough-featured face of blotchy complexion betrayed his liking for 'shumpine' (champagne). He was truly a parody: a clergyman in 'clerical dress' in accordance with the self-importance which had long since earned him the nickname 'Bishop Lang'; and a worthy successor to his famous uncle, the blacksmith priest Joseph Paisley. Formerly a Scotch pedlar, and, according to the *Dumfries Weekly Journal* of 1805, a tobacconist who 'had long been in the habit of marrying persons who came to him' was now, ironically, a pedlar of lawless English marriages. 'Beyond seventy-five years of age',[8] he appeared a crude fellow, with a shrewdness and air of familiarity, acquired during his many years in this dubious profession. He was only too aware of the debt owed to him by those of a superior rank who, albeit unwilling, acknowledged the power which his performance of so important though clandestine a ceremony gave him.

Lang stood before them, marrying them as he had married many hundreds before. With mock solemnity he asked the couple whether they took one another to be man and wife, as was the mode in Scotland, whereupon they both answered 'Yes', Ellen very distinctly. Then Lang, taking the ring, slipped it on to the slender finger – of the second Mrs Wakefield.

5

Thou Can Love a Lass . . .

The first Mrs Wakefield, Eliza Anne Pattle, as Edward Gibbon must have been well aware, was both an heiress and a ward of court. However, it would be churlish to suggest that he wanted her less for herself than for her money. She was to become, indisputably, the love of his life.

At the beginning of June 1816, told by Eliza that her mother was taking her away for the summer season, he determined to follow her. Mrs Pattle had begun to suspect that her daughter had an admirer, 'but she did not know the character or family of the lover', being aware only 'that an attachment existed'.[1] It might well be for this reason that she had rented a villa in fashionable Tunbridge Wells, some thirty-six miles from London, where she had friends and relations. A few days later, Edward Gibbon had watched from a window of his employer's house, opposite that of Mrs Pattle, as her daughter Eliza and a whole retinue of servants were driven away by Robert Latimer, their coachman. Soon Mrs Pattle and her daughter would be engaged in the familiar round of renewing acquaintances and enjoying the society of Tunbridge Wells. Edward Gibbon had lost no time in pursuit of his beloved, using his customary charm to form valuable liaisons with Mrs Pattle's manservant, Clanton, and the cook, Charlotte Woodbine. With their help he would not only maintain contact with Eliza, but also plan their elopement.

Early on the morning of 13 June Mrs Pattle sallied forth on a visit to Tunbridge. Meanwhile, back at her villa, a chaise and four, followed by a stylish gig, drew up at the door. Confident that Mrs Pattle would be away for some time, her daughter's young suitor 'handed his fair charge into the gig'. No sooner had Mrs Pattle departed than Edward

Gibbon's careful plan had been put into operation. 'Into the chaise was handed with great ceremony, Clanton, the manservant, and Woodbine, the cook, both very genteelly dressed, and while this vehicle drove off with the blinds up, by one road, with all possible despatch, urged by the apparent anxiety of the inmates',[2] Edward Gibbon, 'leisurely, without any show of grandeur', Eliza safe within, ordered the gig to drive off in the opposite direction.

Soon after her return at ten o'clock, Mrs Pattle sent for Eliza. Great was her alarm to be 'apprised that her bird of paradise had flown';[3] moreover, she was to learn that neither her manservant nor her cook was anywhere to be found. Fearing the worst, Mrs Pattle lost no time in appealing to her close friends Mr Becher and Colonel Tweedale for assistance. They set off immediately, but unfortunately in the wrong direction. Eliza's hysterical mother, having given orders for her coach to be prepared without delay, drove off in hot pursuit of the chaise which she believed to be carrying her daughter. She had not travelled far before she became aware of the ominous shuddering of the sorely pressed vehicle. Pulling the horses to a halt, her servant jumped down to see what was amiss. Although assuring Mrs Pattle that the coach was not in a dangerous state, he advised that it would be unwise to proceed. Patiently bearing the brunt of his mistress's anger and despair at this ill-timed misfortune, he ventured to inform her, when the tirade abated, that Mr Wakefield had been 'doing something to the chaise the night before, and this may have accounted for the mishap'.[4] Later it transpired that Edward Gibbon Wakefield had bribed Mrs Pattle's servants to help him, and that her coachman, Latimer, had provided the transport for the whole escapade.

As the drama unfolded, the lovers drove on in the opposite direction, as had always been Edward Gibbon's intention, making for London, where in Brompton they posted a letter to Mrs Pattle. The letter, purporting to have been sent from Calais, was designed to further confound their pursuers.

Calais, 14th June 1816

My dearest Mother,

Trusting the almost unwarrantable step I have taken has not occasioned me entirely to forfeit your affection, I hasten to inform you of my safety, also 'ere this reaches you I shall be a wife, whose I need not say for You perceive by my date we are across the water but do not write to me as we are still moving, our destination is uncertain. This will be a great privation to me but it must be so for a short time, therefore for God's sake do not let my hope of your forgiveness prove deceitful for 'til then I must remain your unhappy but affectionate daughter Eliza.

P.S. Tell my beloved uncle how great is my feeling of regret at not being able to write to him, but I am unable to do so from extreme anxiety and want of time. Oh! for heaven's sake, then I shall be quite happy, it only rests with you, everything promises me happiness. I will soon write and give a full account of a great deal more to you and my dear uncle Nat & G. Templar.[5]

The contents of the letter served only to increase Mrs Pattle's distress; the news that her daughter had been carried across the Channel and by now would be the wife of this adventurer was more than she could bear. The letter, though in Eliza's hand, was clearly the work of her bold admirer, written to throw their pursuers off the scent. Despite her daughter's reassurances, Mrs Pattle lost no time in seeking the intervention of the Lord Chancellor.

Edward Gibbon, it was found, had disposed of the gig soon after leaving Tunbridge: 'from that time their journey throughout was one of the most romantic and adventurous in the records of hymeneal fugacity.' Meanwhile, everything possible was being done to trace the runaway couple:

They had not proceeded far when he found a price was set on his head and advertisements and placards put out all over the country giving a description of his person as the abductor, abducer of an heiress, a ward in Chancery and offering a large reward for his apprehension. At every turn they dreaded the appearance of peace officers and the interrogatores of all whom they met.[6]

Although the original intention had been to head for Gretna, the runaways' fear of discovery had led them to travel randomly, using the most 'unfrequented by-roads, petty towns, villages, and hamlets; and thus they traversed the whole country making an occasional stretch northwards'.

Although Edward Gibbon's employer, the Hon. William Hill, had been most generous, confessing to having advanced him a year and a half's salary, besides paying him some arrears, a sum therefore of about £250, Edward Gibbon was well aware of the need to conserve funds in order to accomplish his aims.

Their difficulties increased daily, but their spirits it appeared bore up against them, and the young lady, who it might be said had never before been required to set her foot upon the ground beyond a short walk and had enjoyed the ease and comfort of a carriage, even when she took an airing, was now reduced by necessity of walking many a long mile on the public road with her companion. On some occasions they were together on top of a coach or wagon, and rested at the most humble houses of entertainment on the wayside. In this manner, and partaking of the most common fare, they journeyed for many hundreds of miles together . . . until their dress, their funds and, almost their hopes were reduced to the lowest ebb.

If proof was needed of the love and commitment which this seventeen-year-old girl had for Edward Gibbon, then surely this would serve; equally, his affectionate and brotherly treatment of his prospective wife confirmed his own honourable intentions. It was to be a further three weeks before they reached their destination:

After a variety of suffering consequent upon their romantic adventure and many hairbreadth escapes from detection, they arrived at Edinburgh . . . in total destitution, Mr Wakefield was necessitated to leave his bride at an obscure lodging until he besought her the relief which her immediate wants required.[7]

Leaving Eliza at their 'obscure lodgings' in Leonard's Hill, Edward Gibbon set off for the house of his father's friend Mr Gray. Four years had elapsed since his departure – homeward bound from a brief encounter with yet another educational establishment – but he was unprepared for the suspicious reception he received from their maidservant. Casting her eyes over his shabby if genteel attire, she was clearly disinclined to be hospitable, only the earnestness of his entreaties finally persuading her to refer him to her mistress, Mrs Gray. When she appeared, at first that lady seemed no more impressed than her servant. However, recognition finally dawned as Edward Gibbon, after asking if she had received a letter from his father, identified himself, and, 'despite the disguise wrought by the journey of the last three weeks', she was 'moved to joy when she realised that he was none other than her former young friend himself'.[8]

Although his tale was indeed one to stretch the imagination, Mrs Gray heard him out. Prior acquaintance with this headstrong young man had prepared her for some such episode, but experience of his former romantic attachments meant that her credulity was somewhat strained when presented with his description of a young lady of 'great respectability'. Furthermore, she could not hide her surprise at the state of her young friend, whom she knew to have been most particular about his dress. Edward Gibbon continued that not only was he destitute, but, worse, his companion was in desperate need of new clothes. Consequently, the lady sent her son back with him to ascertain the true state of affairs in respect of this 'virtuous young lady'. He found her

> the most beautiful young creature he had ever beheld and her language and accomplished manners were such as at once convinced him that she was a virtuous young lady of rank and education. She was withal . . . so dejected by fatigue and anxiety of mind, that he hastened with a report to his parents.[9]

Reassured by his words, the lady and her son insisted that the young lovers leave their 'obscure lodgings' to come and live under their roof, even advancing them sufficient funds to enable the couple to appear as became their rank in life. Mr Gray, the gentleman of the house, after making numerous enquiries, discovered that the young lady, who was a ward of court and heiress to the fortune of her deceased father, had eloped with Edward Gibbon, who was himself not yet of age. However, he accepted that the couple were deeply in love, earnestly believing that Edward Gibbon had no idea of Eliza's 'high expectations'.

Despite the reward offered for the apprehension of Edward Gibbon, he decided to hasten the legal marriage of the couple in order to protect Eliza's reputation. Two weeks before the ceremony took place, news of the couple's elopement reached Edward Gibbon's grandmother, Priscilla. Staying with her daughter in Ipswich, she recorded in her diary that she had received 'news of the arrival and departure of two fugitives in whose welfare I am deeply interested'.[10]

Edward Gibbon and Eliza Pattle were married on 27 July 1816, by a minister of the Church of Scotland in the presence of Mr and Mrs Gray and their son, of St Leonard's Hill; soon after, news of the event reached the Wakefield family. The newly married couple then travelled to London, where on 7 August they met Edward Gibbon's father and two of his brothers, William and Felix. Priscilla, still in Ipswich, responded to a letter from her grandson, Arthur, declaring she was charmed with his account of Eliza and pleased that the young bride had been introduced to their Tottenham friends. She added, however, that she felt hurt that Edward Gibbon had not seen fit to take his father, who had done so much for him, into his confidence – all thoughts of her son's failings as a father apparently forgotten. Priscilla finally met Eliza in the autumn, declaring herself greatly pleased with her. Clearly, the Wakefield family was delighted with Edward Gibbon's choice of bride. Writing three years after his daughter-in-law's death, Edward Wakefield still spoke of her gentleness, her 'excellent acute sense, and her kind, reserved way; she never forced it on you but left it to you to find it out'.[11]

William Hill worked hard to effect a reconciliation between Mrs Pattle and Edward Gibbon. This, together with the young bridegroom's unfailing charm, carried the day: Mrs Pattle, her protective instincts breached by this charismatic Lothario, was persuaded that it was indeed a love match. Lord Chancellor Eldon, who had himself contracted a runaway marriage, and may well have been sympathetic, was convinced by the petitioning of Mrs Pattle and William Hill, and probably of Edward Gibbon himself, of the propriety of the Scottish marriage. To the pleasure of all parties, the couple were married again in London on 10 August. By 26 August an award had been made in Chancery of £600 per annum to Edward Gibbon from the late Thomas Pattle's estate. During the course of a single month his fortunes had been reversed.

When David Lang invited Edward Gibbon to 'embrace the bride',[12] Ellen 'met Mr Wakefield very pleasantly',[13] and Lang shook hands with them both, wishing them well. The marriage certificate was duly completed, the two witnesses John Linton and William Graham adding their signatures to those of Ellen and Edward Gibbon. Lang, having added his own signature to the certificate, was drawn to one side by Edward Gibbon, who paid him the sum of £30. Hastily, the wily old man pocketed his fee and, pressing home his advantage, turned to Ellen to explain that he was accustomed to receiving a present of money from the bride, which might purchase him a new pair of gloves. Ellen dutifully responded with a gift of twenty shillings.

Formalities concluded, the wedding party, now in high spirits, sat down to dine. Lang, who had declined to eat with them, was cordially invited by Edward Gibbon to partake of some wine, and when asked for his advice did not hesitate to recommend the 'best of shumpine'.[14] Edward Gibbon, evidently not averse to indulging the rascally old 'clergyman', invited him to join them for a drink of 'his favourite tipple' and after waiting downstairs while the party dined, he returned later to help them finish the wine, before wishing them good day and departing.

By late afternoon the wedding party was ready to leave, the newly-weds holding hands affectionately, talking and laughing together as they waited for their coach. Standing happily on the steps of Gretna Hall, the group's easy air belied the fact that but thirty-six hours ago Ellen Turner had been taken from her Ladies' Seminary in Liverpool; a fifteen-year-old ingénue, preparing for yet another routine day of a school designed in some degree to prepare her for marriage to a suitor of her father's choosing – 'some said Mr Turner considered her a fit match for a noble duke'.[15] Leaving Gretna for Carlisle, the coach now carried not 'a fifteen-year-old ingénue', but a wife and furthermore the wife of an unscrupulous adventurer.

The wedding party retraced their journey, arriving at the Bush Inn, Carlisle, at six in the evening as darkness settled. Thanking their post-boy, William Graham, for his sterling work, they followed Thomas Atkinson, the head waiter, up to the parlour. There they rested for several hours, taking tea, while Edward Gibbon wrote a letter and Ellen and William played draughts. Despite the tiring and exacting circumstances of their journey they were in high spirits, particularly Ellen, who had been assured by Edward Gibbon of her father's safety, now no longer a fugitive since receiving intelligence from the post-boy of his daughter's marriage. Furthermore, the marriage certificate would satisfy the Sheriff's officers that they had no further claim on him. This welcome news confirmed that she had made the right decision: Ellen 'felt that she had rendered a service to her family beyond what she ever hoped she could have the opportunity of doing';[16] and she was delighted to learn that soon they would meet her father, either at Shrigley or, if business had taken him there, in London.

They left for Penrith in a post-chaise: the green barouche, purchased three days earlier in Manchester for £40, and which had carried them safely for more than 200 tortuous miles, now lay broken. James Hamilton of the Crown Inn knew the Wakefields by sight having seen them that morning coming from Shap on the Kendal road, and he particularly remembered the elder gentleman, for whom he had changed a £50 note. The chambermaid, Margaret Dunwoods, who was convinced that they had just returned from Gretna, was surprised when asked by Edward Gibbon to make up three separate beds, in different rooms. Later she overheard Wakefield saying to his young bride, 'I must see where you are going to sleep my dear'. Attending Edward Gibbon, early the following morning she found him alone and not yet dressed, and, as is the wont of curious chambermaids, later confirmed for herself that all three beds had been slept in, and that there was no evidence to show that more than one person had slept in each. Nevertheless, she saw nothing pass between Edward Gibbon and Ellen 'but what was loving on both sides'.[17]

Edward Gibbon Wakefield had gambled much on the success of the abduction of the young Ellen Turner. Having rehearsed this criminal escapade ten years previously, he was well acquainted with the law, and no doubt the arousal of Margaret Dunwoods' curiosity was astutely sought. He knew full well that to consummate this 'illegal' marriage in England would constitute a felony, and the chambermaid's evidence would be vital in demonstrating that, even on his wedding night, his behaviour had been beyond reproach. Having previously secured the compliance of his dear Eliza's mother, her guardians, and even the Lord Chancellor, in the matter of their Scottish marriage, it only remained for Edward Gibbon to procure the assent of the bride's father – the formidable Mr Turner.

The die was now irrevocably cast. I now had three objects in view, to keep my engagements at Calais, to inform Mr Turner as soon as possible that his daughter was legally married . . . and if possible to keep from my wife that I had in any degree sinned against her father.[18]

After arriving in Leeds, the Wakefield brothers and Ellen waited in the Bull and Mouth in Briggate for the coach which would take the married couple on to London. Edward Gibbon explained to Ellen that it was possible that her father might have gone there, promising her that if they failed to find him they would return to Shrigley. William left them in Leeds, though he had not yet served his purpose, for he was to provide a final service for his brother prior to organising his own wedding in Paris to Emily, the daughter of Sir John Sidney. William was to travel to Shrigley with clear instructions to conceal nothing of the events of the past two days from Mr Turner, but to urge him to avoid at all costs a public scandal by accepting the marriage of his daughter to Edward Gibbon Wakefield. In Ellen's interest he was to be persuaded that Edward Gibbon was an honourable man and a fitting husband for his cherished daughter, for regardless of whether the marriage was upheld, according to the social conventions of the time, Ellen was now in a very precarious position: even though it might be successfully argued that she had been 'blackmailed' into the Gretna marriage, any future marriage prospects would be damaged. In light of this, William had every reason to hope that Mr Turner would allow himself to be persuaded as to the propriety of the marriage. He was to discover, however, that her father was made of stronger stuff – William Turner, prospective High Sheriff of Cheshire and a 'self-made country gentleman' was reputed to nurture high hopes for his only daughter and heir.

The newly-weds proceeded by public conveyance to the capital, though there are 'no entries in the post horse duty books of any Leeds posting house, of a carriage being ordered in the name of Wakefield'.[19] As Edward Gibbon travelled south with Ellen by his side, he had considered the words of her father's enemies and her detractors: that she was 'ugly, ignorant, awkward and vulgar'.[20] A great beauty, he owned, she was not, but neither was she plain: there was a generosity of mind and spirit, displayed by this comely, indeed handsome young woman – the charge of ignorance was insupportable. Under the trying circumstances she had but recently endured, Ellen had steadfastly retained her dignity and composure; at all times she had conducted herself with intelligence and sensitivity. As for 'awkward and vulgar', how could anyone so misrepresent her? Throughout the time they had been together, while he, a man of some thirty years, had flagrantly dissembled, this fifteen-year-old schoolgirl had met all his deceptions and evasions with a grace and candour belying her years, and a touching artlessness that would put him in mind of Eliza.

> Young as she was, Eliza possessed a gentle courage, a quiet steadiness of purpose, a clearness of vision, a delicately balanced judgement and sense of responsibility . . . and possessed both strength of character and wisdom beyond her years.[21]

Perhaps for the first time since the death of his former wife, Edward Gibbon's senses were stirred by a woman. This bold venture might yet provide more than merely the standing and influence he craved; more important than these was the possibility of regaining the only truly meaningful and joyous period of his life – his four years of marriage to Eliza.

6

And Thus the Whirligig of Time Brings in his Revenge

Those four memorable years had been spent in Italy, where Edward Gibbon was attached to the Hon. Algernon Percy at the British Legation in Turin, the Piedmontese capital. Nestling in the Alpine foothills at the base of the Valle d'Aosta, amid Roman ruins and medieval palaces, it was the 'Paris of the South' and as such was most agreeable to Edward Gibbon, whose appetite for the French capital had already been whetted during his sojourn there as a King's Messenger. Although based in Turin, Edward Gibbon and Eliza seem to have passed much of their time in the Mediterranean city of Genoa, where they stayed with the Hon. William Hill, who also extended his hospitality to Lord Byron during this period. Soon Hill was writing to Edward Wakefield senior, reporting that Edward Gibbon and his wife were well and doing everything a father could wish, having rented a house nearby until they were able to establish more permanent quarters in Turin. 'Houses and furniture are much cheaper here and you will be glad to hear that he weighs all these things in his mind and has begun his new life in the true spirit of economy.'[1] Hill concludes his letter by praising Eliza: 'you are most fortunate in your daughter-in-law, for although I have not been able as yet to see much of her I am quite convinced she is a most amiable and excellent person.'[2] The recipient, under the terms of the settlement agreed by the Lord Chancellor, of interest and dividends from the £70,000 trust fund set up from the proceeds of the estate of Eliza's father, Thomas Pattle, Edward Gibbon appeared to be financially secure.

This was the high life Edward Gibbon adored; for though Eliza had secured his heart, he remained the most mundane of young men. With that comfortable life interest behind him, and the prospect of Eliza's legacy, he felt equal to anything – and the equal of anybody. His official position was prestigious, entailed mixing with the élite of all nations and appearing, resplendent in uniform, at state balls and banquets. Nevertheless, when more responsible business was delegated to him, he discharged it with an efficiency that both surprised and pleased Mr Hill. Ironically, Edward Gibbon's father, who, despite the entreaties of his mother Priscilla, had been so absent and remiss during his children's formative years, was now bent on supervising the activities of his maturing son. Perhaps this attentiveness, coming so late into his eldest son's life, was not welcome: Edward Gibbon, somewhat irritated by such unprecedented interference, begged that he and Eliza should not in future be the subject of correspondence to Mr Hill. 'Why am I to be looked upon as a fool or a baby because I have been unwise or foolish enough to marry – you did not interfere with me for the last two years; why should you do so now?'[3]

However, within a couple of months, Edward Wakefield was to be drawn into his son's affairs. Francis Place contacted him regarding the plight of a certain Mr Wilson, who claimed to have been shoddily treated by Edward Gibbon. In a letter to Francis Place, dated 16 December 1816, Wilson recounted the service he had performed for Edward Gibbon at the time of his elopement with Eliza Pattle, in conveying the young couple to Scotland where they could marry, having first driven them to his brother's farm in Hertfordshire 'where we remained three or four days until the affair blew over'. There Wilson had been promised by Edward Gibbon

a handsome present and such provision that I should never want again. . . . We reached Scotland in safety and returned in safety likewise . . . out of twenty-seven days I was gone I had my clothes off only four times. I rode outside the post-chaise the whole way nearly there and back and it rained incessantly the whole of the time. My stockings were completely ground on to my feet and I had not a clean shirt until our return . . . Mr Wakefield was very often kind enough to say he was well pleased with my endeavours that he would do something handsome for me when we came to London.[4]

Accordingly, Wilson claimed, they had met at the house of Edward Gibbon's father in London. There he was assured that a position had been secured for him as Land Steward on Edward Wakefield's estate in Devon where he would be very comfortable. Edward Gibbon also promised him various sums of money before leaving for Genoa, which he had never received, and to his 'great mortification' he had found that a dispute regarding the Devon estate meant all 'prospects lost, left without a shilling', adding that 'he had assisted Mr [Edward Gibbon] Wakefield in getting a large fortune and in justice, he ought in some measure to provide for me'. Furthermore, he added plaintively, 'Had I turned villain and while Mr Wakefield and Miss Pattle were at my brother's I had informed her guardians in Town and received six hundred pounds reward I might have done such a thing.'[5] Edward Gibbon's father, learning that his offspring had fobbed off the unfortunate coachman with the meagre sum of five pounds, while admitting that his son ought to fulfil his promise, added cavalierly that 'in law he was only an infant'. It can only be imagined what Place, the exasperated middleman in this shabby affair, thought of this 'giddy boy'[6] and his indulgent father.

Meanwhile, Edward Gibbon was enjoying the company of his younger brother William, who had been appointed to assist Mr Percy in Turin. Less welcome was the presence of Edward Gibbon's mother-in-law, Mrs Pattle, who was now living with the young couple. In a letter written on 23 November 1816, Edward Gibbon complained to his father that

Mrs Pattle has expressed not only a great inclination, but a decided will to go to India and she has spared no pain to induce me to accompany her. Miss Lawes goes on worse and worse, she has been playing the devil during my absences from Genoa and her influence on Mrs Pattle increases daily – all Mrs P's Indian speculation proceeds as far as I can judge from Miss Lawes . . . Mrs P will remain long with us, *if only I can* get rid of Miss Lawes. The difference between my marriage being a good thing and a very indifferent one depends upon the temper of Mrs. P.[7]

Minor disagreements with her daughter invariably enabled Mrs Pattle to reproach her, with sarcastic references to her past duplicity at Tunbridge Wells. However, Edward Gibbon was not so opposed to

Mrs Pattle as to her friend, the formidable Miss Lawes, though he still managed to retain a sense of humour despite his predicament.

> Miss Lawes was accustomed to immense quantities of laudanum, which she drinks as I do water, as she does brandy, she took poison because I would not introduce her at court. It had not a very serious effect and the apothecary would not sell her enough to kill her.[8]

A weakness in Mrs Pattle's character, an inclination to be swayed so readily by those stronger in purpose than herself, had worked in Edward Gibbon's favour when prising his Eliza from the side of her doting mother; in these new circumstances, he found it to be less welcome. By January the following year, he was pressing Miss Lawes' family to recall her to England; it had become obvious that Mrs Pattle was in awe of the troublesome Miss Lawes, she 'dare not dismiss her'. For Edward Gibbon she was yet another burden to add to his list of growing concerns: the furniture and effects had eventually arrived, but had been damaged in transit; though less important than it might seem, his uniform, to him a very necessary visual symbol of his status, had still not arrived: 'my helmet is at Westons in Bond Street and a helmet at Wagners – I am in great want of them'.[9] And while welcoming a visit from his younger brother Daniel, this too was fraught as the young man was in a poor state of mind and health and would require care and attention to help him recover from the effects of 'bad company and bawdy houses'.[10] To add to Edward Gibbon's woes, Mrs Pattle had to keep Eliza company during his absence and the dreaded Miss Lawes had to be left by herself at his mother-in-law's house, costing Mrs Pattle at least £600 a year and, he believed, 'her beastly family should know it'.[11]

Turin was found to be full of English, enabling Edward Gibbon to renew his acquaintance with a number of his old school fellows. Writing to his grandmother Priscilla in February, Edward Gibbon assured her that they were all well and that life in Turin was suiting them admirably. He enthused, 'the climate here is most refreshing, for although close to the Alps we have fine English weather . . . the whole . . . of Piedmont is covered with snow like the month of April'.[12] He confessed to be most pleased to report that Mrs Pattle 'greatly improves on acquaintance',[13] and, with undisguised glee, announced that Miss Lawes had left for England. By now, Edward Gibbon was enjoying a truly amicable relationship with Mrs Pattle. Undoubtedly his position at the British Legation contributed to her growing attachment to him, requiring as it did that both he and his family enter fully into the glittering diplomatic world of grand balls, soirées, fêtes, endless visits and elegant pursuits. Mrs Pattle relished the opportunity to mix with the social élite. The presence of the Princess of Wales caused great excitement when she visited Turin that month. Princess Caroline, bent on disgracing the Prince Regent, had been

> carried through the streets of Genoa in an illuminated phaeton, made in the form of a conch shell, decorated with mother of pearl. Within sat a vast woman of fiftyish, short, round and high in colour, wrapped in a gauzy décolleté gown with a pink bodice. The pink feathers of her headdress floated in the wind, and a short white skirt came scarcely past her knees, leaving on view fat pink legs.[14]

Dazzled by this daring and outlandish display, Mrs Pattle and the ladies of the day awaited her arrival with eager anticipation: Edward Gibbon, clearly less impressed, thought her – 'quite mad'![15]

Not surprisingly, Edward Gibbon was now living beyond his means, the cost of setting up his household, and the necessity of supporting Mrs Pattle, outrunning his finances. Furthermore, he was hoping to buy a large estate, preferably far from London, 'capable of giving him influence and standing'.[16] To this end, and concerned about his future inheritance should his mother-in-law outlive him, he urged the lawyers swiftly to conclude the terms of his settlement. In seeking to commandeer his young wife's fortune, albeit to protect their joint future, he found himself hindered by the profligate Mrs Pattle. Moreover, his brother Daniel was once again beset by misfortune, having been kicked by a horse just as he was planning to leave the Wakefield household. Yet there were compensations, notably a ball in Naples which served to raise Edward Gibbon's spirits and those of his womenfolk. At last the wild and wayward young Edward Gibbon looked set for a promising and settled future; beside him a beautiful and talented young wife, admired for her gentleness and wisdom. But it seemed the gods were not yet prepared to smile upon him – within days he was to be brought down, under the hooves of his own runaway horse.

I was riding full gallop on a road near Turin, when a fool who was showing off [chased] his horse across the road. In order to avoid killing him and myself I was obliged to pull up at once from a gallop to a dead stop[;] in doing so I was forced to cling to the saddle and use any effort to prevent a fall. Before I was well reseated I fell.[17]

Brothers in adversity, within days Daniel was to fall over one hundred feet into the sea near Pozzalo. Together they convalesced, but Daniel recovered far sooner than Edward Gibbon, who was still lame five weeks later. The tendon of his hip joint was so badly damaged that the physicians and surgeons he had consulted in Turin ordered him to be confined to bed for two months. He was to be treated with hot baths, and was urged to consult the King's physician Dr Audiberti, who had studied at Edinburgh and enjoyed a fine reputation in Turin. There were further consultations with Audiberti, Professor Gesi and a Professor Rossi, who was one of Napoleon's surgeons, but such was his incapacity that he had to be lifted in and out of bed by his servants. Though his condition had improved by the end of May, he was still by no means well, while Daniel had fully recovered. Since he had decided to remain with them he now needed steady employment, which he found with the ever beneficent Mr Hill.

By June, Edward Gibbon and Eliza felt sufficiently confident to announce to their family and friends that Eliza was with child and due to lie in in November. Edward Gibbon, still abed and prostrate, was cheered by Eliza's well-being. However, now they were to become a family, it seemed even more pressing that they should find a suitable estate in England. The suggestion that they settle near King's Lynn made him uneasy. Mindful of the health both of his wife and future child, he had no wish to live in the damp climate of the Fens. He speculated that land values in England would drop because of the effect of abundant harvests on the Continent, and hoped that a wider choice of more affordable properties would soon become available.

Several financially advantageous marriages presented themselves to Mrs Pattle, but all, much to Edward Gibbon's dismay, were rejected, and his mother-in-law continued to be a drain on his resources. Moreover, he was increasingly concerned by the interference of her brother, John Middleton, in the authorisation of the settlements due from the estate of Eliza's father. Soon Edward Gibbon found himself no longer able to support his mother-in-law and was forced to resort to asking his grandmother, Priscilla, to lend him money. Nevertheless, Eliza's pregnancy progressed and despite his problems, Edward Gibbon afforded her every attention. Though he was sorely missed by Mr Hill, in his absence Daniel was evidently working hard.

After three debilitating weeks spent in bed following a bilious attack and describing himself as 'weak as a cat',[18] Edward Gibbon was at least temporarily encouraged by the signing of the 'financial settlements', despite Mrs Pattle, without friends or occupation, proving expensive to keep amused. Money difficulties prevailed, but Mr Hill was determined that they should maintain their style of living in order to keep up appearances. As Eliza's confinement drew closer her husband's monetary worries increased. A foreigner, he was finding it difficult to borrow locally; not only was there the expense of his illness, but his mother-in-law was showing 'a want of prudence as well as of money', and was suspected either of having interfered with her late husband's will or at least of having 'used undue influence on it'. Edward Gibbon, still unable to work for Mr Hill, proposed a move to Genoa, for his own sake as well as Eliza's. He had been told by the surgeons that the cold of Turin would be very 'hurtful to his hip', therefore they should travel to the warmer climate of Genoa where it hardly ever froze and snow was unknown; 'at Turin twelve weeks of uninterrupted frost and snow are not called a severe winter'.[19] There was the added bonus that everything in Genoa was cheaper, and Edward Gibbon would be able to sell his carriage horses, which, though indispensable to Mrs Pattle in Turin, would be useless in Genoa. These would realise £150 while the change of air would probably suit his mother-in-law, who was proving both troublesome and unwell. Fortunately, there would be some lords and ladies in Genoa, who would 'pay fine attention to Mrs Pattle',[20] whom he believed to be most reluctant to leave Turin during the carnival, complaining that accompanying her daughter would be very dull. Eliza, in the advanced stages of her pregnancy, would be carried by sedan chair, which Edward Gibbon regarded as an easy mode of travel; and Daniel, who was still working for Mr Hill, hoped to join them soon as he found the cold of Turin disagreeable. For his part he would have preferred to return to England, but could not because he too was in debt and could live more cheaply abroad. Eliza would have welcomed the opportunity to hire an English nurse for her infant, now to be born in Italy, but conscious of their financial situation, she did not press the point.

Meanwhile, in spite of mounting debts, his inability to borrow money in London and his promise not to draw from his bank for the next nine months, Edward Gibbon was still actively seeking an estate in England. He was advised to secure a property in Wales, and expressed an interest in two estates shortly to be sold by Mr Hill's brother. He had heard from Lord Kensington, 'a gigantic Welshman'[21] living in Genoa, of a property in Carmarthenshire, and believed that nowhere was land to be bought so advantageously as in Wales, where at least a dozen large properties were for sale. It was no longer the fashion to buy and build in Wales, since nobody of any consequence wished to live more than sixty or seventy miles from London.

The Wakefields arrived in Genoa on 3 November, and Edward Gibbon wrote home that they would

remain [here] for some time, the climate is most delightful and agrees with us all. Eliza is very well and will I suppose have hardly a month before her confinement. What she wants is an English maid – but English servants are such devils that she is afraid to ask for one – they all give themselves great airs when abroad.[22]

There, news reached them of the death in childbirth of the Prince Regent's daughter, Princess Charlotte. Years later, Edward Gibbon could still recall the grief of the British diplomats at the news; so great was their dismay, they burst into tears. This would have been an unwelcome but timely reminder to Eliza of the not inconsiderable dangers of giving birth. For Priscilla Wakefield it clearly gave rise to concern. Shortly afterwards she wrote to her grandson, 'I long to receive an account of a happy increase at Genoa . . . the fate of the poor princess makes one more anxious'.[23]

By now, Edward Gibbon was reaching the end of his tether with regard to the incorrigible Mrs Pattle. She no longer had the income to support her lavish lifestyle and, having lived with him for a whole year, had created heavy expenses: the provision of a carriage, various amusements and extra servants meant that she now owed him a great deal of money. His resultant debts and inability to support her financially added to her discontent and his embarrassment.

On 4 December, Eliza was safely delivered of a daughter, Susan Priscilla, thereafter known as Nina – a name believed to have been given to her by her nurse. Mrs Pattle had witnessed Nina's birth, and Edward Gibbon was hopeful that she would prove to be in better humour as a grandmother, but was secretly doubtful of his own prospects as a father – he wrote of the infant Nina, 'I love her so much that I am almost sure I shall be deprived of her'.[24] Shortly afterwards Eliza's mother decided to pay a visit to London, where Edward Gibbon was pleased to be able to send her word that 'Eliza is accountably well and the baby cannot be better'.[25] Relaxing with his wife and newborn daughter in the agreeable climate of Genoa, he was able to turn his thoughts to the future; his proclaimed ambition was now to acquire a seat in the British Parliament, although in his present impecunious situation this aspiration was unrealistic. His old problems continued. It had become increasingly apparent that the money he had received from Thomas Pattle's estate had been unwisely invested, forcing him early in the new year to give instructions 'to sell if the market is up, at the shortest possible notice'.[26] Although he was able to report that the 'baby flourishes greatly',[27] clearly his fortunes did not.

After the birth of Nina, his relationship with his father revived. He thanked him for his offers of help, but now, as a father of a family of his own, acknowledged that he must shoulder his responsibilities. Informing his father that he had forwarded a packet through the Foreign Office containing some 'worked' dresses for his sister Catherine and grandmother, and a present from Eliza, he added that he was concerned that some of his letters had not reached him, the contents of which might not be favourable and should not be divulged. 'Pray, look well at the seals and either burn them carefully or hide them – a lock and key are not sufficient unless *very good*. I am afraid some of your present clerks are pilfering intelligence from the contents of your drawers.'[28] He intended, he informs his father, to send letters in future by private hand, but it was proving difficult to find suitable carriers as 'they are scarce for England'.[29] The previous month he had sent a packet by 'a blackguard Captain of Marines, whom I do not much trust, but as he returns to Genoa for his own private affairs I suppose he will hardly dare to purloin it.'[30]

By the end of December Edward Gibbon was writing to his father once again, agreeing that if he were to remain abroad, it might hamper his advancement. Until he could be sure of better prospects in England, however, he felt he must stay, from a mere motive of economy.

> I should not think of bringing my family to England for till I have more fortune I can take advantage of, but few of the benefits attending a seat in Parliament . . . without proportionate fortune I cannot introduce my wife. I feel confident of a certain part of speaking in public if my lungs are strong enough, and look forward to a seat in Parliament as the only thing to raise me and my family to anything like what my ambition prepares for them.[31]

In February 1818 as his brother Daniel prepared to return home by sea, Edward Gibbon sought a publisher for his treatise, 'An account of the political state of the Duchy of Genoa since its cession to the King of Sardinia'. He confessed, 'although full of very curious facts, it had not cost me much time or labour as my opportunities for gaining it have been excellent'.[32] Edward Gibbon, with his inherited Quaker precepts and memories of an early life filled with battles fought on behalf of the oppressed and good causes supported by both his father and grandmother, empathised with the Italians of the north, living as they did under the despotism which had resulted from the terms agreed at the Congress of Vienna in 1814. At the end of April disquiet approached from another quarter and Edward Gibbon was writing that 'everybody here is alarmed at the possibility of a war with America. Of course, I dread such an event as much as anybody, I see the funds falling rapidly.' Four months later he was still worried about the effect of the 'damned squabble'.[33]

By mid-summer of 1818, Eliza was far advanced into her second pregnancy and all appeared to be well, but the child, a son named Edward, died within a few months of his birth. The young mother felt the loss keenly; eighteen months later she was still thinking of her dead son. In her diary of 1820 she was to write, 'Little soul, thou art happy, and yet thy selfish mother wishes thee in her arms again'.[34] Looking back over the year, Edward Gibbon was at least able to take comfort in the knowledge that his career was proving both rewarding and successful, Mr Hill acknowledging his zeal and enthusiasm. As Britain's official representative at a fête in honour of Grand Duke Michael of Russia and the Prince de Carignan, held shortly before Christmas, Edward Gibbon took it upon himself to challenge one of the 'less prestigious' guests, a Mr Thomas. Outraged both by the linen draper's 'improper dress, and still worse his ingratiating behaviour with the Highnesses and Excellencies', he had taken the draper to task, pointing out that not only 'had he no sword and was not dressed correctly but was also attracting unwarranted attention by his embarrassing behaviour'.

So enraged was the linen draper by Edward Gibbon's attack that the following morning he called him out. While having no objection to fighting a duel, Edward Gibbon was loathe to demean himself by 'taking a bullet' from a mere linen draper; in this opinion he was supported by his peers, one of whom, Prince Kossloffsky, scoffed at the idea of a gentleman – giving satisfaction to *un marchand de drap, chez qui on va acheter deux palmes de perkale* – a linen-draper to whom one goes to buy a couple of lengths of calico'.[35] As a result, and in the throes of what Mr Hill described in his despatch to Foreign Secretary Lord Castlereagh sympathetically enough as a 'Welsh passion', Mr Thomas insulted Edward Gibbon publicly. Believing he had no choice but to accept the challenge, Edward Gibbon approached Prince Troubetskoy, a member of Grand Duke Michael's entourage, to be his second, judging him to be of suitably exalted rank, and therefore able to lend some *ton* to the occasion. Fortuitously, Mr Thomas, persuaded by his friends, had decided that discretion was probably the better part of valour and cancelled the duel. The matter was finally put to rest by Mr Hill's somewhat conciliatory letter to Mr Thomas, who was thus appeased.

This minor incident apart, Edward Gibbon had distinguished himself in the employ of the Hon. Algernon Percy and Mr Hill. Indeed, Mr Hill was exceedingly fond of Edward Gibbon, whom he had supported in his elopement with Eliza, describing him as possessing 'an excellent acute sense', and praising her 'gentleness'[36] and the impression she had made upon all his friends. He was to remain a friend of the young couple for some years to come. In October 1819, the family left Italy. While they rested in Dijon, Edward Gibbon wrote to his father to tell him that they expected to join him in Paris within the week; assuring him that, despite the arduous journey, 'We are all tolerable well, Mrs P is lame but still better than expected, the child is not the least hurt by the travelling'. Evidently, Edward Gibbon was still anxious to keep Mrs Pattle in good humour, concluding his letter to his father with detailed instructions as to the preparations for their accommodation:

Mrs Pattle should be given the best bedroom; a tub specially installed, and the looking-glass changed; her portrait is to be displayed in the dining room; and Mrs Rich must employ an extra cook, as Mrs P is very particular; Mrs Rich must wait on Mrs P a good deal, and have an additional young woman to wait upon everybody for neither Mrs P. nor Nina can manage without somebody to wait on them. I wish to make them as comfortable as I can.[37]

He added that Russi, the surgeon at Turin, 'gives but poor hope of Mrs P's ever walking properly and she is altogether much shook and altered'. The cause for Mrs Pattle's decline is not known, but judging from her symptoms it is possible she had suffered a stroke.

Eliza was almost three months pregnant when the family, now settled in England, visited Priscilla to celebrate the New Year in Ipswich. Eliza and her husband seemed as happy together as ever, for at the beginning of her diary for 1820, she wrote, 'Dear Edward, Would that I could make thee as happy as I desire and your kindness deserves and grant that this New Year may end as it has begun'.[38] At his grandmother's they attended a lunch *en famille* – a large party to celebrate Priscilla and Edward's forty-ninth year of marriage. Eliza was filled with admiration for Edward Gibbon's grandparents, and was flattered by the attention of such a personage as Priscilla Wakefield. 'Will Providence give us such a spell of happiness? God grant it may be so.' Back home the family were all suffering from colds, Eliza, very concerned that Nina's was a bad one, and that she 'requires the mercury'.[39] Moreover she had the additional worry of her mother's state of health, since Mrs Pattle's leg showed no improvement. For poor Eliza, who had such a dread of weak health and illness, their maladies made her dwell once again on her dead son, about whom she 'cherished the slightest recollection'. To her dismay Nina's cough continued to worsen, and Eliza was loath to leave her, going out against her will only 'to please Edward'. Eventually it was confirmed that Nina was suffering from 'that fearful disorder, the whooping cough'.[40] Although considered delicate, Nina was eventually to recover, but thereafter was always to suffer from a weak chest.

Three weeks into the new year, during the evening of 29 January, George III died, ending a reign of sixty years during which America had declared Independence and England had confronted both the threat of foreign invasion and the fear of revolution at home. In the aftermath of the French Wars abroad and increasing industrialisation at home, the country faced great social and economic upheaval. For the King, it had been a merciful release from the terrible treatment administered by his physicians, as, blind and senile, he descended into madness.

On 5 July 1820, life dealt Edward Gibbon Wakefield a blow from which he would never fully recover – his beloved Eliza was dead. Ten days earlier, on 25 June, she had given birth to a son, Edward Jerningham. The infant was healthy, but it soon became apparent that the birth would cost Eliza her life.

According to his great granddaughter and biographer, Irma O'Connor, the stricken Edward Gibbon

> could not bear to look at the face of his infant son, against whom his grief imposed an invisible but impassable barrier which he was never afterwards entirely able to dissolve; and to the end of his life he never mentioned his wife's name to anyone, drawing an impenetrable curtain of reserve between the outside world and that Holy of holies in which his love and memories of her dwelt secure and alone.[41]

The terrible blow he felt is borne out by a letter to his sister Catherine, written on mourning paper, shortly after Eliza's death. It is a powerful and moving tribute to her:

I was oppressed by blue devils to such a degree that I knew I should only fill my letter with melancholy topics . . . I begin to suffer deprivations of all kinds from the want of my happy home, the future presents itself in dismal colours. . . . These uncomfortable feelings *unsettle me extremely*. . . each view of my future existence presents the same dreary prospect, the same hourly want of that cheerful face, lightened up as it was, by a temper, manners and habits so exactly suited to my taste and inclinations . . . one who combined so many of the qualifications which to a fastidious person like me are absolutely necessary towards the maintenance of an affectionate intercourse.

If my wife had deceived me, if she had ever made me feel ashamed of her, if she had conscientiously held opinions adverse to mine, if she had not evinced for me at all times the most ardent affection, if she had not anticipated all my wishes, if she had not possessed any one of those qualifications which in my eyes are necessary towards excellence in a wife, I should not have given her full credit for the rest and we shall have been less happy than we were. And she *did* possess *all these* qualifications, love they say is blind. I may be so to her defects, but I cannot bring one to my recollection. I am not now speaking in general terms but mean *defects* in *my eyes*.

Her ready cheerful submission on occasion when I was clearly in the wrong and where by opposing me she would probably have fulfilled a duty more important perhaps than that of obedience to her husband would to some men have been a signal fault. But I could not love a strange woman, but because she became my own creature, whose mind would in time take just what impressions I pleased. I ask more, in this respect, than ninety-nine men out of a hundred; yet I obtained all that I could desire . . . the degree of knowledge which she possessed and the calibre of her mind were exactly suited to my temper and taste. I could not bear a wife who would instruct me; but I could not suffer one who was unable to understand me. This to anybody but you (and it is for you alone) would be vanity; but you know me well enough to tell that is a fact, silly and presumptuous though it may be.

I feel that in everything which regarded me, particularly my dear Nina, was perfect. The good sense and wisdom she displayed in the management of her mother, her kindness and warm affection towards those whom I loved, her adoration of our children and admirable manner of treating them, her knowledge of the world, displayed in a nice and instantaneous discernment between good and bad people, her correctness of conduct, her prudence, modesty and discretion form a combination of virtues which I never met before and never expect to see again. . . .

I have had some pleasure in the recapitulation of my poor darling's virtues and yet the recollection of them adds to the bitterness of my misfortune. Time our oldest enemy, will, I suppose prove my best friend.[42]

There can be no doubt that theirs had been a love-match, a union which the undiscerning might have deemed unlikely: on the one hand, Edward Gibbon Wakefield the adventurer, headstrong and impetuous, on the other, Eliza, gentlewoman, prudent and sensible. But it was also a fine, balanced partnership: for Eliza, though brief, the marriage had evidently been both happy and fulfilling; for Edward Gibbon, it was a union which bestowed purpose and a sense of responsibility and direction on his life that hitherto had been lacking. He had, despite a loving and positive family influence, been a wayward youth; now, deprived of the love of Eliza, which had exerted so stabilising an influence, he reverted to the headstrong waywardness of his earlier years. In his despair, love turned to anger, responsibility gave way to recklessness. Though able to glean some comfort from his closeness to his young daughter Nina, the existence of his infant son on the other hand served merely to deepen his intense grief and sense of loss. Two years later, his antipathy for his son remained; writing to his sister Catherine, he professed, 'I shall love him bye and bye, I suppose, as much I do his sister.'[43]

Yet only a year after Eliza's death, it is clear Edward Gibbon could not see a future for himself and his children unless he contracted another marriage. Not for the first time he was motivated by his financial situation and his wish to re-establish a settled family life for his two young children. Despite professing to his sister that Eliza could never be replaced – 'I shall never see her like again' – while staying at Presteigne in Wales, he had met a lady of a 'most amiable disposition', who was 'well informed, perfectly ladylike in her manners' and 'totally devoid of affectation'. He confessed himself attracted by her 'mildness, submissiveness and tenderness' and her passionate love of children. Obviously contemplating marriage, he was certain that this lady would 'fall in with his views' and that love was not out of the question, with, he added significantly, 'an amiable person with a very large fortune' who 'is willing to embark in the lottery of marriage with me. I shall be happy in such a marriage.' So he assured Catherine, concluding, 'I have not a doubt of it, at least, as happy as I can *ever* be – with daily regrets for the treasure I have lost and a conviction that she can never be replaced.'[44] Writing to his sister shortly afterwards, from 'the solitude of a dirty Welsh inn' on 'a pouring wet day', he confided that he could make himself a home in 'this delightful country' among 'the hearty and friendly inhabitants of this out of the way part of the world'.[45] His sister, however, did not approve of his 'late precipitate conduct', fearing his children might be neglected. For whatever reason, perhaps Catherine's misgivings, the marriage never materialised.

Ellen, the schoolgirl at his side, was little older than his own daughter, Nina. Edward Gibbon Wakefield was not a man without conscience, but he had long since travelled, literally and metaphorically, beyond the point of no return – within the hour, they would reach London.

7

Out Upon it! I Have Loved

Late on Friday evening, 10 March 1826, Ellen and Edward Gibbon entered the great city of London. The lights and shadows, shouts and laughter, glistening cobbles and glimmering gas lights – a veritable kaleidoscope of sights and sounds – they swept into Hanover Square. Desperately tired, but restored by the atmosphere of the metropolis, they swung into the courtyard of the Brunswick Hotel in the post-chaise that had carried them safely on the last stage of their journey from Barnet. It was here that Edward Gibbon planned to draw his carefully plotted scheme to a satisfactory conclusion. His brother William, entrusted to deliver the '*fait accompli*' tale to Shrigley, should by now have achieved his purpose. It was time to take stock, to devote himself to the welfare and well-being of Ellen. Edward Gibbon asked to be shown to the family rooms which his servant Thevenot had arranged for them on his return from Halifax, but Jalley, the hotel waiter, surprised him with the news that his brother awaited him. Filled with apprehension, he followed Jalley to an upstairs room where to his relief he found not William, but his father's friend Mr Mills. Ensuring that Jalley was out of earshot, the latter nervously conveyed a message to Edward Gibbon from his father, desiring that 'he remain in London not a single hour, for he would be liable to be apprehended and brought to justice'.[1] This was hardly the denouement that Edward Gibbon either desired or expected, but, true to character, he quickly concocted a tale to reassure the tired and justifiably fretful Ellen; her father, he informed her, had left on urgent business for Calais, and they must follow him to France. A tearful Ellen returned to her bedroom while Edward Gibbon sought out his servant, Thevenot, who had already retired to bed. In the early hours of Saturday morning Edward Gibbon Wakefield, having once again employed his tried and trusted skills of tact, diplomacy and duplicity, carried Ellen into Dover, a distance of some fifty miles.

The journey had been uneventful, the night sky clear and starlit, the air cold and frosty; within the coach the couple drew closer together, sleeping fitfully between stages. As they entered Dover, Edward Gibbon entertained Ellen with promises of the many diversions of the land across the water. Events conspired to aid him in the form of a group of friends encountered in one of the inns fronting the harbour. As ever, undaunted and with his customary charm and aplomb, Edward Gibbon introduced them to his new bride. They did not have to wait long for a passage for there were steam packets aplenty. Together they boarded, the newly-weds and their companions settling down for the four-hour crossing.

This was a journey which he had contrived ten years previously in order to throw his pursuers off the scent; then he carried his young bride-to-be, Eliza Pattle, to Edinburgh; now, with his second bride, he entered the troubled waters of the Channel; and in England, the peaceful hamlet of Shrigley was brewing a storm of its own. The father of the bride, preparing to alight from the London to Macclesfield mail coach, was met by his good friend and lawyer, Thomas Grimsditch, clearly much agitated and brandishing a newspaper. Tired and bemused, William Turner climbed down stiffly from the carriage, his feet barely reaching the ground before the distraught Mr Grimsditch accosted him. Not until Ellen's father read the words for himself could he truly take in the preposterous news which had tumbled from the mouth of his solicitor.

On the 8th, Edward Gibbon Wakefield Esq, to Ellen, only daughter of W. Turner, Esq. Of Shrigley Park, in the county of Chester.[2]

William Turner and Thomas Grimsditch had left Macclesfield during the evening of Monday 6 March to attend to business in London, returning separately to Macclesfield on Friday 10 March. Within a few hours of his departure, Ellen had arrived in London; ironically, her father, whom she had so earnestly sought for three days, had probably passed her on the road as he travelled north. In a state of shock and disbelief, William Turner begged Grimsditch, his confidant and attorney of the last eight years, to accompany him on the short journey back to Shrigley. He was stunned by the news, his mind stumbling in search of reason and action: it was inconceivable that his young daughter, whom he had safely delivered only three weeks previously into the hands of the Daulby sisters in Liverpool, was now a wife, and, moreover, the wife of a man of whom he had no knowledge, and whose name he had never encountered. The inevitable repercussions of this astounding announcement assailed him, and he dreaded to think of its effect upon his already ailing wife. Almost ashamedly, he also considered the effect of this catastrophic news – were it to be proved true – on his own standing and ambitions – his 'self-made' status of country gentleman and his forthcoming investiture as High Sheriff. These thoughts offered him momentary reprieve – could it be nothing more than a cruel hoax? The 'New Squire' was not without enemies in the county; he was 'an object of jealousy to the old established gentry and of envy to the numerous manufacturers of the neighbourhood',[3] where he had but recently settled.

As his horses struggled up the last steep incline, the sight of Shrigley Hall served temporarily to lift his spirits; his fine new mansion attesting to his self-worth. And indeed at Shrigley there was every appearance of normality: his footman Broster, waiting in the hall, informed him that his wife was resting, and by the time Mrs Turner, accompanied by her niece Margaret, joined her husband and Mr Grimsditch in the drawing room, he had visibly composed himself. Mindful of his wife's delicate health, he took pains to break the news as gently as he could: their daughter, he informed her, had, inconceivably, been reported by a London newspaper to have been married. Hastily he assured his wife that in all probability this was an absurd error which he would lose no time in rectifying. Meanwhile, together with Mr Grimsditch, he set about devising a course of action, prevailing upon his niece Margaret to write to the Daulbys, seeking to verify that his daughter remained in their care. Having received the enquiry on Sunday 12 March, Miss Elizabeth Daulby set forth for Shrigley the following day. Her arrival was to confirm the Turners' worst fears: their daughter was no longer in her care. Furthermore, she had in her possession evidence which was to prostrate Mrs Turner and devastate her husband. Deeply embarrassed and troubled by the developments of the last twenty-four hours, and the evident distress of the distraught parents, Elizabeth Daulby surrendered the letter which purported to have come from Mrs Turner's doctor; the letter which had succeeded in persuading the Daulbys to give up their charge to complete strangers.

Ironically, while Turner and Grimsditch laboured to unravel this sordid affair, there was another, close by, working equally hard to secure the enterprise: Frances Davies, daughter of the respected clergyman and headmaster of Macclesfield School, who had contracted a secret marriage three years previously with Edward Gibbon's father. Stepmother to the Wakefield brothers, she had played a key role in the abduction, and even now was carefully monitoring developments at Shrigley in order to ensure that matters were brought to a satisfactory conclusion. William had sent word that he had been unexpectedly forced to return to France to attend Emily, his bride-to-be, and therefore his visit to Shrigley to assess Mr Turner's reaction to the marriage would be delayed. In the meantime, Frances hoped to engineer a means of persuading Ellen's father to acquiesce to his daughter's marriage. Fortuitously for Frances, her father, Dr Davies, who seemed to have assumed the role of her unwitting informer, had accidentally met Mrs Critchley, Ellen's aunt, and had learned of the marriage. On receipt of this valuable information from her innocent father, and encouraged to learn that Mrs Critchley appeared to be kindly disposed to the union, Frances wrote to her stepson William, apprising him of this turn of events. 'You must not let a foolish account of the affair get into the papers. It would annoy Turner I'm sure,'[4] – an understatement indeed, in view of the subsequent reaction of Ellen's father and the British press.

Although reluctant to leave his wife, by now 'in a state quite indescribable', William Turner was 'decidedly of the opinion that if she did not see her daughter in a few days, the shock she had sustained would be fatal to her'.[5] Consequently, accompanied by Thomas Grimsditch, he set off immediately in pursuit of Ellen, travelling directly to London where they were to join his brother Robert and his brother-law Henry Critchley. In the early hours of Tuesday morning, upon learning 'of the true character of the affair',[6] Mr Grimsditch informed William Turner that Edward

Gibbon Wakefield and his daughter had left the country and were now believed to be in Calais. Without delay, a warrant was obtained from Sir Richard Birnie, the chief magistrate at Bow Street, who 'at once acquiesced to the wishes of the distressed relatives and appointed two of his principal officers to accompany them to France'.[7] One of them, Ellis, was directed to 'execute his commission with prudence, discretion and the greatest delicacy',[8] Birnie explaining that he had no doubt his warrant would be obeyed in most parts of England, but within the French capital he could exercise no jurisdiction, although instances had occurred where persons had been given up at his request for crimes of forgery and other similar offences. Later in the day Grimsditch collected a despatch from the Foreign Office in which Canning instructed Granville, the British Ambassador in Paris, 'to give all the countenance and support that you may have it in your power to afford . . . for the apprehension of the culprit Wakefield'.[9] That evening, Mr Grimsditch, Ellis, a Bow Street Runner, Robert Turner and Henry Critchley, Ellen's two uncles, left for Calais. Mr Turner did not accompany them as 'he was unable to go any further'.[10] The shock of the last few days had finally taken its toll, and he was content to leave the pursuit to his trusted friends and relatives. While the rescuers were en route, these details reached Liverpool when Grimsditch's partner, William Hopes, wrote to William Roscoe, the friend of the Daulbys. 'Several friends have proceeded to France with the authority possible for the recovery of [Mr Turner's] daughter.'[11]

Calais was a popular destination for those of modest means or those who had fallen on hard times, some famous, others notorious, among their number Emma Hamilton, Nelson's paramour, and the bankrupt Beau Brummell. Soon Mr and Mrs Edward Gibbon Wakefield were happily ensconced in the Hotel Quillac, an establishment renowned for its English comfort, cleanliness, good living and moderate prices. Edward Gibbon had rented a salon and two connecting chambers, each with a bed, the mode of accommodation regularly occupied by married couples staying in the hotel. Introduced by Edward Gibbon to Monsieur Quillac as his wife, Ellen was known as 'Madame Wakefield',[12] her new husband devoting himself to her welfare and happiness.

Calais, though a wretched place was full of novelty and amusement to her. There we passed nearly a week like any other newly married couple, and as if neither I nor she had any reason for anxiety.

Although desperate for news of Mr Turner's reaction to his daughter's marriage from his brother William, Edward Gibbon nevertheless succeeded in affording his young bride every attention.

I was so fully occupied in teaching, dressing, amusing and caressing the high spirited and affectionate girl whose happiness, whatever might be the conduct of her family was now become the first object of my existence, that I was indifferent to almost everything but the actual enjoyment of the moment [of] which no one can imagine the intoxicating nature, who has not by rare good fortune been the first object of a young heart's legitimate tenderness; and the revolution in her situation was so complete – converting her one day from a scolded or neglected and always restrained school girl into the earthly idol of a passionate and romantic husband – that it is not fair to wonder at her having under its happy influence preferred the Vaudeville – even of a Calais Theatre, to the die-away songs of a Liverpool Concert – the hasty productions of a tenth rate *marchande-de-modes* to the little coal scuttle bonnet and scanty pelisse of a Macklesfield [sic] dressmaker, and my poor company to that of her governess.[13]

If Edward Gibbon's account is to be believed, the days Ellen spent in Calais awaiting the arrival of her father were not those of a frightened, abducted ingénue – quite the contrary. Doubtless, to be fêted by a sophisticated man of the world such as Edward Gibbon would have been a heady experience for any woman; for a young inexperienced schoolgirl it must have been a dormitory dream come true. The purchase of a new ring to replace the ill-fitting one given to her at her Gretna marriage signified the reaffirmation of the hastily contracted marriage, and her letter from Calais to her mother, signed Ellen Wakefield, was surely further confirmation of her acceptance of her newly acquired status. Encouraged by Ellen's response, yet mindful of her longing to see her father, Edward

Gibbon evidently felt emboldened to approach Mr Turner by letter in which he informed the father of his daughter's welfare while also showing concern for their relationship:

Calais, March 13th 1826

Dear Sir,

I cannot help feeling that I ought to write to you, and yet I am so completely at a loss to know what to say, that I begin a letter upon the chance of finding words as I proceed. Nothing that I can say will give you pleasure, excepting an assurance which I rejoice to be able to give, that your dear child is perfectly well, and would be completely happy but for her separation from you and her mother.

I know, Sir, I have done you an almost unpardonable injury; and I feel, that in your situation I should be furious with the man who had dared to marry my daughter without my consent; still I hope that in a similar case I should suspend my judgement til I could learn all the Facts, and til I could ascertain whether my child's prospects of happiness had been seriously affected by such an event. It is with this feeling that I have ventured to beg that you will take the trouble to know me, and learn from all my friends whether or not your daughter has made an unhappy marriage. I trust in God, and firmly believe, that she has not; and if I shall succeed in making her completely happy, you must be satisfied; at least that would be my feeling in your situation. I acknowledge the full extent of the wrong that I have done you, but I may be able to repair it, unless you put reparation out of my power, by refusing to give me the opportunity. At all events, I have incurred towards your child the most sacred of obligations; and I feel that, come what may, even though you should entertain towards me the most unrelenting hatred, she has a claim upon my devoted tenderness, such as few women could ever make before. Promises would be thrown away in such a case. In respect to her, I desire to be judged not by words, which it is easy to string together, but by facts, which time alone can shew. I must tell you, that she pines to see you, and watches the arrival of every packet, as if her life depended upon seeing you in it. She is a dear affectionate excellent creature, and well deserves from you as much affection as she feels towards you.

I remain, Sir,
Your obedient,
E.G. Wakefield[14]

Indeed, although no doubt enjoying her honeymoon, Ellen must have longed to see her father again. Knowing how much he cherished her, she must have anticipated the joy of that meeting at which she would be able to reassure him, not only of what she still misguidedly believed to be her successful fulfilment of his wishes but of the enhancement of her own happiness. Dutifully she went each day to the quay to await the arrival of the Dover packet in the hope of seeing him. At her side Edward Gibbon, too, anxiously awaited an arrival, that of his influential friend and former employer Algernon Percy, from whom he would entreat support in his encounter with Mr Turner. But about Mr Turner his brother William was still unable to furnish any information.

On the fourth day, in the late afternoon, the Dover packet brought both Ellen's liberators and Algernon Percy to the pier head in Calais. When Ellen told Edward Gibbon that she thought she saw one of her uncles disembarking, he quickly ushered her back to their hotel, conscious of the need to conduct the forthcoming negotiations on his own terms, away from the prying eyes of the public. Settling Ellen into Madame Quillac's private drawing room, he withdrew before hastening to the hotel courtyard to forestall her uncles. Edward Gibbon had considered flight, for he had both a carriage and passports ready and could 'have escaped to the world's end with [his] wife',[15] but he had rejected this option. Man and boy he had always achieved his aim, whether it be a determination to quit his school, or to take a wife; surrender and defeat were not in his vocabulary. He already possessed a blueprint for success: Eliza and her guardians had succumbed; Ellen too had fallen under his spell; he would have had few qualms as he awaited the final onslaught.

Directed from the Hotel Meurice, and accompanied by Mr Grimsditch and Ellis, the Bow Street Runner, Ellen's uncles were accosted by their quarry as they entered the courtyard. Promptly taking charge, Edward Gibbon led Mr Grimsditch and Ellen's uncle, Robert Turner, to his room, where he requested a hearing before taking them to Ellen. It soon became apparent, however, that Mr Turner's emissaries were not to be deflected and would prove implacable adversaries: Grimsditch, the skilled lawyer and servant, and Robert Turner, avenging brother, determined to wrest his niece and sole heir from this 'ruthless ravisher'. Edward Gibbon, warned only moments earlier by his friend Percy of their intentions, sought to defuse the situation. Taking the initiative he informed them calmly that he understood legal proceedings had been instigated against him, yet he was unable to conceal his agitation when Ellis, the Bow Street Runner, suddenly entered. Dismissing Ellis, Grimsditch demanded that they be allowed to see Ellen, warning Edward Gibbon that the 'strongest measures' would be taken against him and, with a flourish, producing the warrant and despatch from Canning, declaring that the act committed was

> a very atrocious one, that he had taken away Miss Turner, a mere child by means of a forged letter, that he had struck a blow at the peace of the family, the effects of which he never could repair; that I thought it would be the death of Mrs. Turner, if she were not dead already; and that we had left Mr. Turner in London broken-hearted, and unable to go another yard after his lost child.

In his view, concluded Grimsditch, Edward Gibbon 'deserved to be shot'.[16]

Sensing the growing strength of the opposition when Ellen's other uncle Henry Critchley joined them, Edward Gibbon had recourse to all his skill and experience as His Majesty's diplomat and resumed the offensive. He assured Grimsditch that he would not attempt to justify his conduct; he had a daughter of his own, and if any man were 'to take her off in the same manner, he would send a bullet through his head'. Grimsditch countered that his actions were illegal; under British law his marriage was void, and as a consequence he was liable to be severely punished. Dismissing any attempt by Edward Gibbon to discuss the matter further, he asserted that they would take Miss Turner home: 'take her back we will.' Having delivered this *coup de grâce*, Grimsditch left the room, while Critchley, no longer able to contain himself, angrily demanded to know 'what had induced him to commit so cruel an act as to carry away so young a child, whom he had never seen'.[17] Quite unabashed, Edward Gibbon informed Critchley that although he had never met Ellen, he knew a great deal about her due to his close connections with the family of Dr Davies of Macclesfield – she had frequently been the subject of their conversations and he had heard that 'she was a fine girl, with a very large fortune'. To the astonishment of Critchley, he continued that he was 'determined to possess himself of her', adding that, 'he had never attempted anything that he did not accomplish'.[18] Critchley then demanded that they see Ellen immediately and 'without restraint', betraying his fear that Edward Gibbon may have exerted his considerable charm and influence on his inexperienced and impressionable niece. Sensing this, Edward Gibbon, anxious to reassure them that they would not find her unduly influenced, assured them that although Ellen might think favourably of him, it was nothing compared to the 'unabounded affection she felt for her parents' – 'I dare say she will fly to you, and from me, when she sees you',[19] he concluded.

To render his words credible, and mindful of the illness of Ellen's mother and the distress of her father, Edward Gibbon realised that he must agree to Ellen's return to England. Since her liberators rejected his wish to be present when they met Ellen, Edward Gibbon begged them 'not to give her a bad opinion of him'.[20] Still confident that the marriage might continue, he asked them not to reveal any details which might jeopardise its future success, urging that 'it would be expedient to withhold them for her sake'.[21] Though unmoved by this disingenuous plea, they nevertheless agreed that he could see Ellen after they had spoken to her. Immediately he went to Madame Quillac's room to fetch her and conduct her upstairs to meet her uncles, while he and Grimsditch remained outside. Anxious to reassure Mr Grimsditch, Edward Gibbon then promised him that the marriage had not been consummated, stressing, 'Miss Turner is the same Miss Turner she was when I took her away'. Initially relieved but disinclined to accept the word of such an unscrupulous deceiver, Grimsditch joined his associates in Ellen's room where he found the party 'in a state of considerable distress and anxiety'. Ellen was understandably bewildered, unable to comprehend the facts which her uncles had just presented to her. However, when Grimsditch told her that she was not married, her reactions – distinctly at odds with Edward Gibbon's perception of their relations – was one of apparent joy and relief. She threw herself into the arms of her uncles and cried, 'Thank God for that. Oh he is a brute, he has deceived me and I never called anyone a brute before.'[22] Her uncles declared themselves quite overcome by their niece's reaction to the news that not only was she the victim of a callous deception, but furthermore the man in whose company she had spent the past eight days was not in fact her husband, but a charlatan. It is difficult to ascertain the true state of Ellen's feelings when she learned of Edward Gibbon Wakefield's deception. If his account of their relationship is to be believed – and judging by Ellen's behaviour, although there had been early occasions of anxiety, she appeared to have settled happily into her new role – the fact of his deception must have been truly shocking. 'Oh he is a brute, he has deceived me', are the words not of someone brought to safety but rather of one brought to the painful realisation of an unpalatable truth.

Some fifteen minutes later, the group's composure regained, Grimsditch sent for Edward Gibbon. 'We find that you have practised upon this poor child the most extraordinary deception ever heard of.' Not only would he return Ellen to England, but he would place Gibbon in the custody of Ellis, the Bow Street Runner who would convey him to England also. Edward Gibbon, who by then had had time to regain his wits and composure, was quick to point out that he was 'on the wrong side of the water for that'. Undeterred, Grimsditch assured him that the French police would assist their cause; whereupon Edward Gibbon countered that the gendarmerie would more readily assist him in ensuring that his wife remained with him in France. With a triumphant flourish, Grimsditch then produced both the despatch from Canning and the warrant for his arrest. Unabashed, Edward Gibbon replied calmly and, as it turned out, correctly, 'that the warrant could not be enforced in France'. 'You may know the law of England, but I understand international law better than you do.' Considerably discomposed Grimsditch blustered that he would arrest him, 'right or wrong'.[23] There then ensued a war of words between the two:

Grimsditch invoking the authority of the statutes of Philip & Mary and Henry VII which imposed a severe penalty for abduction, Edward Gibbon rejoining that in law Ellen was his rightful wife. Critchley protested vehemently against the legality of the marriage, whereupon Ellen, speaking for the first time in the presence of the unmasked Edward Gibbon, said, 'I am not your wife. I will never go near you again. You have deceived me.' She promptly threw her arms around her uncle's neck 'in a sort of wild agitation' and added, 'I will go with my uncles'.[24] These are the words of a 'woman scorned', certainly not those of an abducted schoolgirl. By all accounts their marriage had been followed by a honeymoon period, albeit unconsummated. How revealing were her words – 'I am not your wife. I will never go near you again. You have deceived me'; are words of regret, not relief.

Reassured and emboldened by his niece's declaration, Critchley vowed that he would only 'part with her with his life'. Grimsditch, determined not to be outmanoeuvred by this Ulysses, reminded Edward Gibbon that a marriage contracted by force was illegal, and, knowing that Edward Gibbon had moved in the best society, asserted he could not be ignorant of the laws of his own country. Edward Gibbon strongly refuted this but the equally shrewd Grimsditch retaliated, reminding him that he had 'got possession of her by means of a forged letter, and carried her away, a mere child by deception and fraud, from beginning to end, and hurried her off in a carriage and four that so young a child could not resist', and had 'great power over her', adding once more that Edward Gibbon deserved to be shot. Executing a timely volte-face, Edward Gibbon enthusiastically reiterated that he 'believed that he too should have shot the man who had taken his daughter, unless reflection at the moment had restrained his passion',[25] adding cogently that Ellen was returned to them 'a pure and spotless virgin'.[26] Undaunted, Grimsditch the lawyer declared in his most lordly fashion that 'he would parley no longer'.[27] Accompanied by an interpreter, he straightaway sought out the Mayor of Calais, leaving Ellen in the care of her uncles. On his departure, seeking to offer some comfort to Ellen's unhappy uncles, or perhaps hoping to gain their favour for his enterprise, Edward Gibbon solicitously invited them to follow him to their niece's bedchamber, assuring them that it was the first time he had entered it. When asked by Robert Turner whether he would have any objection to confirming in writing that Ellen remained unsullied, Edward Gibbon readily agreed, turning the request to his own advantage by answering, 'not in the slightest, if you think it will be a comfort to Mr and Mrs Turner'.[28] There was then further 'desultory conversation' about arresting Edward Gibbon, while he, knowing that this was now out of the question, offered to accompany them to London on condition that bail was arranged for him. Since such an assurance was hardly forthcoming, Edward Gibbon declined to return to England immediately. However, he assured Critchley and Turner that he would travel there very soon to 'meet manfully though submissively the worst consequences of what he had done'.[29]

Upon the departure of Ellen and her uncles for England, the silver-tongued Edward Gibbon Wakefield, thwarted by the assumed deafness of the implacable Grimsditch and unable to accept that 'his prize was entirely lost', was obliged to launch an alternative offensive – no man embodied so neatly the epithet, 'the pen is mightier than the sword'. Scripting what he considered an invincible argument for the preservation of his marriage to Ellen, Edward Gibbon in his second letter to Mr Turner sought to bend him to his will. Hoping to disarm the injured father, he threw himself upon his mercy, entreating him to attach no blame to his daughter in respect of their marriage, and fully accepting responsibility for the pain and injury he had caused her family. He professed that his overriding desire throughout had been to secure the love and happiness of his daughter, and as a father himself of a young daughter, he understood the pain his actions must have occasioned. Moreover, he did not seek release from the consequences of his behaviour nor did he resent the measures already taken against him nor those that might assail him in the future. Well aware that Mr Turner was probably still too angry to entertain a single positive thought towards him, he begged him to ascertain from those who had known him for years how well he had performed the duties of a husband to his late wife; he was convinced that such information would furnish incontrovertible proof of his capacity to make Ellen happy. Edward Gibbon reluctantly acknowledged the fact, put to him so forcefully by Robert Turner and Henry Critchley, that only an Act of Parliament could decide the legality of the marriage. All too conscious of Turner's determination to prove the marriage illegal, Edward Gibbon exhorted the father to consider whether this would be the best course of action to ensure his daughter's future happiness, convinced as he was that Ellen had accepted him as her husband. He assured her father that his treatment of Ellen had been 'punctiliously delicate'; not only had he abstained from enjoying the rights of a husband, taking not even 'the slightest liberty with her person',[30] but even their conversation would not be deemed 'unfitting from a brother to a sister'.[31] No doubt quite confident of the power of his prose, Edward Gibbon boldly concluded his letter:

> There is one subject which I hardly dare to mention; it is the state of Mrs Turner's health, of which today I received so lamentable account; but I will not harass you with expressions of regret and anxiety on her account. They would be worse than thrown away. Begging you to believe in the respect which your affliction obtains from me.[32]

It was a cogent argument, and one which could be fully substantiated: despite the scandalous manner of his abduction of Ellen, and the subsequent deceit employed to persuade her to the altar, he had remained in many ways a man of honour: *Sans peur et sans reproche; integer vitae scelerisque purus* [a pure life free of wickedness].

8

A Wife but Not a Wife

'They took off her ring and gave it to me. I shall preserve it carefully; they should have thrown it away.'[1] Edward Gibbon Wakefield was not discouraged, for already, within the brief space of eight days, he had taken, wedded and persuaded Ellen to love him – or so it would seem. Now, safe in the knowledge that ten years previously his former wife Eliza and her irate mother and uncles had all succumbed to his powers of persuasion, he probably never doubted that he would re-possess himself of his young bride and gain the consent and, moreover, the co-operation of her doting parents.

Before preparing to depart for Paris where he would be reunited with his children, and with a need both to rationalise the events of the last few hours and to acquaint his brother with its details, Edward Gibbon wrote to William of the arrival of Ellen's uncles with a warrant for his arrest. He recounted how, frustrated by their inability to return him to English shores, they had left with Ellen, and how he had assured them that as soon as he had seen his children and settled his affairs, he would return to England to face any charges. 'The grand question is, is the marriage legal. They said, no, and quoted the statutes of William and Mary upon me, till I was tired of their Majesties' names.' He confessed to William that the whole proceedings had been hostile, and although he could easily have escaped with Ellen, he had been reluctant to do so because of the extreme distress of Mr and Mrs Turner. He owned that he was 'in a stew'[2] about William's situation, hoping that he was safe. That the law could punish them, he was in no doubt, but although he would meet it, come what may, he prayed that his brother would get away as soon as possible, warning him not to say anything to anybody, but to leave all communication to him.

Doubtless, it was with great satisfaction that Ellen's uncles snatched her from Calais, and the 'insidious grasp of the conspiring and perfidious ravisher'.[3] Whether Ellen shared their feelings can only be surmised. She would have been overjoyed to learn that not only was her father's future secure, but it had, in fact, never been in jeopardy; however, the discovery of the perfidy of her hitherto charming deliverer, and dear husband, must have been a bitter blow. The 'honeymoon' was over; Ellen was no longer a cherished wife but the child victim of a cunning and heartless conspiracy. It is clear that during her adventure with Edward Gibbon she had been quite unaware that she was the subject of the 'foulest calumny'.[4] Moreover, had she at any time felt unsafe or unhappy there had been numerous opportunities for her to seek assistance, 'In the packet going to Calais, a whisper, a look, a sigh would have roused the gallantry of all the male passengers of a chivalrous age'.[5]

Within forty-eight hours of Sir Richard Birnie issuing the warrant for Edward Gibbon's arrest, Ellen was in Bow Street. From there, she was hurried back to Shrigley to be reunited with her distraught parents. Despite the passing of only a few days, news of this 'calumny' had already appeared in the press. On the very day Ellen was restored to her parents, the *Manchester Courier* reported the abduction, describing her as 'the fair inamorata . . . just fifteen years old'. The piece continued, 'that a child should be carried off in open day from the protection of her instructress, by a man of upwards of forty years of age [he was in fact thirty years of age], may appear singular to the unlearned in ladies' schools'.[6] Restored by the return of his daughter, and the consequent improvement in his wife's health, William Turner's innate strength and resolve returned also. Ever a man to be reckoned with, he would now prove a formidable adversary for the adept Mr Wakefield. On receipt of Edward Gibbon's second ingratiating communication, Turner responded by obtaining a warrant against him for capital felony, promptly meeting the local magistrates to secure the best means of bringing him back to England to face charges. One of those magistrates was Thomas Legh of Lyme Hall, whose estates adjoined those of Shrigley and who was to prove a good friend and ally to William Turner.

In France, Edward Gibbon journeyed to his home in Paris, where he had, at the time of the abduction, resided with his two children for several years, although it is not clear whether he still held a diplomatic posting. In 1823, three years prior to the abduction, Sir Charles Stuart had asked for him to be attached to the Paris embassy, and there is evidence that he was a second in a duel fought in the French capital that year. The same year his father had written that his son's ambition was still to enter English politics:

> In all probability you will see both me and Edward [Gibbon] members of the next Parliament. His suit will I hope be determined by the course of a few months and parliamentary office one of his first objects. He will go into support Mr Canning with the full expectation of holding a considerable official situation.[7]

Left in the care of their governess, Nina and Edward Jerningham had been told of their new stepmother by Mrs Bathurst, a loyal friend of their father's, to whom he had written seeking her support and protection for his young bride when he should bring her to Paris. Without delay, Mrs Bathurst had made arrangements with the children's governess for the reception of the newly-weds, and at her instigation the children prepared flowers and nosegays for their young stepmother.

Phyllida Bathurst was a colourful and prominent member of the fashionable set in Paris, to which Edward Gibbon, his brother William and stepmother Frances Davies belonged. The stepdaughter of the Bishop of Norwich, she was the widow of Benjamin Bathurst, a British diplomat who had mysteriously disappeared in Brandenburg seventeen years previously, having stepped behind the horses of his carriage, never to be seen again! Bizarre as this account may seem, it was yet further embroidered by Mrs Bathurst who was much given to over-elaboration of her oft-recounted tales. Her husband, she would claim, was 'supposed to have been murdered by Bonaparte'.[8] As if to teach her a lesson for her self-indulgence, fate had dealt her a second blow that needed no embellishment: her nineteen-year-old daughter had drowned in Rome two years previously, while riding with her uncle by the river. However, these tragedies seem not to have impeded Mrs Bathurst's social life, but rather had enabled her to become somewhat of a free spirit in the idle and stylish circle of the French capital. Furthermore, Mrs Bathurst was a close friend of Algernon Percy, who had been intimate with her deceased sister, referred to by Edward Gibbon as 'Percy's mare'. Losing her eldest daughter in such tragic circumstances might well have inclined Mrs Bathurst to adoption of the Wakefield brothers, developing her talents as a self-styled mother and matchmaker. In the gilded salon of her large house in the Rue Royale, she would hold court, sipping chocolate from a dainty cup, with Lucille, daughter of the French Minister of the Interior, indulging her talent for both gossip and matchmaking. According to Harriet, daughter of Georgiana, Duchess of Devonshire, and wife of the British Ambassador in Paris, 'the climate of Paris was . . . propitious for getting husbands'.[9]

Mrs Bathurst's own attachment, particularly to William, the younger Wakefield brother, is evident in the letter she wrote to him while awaiting the arrival of Edward Gibbon and his new bride. Addressing him as 'My dearest little Willy O', she assured him that she felt 'quite equal to the office of mother towards you, whenever you choose to claim it'. Her involvement in the abduction is clear:

I am fain to confess a more audacious rape of a second Helen no Paris ever undertook. Pity his name was not John – as Jean de Paris might have eloped with this modern Helen and sound better . . . little did I think when we laughed with Miss Davies about Miss Turner and I desired her to get her for you or him, that Edward [Gibbon] would in 2 or 3 days time woo, wed and carry her off, but he is born for odd adventures and certainly had he been a general would have carried everything by *des coups de main*.[10]

A social butterfly she may well have been, but her summing up of Edward Gibbon reveals an astuteness belying the careless and ostensibly superficial lifestyle they apparently shared. Her pleasure in the success of their questionable enterprise, and Edward Gibbon's consequent 'bona fide' marriage to 'a young creature, whose education mental and corporal [would] occupy and attach him',[11] reveals her underlying concern for Edward Gibbon's future happiness. It is tempting to regard Phyllida Bathurst's interest and involvement in the venture as feckless, those of a woman in pursuit of mischief and amusement: but it is clear that this would be ungenerous. Her letter signifying her concern for the brothers' welfare, while relishing the romantic developments in their lives, showed her sensible to the mundane yet essential needs that accompanied their enterprise.

> People in love and their servants must eat must be clothed and housed . . . daily money must be forthcoming to pay for all these vulgar attributes of humanity. . . . My mother used to say when poverty walked in at the door love flew out of the window and romantic as I am I am forced to confess, there is truth in this adage or proverb trite and narrow minded as it seems *que voulez vous mon cheri, nous sommes faites pour cela*.[12]

Nevertheless, Mrs Bathurst could not resist chiding William for failing to apprise her of the outcome of his visit to Shrigley to inform Mr Turner of his daughter's sudden marriage, adding how impatient they all were to meet Edward Gibbon's new wife and to hear news of their father's love affair with Frances Davies. 'You are a most loyal family at the shrine of the saffron coloured mantled god',[13] she tells him. Although Phyllida Bathurst's letter was essentially solicitous, it was still a fine example of her penchant for the *chronique scandaleuse*. Revelling in her responsibility as chaperone to the young Emily Sidney, daughter of Sir John Sidney of Penshurst, cousin of the poet Percy Bysshe Shelley and great-niece of Thomas Coke of Holkham, Earl of Leicester, the agricultural reformer, Mrs Bathurst scolded William for his neglect of his bride elect. Emily, alone once more in Paris, awaiting her bridegroom, was earnestly seeking her father's consent to the marriage. In a state of great anxiety and distress she had spent each day with Mrs Bathurst, who had grown increasingly fond of her – 'the more I see her the better she pleases me'. Mrs Bathurst had noted a certain ambivalence in Sir John towards his daughter's forthcoming marriage, but was hopeful that once it had taken place he would support his daughter and her new husband.

Ironically, as Mrs Bathurst was completing her 'volume' of scandal and speculation for her 'little son',[14] across the Channel in Reading the miscreant's father had been equally presumptious, announcing that he had come into a great fortune, consequent upon his son's alliance with a great heiress. Edward Wakefield, in his role as the anti-constitutional parliamentary candidate for

Reading, had, in consequence, attended a special meeting in the Bear Inn where one Blackall Simonds had proposed Edward Wakefield's adoption on the grounds of his 'strong personal and moral qualities'. According to *The Times* of 21 March, the meeting then descended into 'one of those jolly festivities known to take place in Ireland on the forcible matrimony of some young woman of fortune'.[15] Both Edward Wakefield and Mrs Bathurst were to be gainsaid. At that very moment Lord Granville, the British Ambassador to Paris, was writing to his French counterpart, the Baron de Damas, requesting the help of the French government in apprehending Edward Gibbon Wakefield, who was now believed to have remained in Paris. Advising the Baron that the 'alleged circumstances of the case' were 'most extraordinary',[16] he requested every assistance in bringing Edward Gibbon to trial, following with a letter to Canning acknowledging receipt of a warrant for the arrest of Edward Gibbon Wakefield and other papers regarding his 'nefarious transaction'.[17] Meanwhile, in London *The Times* reported, with undisguised delight, that the celebrations at Reading had been premature:

> We learnt by an evening paper of Saturday, that the affair which had given occasion to so much joy, was a cruel case of abduction; the child who was carried off being only 15 years of age; the father of the intended bridegroom himself, with too great rapidity, published the account of his son's supposed marriage in the Reading paper.[18]

The newspaper concluded by asking its readers if any knew which of the Wakefields had 'made a similar attempt, with better success, on the person of Miss Pattle, and what the Lord Chancellor said on that occasion'.[19]

On the morning of Thursday 23 March 1826, fifteen days after Edward Gibbon and Ellen had been married at Gretna, William Wakefield and Emily Sidney were married by the chaplain, Mr Forster, in the chapel of the British Embassy in Paris. Only three years previously, and in the same chapel, William's father Edward had secretly wed Frances Davies, daughter of the headmaster of Macclesfield School. Algernon Percy, now British Ambassador to the Swiss Cantons, Edward Gibbon's former employer and patron, had joined Mrs Bathurst in giving the bride away. Immediately after the service, William applied for a British passport which would enable him to travel back to England with Emily and, alarmed by the embassy's refusal to issue him one, promptly wrote to Granville seeking an explanation. Conceiving that the objection may have arisen from a fear that he might transfer the passport to his brother Edward Gibbon, William pledged that it would be for the sole purpose of taking his new wife to England. He was dismayed, therefore, to receive Granville's categorical refusal: 'I am sorry that I feel it to be my duty, until better informed than I am at present of circumstances in which your name is involved, to decline giving you a passport.'[20]

Granville must have felt justified in taking so firm a stand, for on the same day he received a letter from Canning in which the Foreign Secretary expressed his dismay at receiving intelligence of Algernon Percy's 'unjustifiable interference in the protection of Mr Wakefield'.[21] He was instructed to inform Percy that His Majesty's government demanded that he instantly withdraw this protection from Edward Gibbon Wakefield. Included in Canning's communication were letters from William Turner and Thomas Legh which gave details of the whole sorry affair. The following day, Viscount Granville wrote again to Canning explaining his reasons for refusing William Wakefield a passport. As the affidavit issued by Sir Richard Birnie implicated William in his brother's abduction of Ellen Turner, Granville assumed a warrant would follow for the arrest of William; however, since this failed to materialise, he no longer felt justified in withholding the passport William demanded.

While those in Paris remained embroiled in the machinations of French and British diplomacy, in Britain the national press and those who would use it as a vehicle for their polarised comment were engaged in their favourite pastime, a national scandal, one which was to entertain the public for many months to come. The Shrigley abduction was every editor's wildest dream, a story that would run and run; its impetus increased by satirists, pamphleteers and its fascination for the public at large. *John Bull*, deliberating on the initial stories appearing in the British press, commented:

During the last week the newspapers have been crammed with accounts of what is called the ABDUCTION of a MISS TURNER, and

The Times, not content with giving a yard and a half of the history, calls public attention to it as something very interesting.[22]

Not surprisingly, attention focused initially on the schoolgirl victim, with various accounts of her beauty, health, wealth and intellect. The *Sun* carried a piece describing her as 'beautiful though of very delicate health', claiming that she was the 'heiress of not only her father's immense property but also that of her three rich uncles'.[23] Not to be outdone in the provision of 'insider information', *The Times* declared that 'it had been hinted that Miss Turner's intellects are not of the strongest kind'.[24] This affront was swiftly countered by a William Broderick whom, it appeared, had met Ellen when she was taken to Bow Street after her rescue from Calais. The following day in a letter to *The Times* Broderick stated that he was 'authorized by an immediate relative of Mrs Daulby, of Liverpool in saying, she "was considered a quick clever girl" and to this I add the testimony of my own observation . . . I am aware the turpitude of the offender's guilt would be only increased by the forgoing assumption; but I think it due to her that the fact should be put forth'.[25] Later that month, and perhaps in part to make amends for their previous derogatory comments, in an apparent volte-face, *The Times* described Ellen 'as a lady of quick and natural talents and no pains have been spent of their cultivation'.[26] The scandal was eagerly followed by the provincial papers too. In Westmorland the public was informed by the *Gazette* 'that Miss Turner a young lady . . . of more than ordinary attractions both of purse and person' was the richest heiress in the kingdom, her father 'the possessor of property, if general report is at all to be relied on, to the amount of more than 1 million pounds sterling'.[27] Opinions were divided as to whether Edward Gibbon and Ellen had been previously acquainted, the *Chester Chronicle* asserting that, contrary to one report, the couple had not met in Harrogate before the abduction, while the *Manchester Guardian* carried a letter from a Mr J. Collier.

Sir, – Various statements have been put forward in public prints, relative to the elopement of Edward Gibbon Wakefield with Miss Turner, the following facts may be relied on. It is not true as stated that Mr Wakefield was a stranger to Miss Turner, previous to the transaction which now occupies the public attention, he having met her at an assembly in Liverpool prior to the elopement and in proof that neither force nor coercion were used on the part of Mr Wakefield to the young lady in question is evident from the circumstance of their having been discovered arm in arm together on the pier in Calais on the arrival of Mr Turner and Mr Taunton, the police officer.[28]

The more erudite members of the public debated the pros and cons of the validity of the Gretna Green marriage. On the same day that Ellen's champion, Broderick, defended her intellect in a letter to *The Times*, W.R. challenged them:

Sir, – In your interesting account of the abduction of Miss Turner, in yesterday's paper you have been misled by your authority on a point of Scotch law, which, by the by, the less you, or he, or any civilized being knows, the better . . . now it is well known to every one acquainted with the Scotch law, that females who have completed their twelfth year may enter into the holy state of matrimony. . . . There can be no doubt, however, that the marriage between Miss Turner and Mr Wakefield is not valid, because, even by the Scotch law, barbarous as it is, to constitute a marriage the consent must be freely and voluntarily given.[29]

In the days and months to come, this vexed question would be contested in homes, taverns, coffee-houses, gentlemen's clubs and courts – even in the House of Lords itself.

In Paris, Edward Gibbon was not slow to respond to 'the various accounts and statements'[30] which had appeared in the copies of British newspapers he had received. On Sunday 26 March, Edward Gibbon Wakefield, the accomplished wordsmith, carefully constructed a letter intended for publication in all the daily papers. He asserted that all the accounts respecting him and Mr Turner's daughter must have emanated from the same source. Furthermore, he could not believe that Mr Turner could have sanctioned them or would have exposed his daughter to the ignominy and distress of such public comments: many of the accounts 'as far from the truth as they could be, without being wholly untrue – and many of them utterly false'.[31] In his present situation, he was not able to furnish any detailed replies to the allegations, all too aware that a man who was out of the country, and 'threatened with a serious prosecution, might be represented, and libelled with impunity'.[32] Furthermore, motives of delicacy regarding Mr Turner and his daughter prevented him from publishing anything without first submitting it for their consideration. Edward Gibbon went on to claim that he had only left England after his marriage to attend to a serious engagement in France, and not because he was afraid; he made it clear that he was fully prepared to return to England to face any charges William Turner might wish to level against him.

His stepmother, Frances Davies, wrote on the same day to Randall, the servant at her husband's home in London, at 34 Pall Mall, asking him to write to her at Buxton where she was spending a few days 'taking the waters'. She was most anxious to know whether her stepson William had arrived back in England and alarmed to discover that a warrant had been issued for his arrest, and that consequently a search might be made of her husband's property in Pall Mall. Though concerned for the safety and welfare of her stepsons, Frances Davies' enthusiasm for the conspiracy now appeared to be waning. Having played a substantial role in the initial planning and preparation of their undertaking, she now appeared fearful of the consequences of what had at first seemed a *coup de foudre* [love at first sight]. Frances' fears were to be confirmed as the proceedings instigated by William Turner moved inexorably forward. Once particulars of the abduction had been formally lodged before the magistrates, warrants were issued for the arrest of Edward Gibbon and William Wakefield on a charge of capital felony. Endorsed by Sir Richard Birnie of Bow Street, they were transmitted to Taunton, the Bow Street Runner in Paris, who was waiting to receive and execute them.

The future was darkening perceptibly for the Wakefield brothers as the press continued to revel in the notoriety of this heinous and seemingly indefensible crime. On the very day that the warrants were lodged with Taunton, who was now in Dover, *John Bull* mischievously wooed its readership with a scurrilous account of the abduction:

Now let common sense try this very interesting affair – a MISS TURNER, worth a million of money sterling, is put out to a seminary for young ladies at LIVERPOOL, to polish her up for the Peerage, to which she is fully entitled, according to the scale of the marriage market. To this school a MR WAKEFIELD – who probably had been led into the pursuit by seeing chalked upon the walls, 'TRY TURNER' – goes in a post-chaise and four, and sends in a message, that MISS TURNER'S Mama had had some sort of stroke, and that he is come to fetch her daughter home – into which carriage, after MISS TURNER has told the schoolmistress that it is not 'Pa's chay', and that she never saw the gentleman who is in it before, the said MISS TURNER is packed. MR WAKEFIELD gallops her about for a certain length of time, and then gallops her to Scotland, where he marries her, and then gallops off to France, and writes to the family from Calais an account of the whole affair.

They, like the FRENCH GENTLEMAN in the story, whose hair came a little through his hat, take a minute or two 'to consider what they shall do', and at last, and after the lapse of a week or ten days, consult that most excellent magistrate SIR RICHARD BIRNIE, who sends off some Bow Street Officers and the girl's uncle to Calais where they find her walking up and down the Pier, arm in arm with her husband.

The minute she sees her uncle she screams out, 'There's uncle – Oh, I'm so glad to see you; take me away from this man I can't bear him,' and back she comes. MR WAKEFIELD making his bow and declaring her a 'pure and spotless virgin'!

Now mark all this – pretty MISS TURNER (and a gentleman of the name of BRODERICK of Bow Churchyard, has volunteered a letter in all the papers to prove that she is no fool) did not the least care about being run away with; for if she had, by speaking to the landlady of the first inn at which she had gone up stairs to put her curls to right, or tie her shoe-strings, or doing anything else she wanted to do, explained the real state of the case, the ravisher in the post-chaise would have been laid by the heels in a twinkling . . . even in Calais itself, her appeal to the high feelings of the French cavaliers would instantly have rescued her from the grip of her persecutor – but No, there she was, walking up and down the pier, hoping something more agreeable would turn up than had yet appeared; and having tried MR WAKEFIELD for a week or ten days, and finding him beyond *our* fancy stupid, and far beyond *her* conception dull, she bounds away from him at the first sight of her uncle a 'pure and spotless virgin', after being married half a honeymoon, and begs to be taken away from the man she does not love.

We are very glad she is well rid of such a thing; but we confess we see nothing either interesting or romantic in the affair, but a good deal of *naivete* on one side and an uncommon quantity of stupidity on the other.[33]

On Tuesday 28 March, only five days after his marriage to Emily Sidney, William Wakefield landed in Dover, where he was immediately taken into custody by Taunton, assisted by Barrett, the deputy constable of Stockport. Meanwhile the well-meaning if exceedingly optimistic Mrs Bathurst had written to Mrs Turner, 'merely as one mother to another', to plead Edward Gibbon's cause, to express her 'astonishment and mortification' at the 'unexpected termination of his nuptials' and her 'indignation at the calumnies which [had] appeared in the public prints'. Commiserating with Ellen's mother, she expressed her deep concern and empathy with the 'anxious suspense' the lady endured 'while ignorant of the fate of her child', hastening to console her with affirmation of the character of her son-in-law.

Mr Wakefield made the most devoted and affectionate husband, and never was a Lady happier in marriage than his first wife . . . and his two children now under my care are quoted in all circles of Paris as models of good and correct Education, his talents are very superior, his heart the best I have ever met with, and as a real steady disinterested friend I have had occasion to know his inestimable value. And allow me to add that I am by no means singular in my opinion of him, there are many most highly respectable people who think in the same manner.[34]

To crown her glowing reference to Edward Gibbon's character, Mrs Bathurst added that 'had Mr Wakefield selected my one and only child as the partner of his life I should have been perfectly contented and have esteemed her a most fortunate woman'. She exhorted Mrs Turner: 'Be noble, be generous; give him your daughter or allow him to try and gain her and your affections.' She concluded with an extract from a letter Edward Gibbon had sent her on his arrival in Calais with Ellen; she made the point that as this letter was certainly never designed to be read by Mrs Turner, it must surely prove Edward Gibbon's honourable intentions.

> If her parents are reconciled towards our union, I shall have nothing to desire; but if on the contrary they are inexorable, I shall look upon myself as doubly bound by honour, affection and gratitude to be her fond protector through life, and in supplying to her those ties I have severed her from, never give her cause to repent the sudden and even rash step I have caused her to take in my favour.

In conclusion, Mrs Bathurst pointed out that she, and having herself suffered the loss of a daughter could share Mrs Turner's distress, must value Mr Wakefield highly 'to take an interest in his fate.'[35]

In Paris, her protégé had been furnished with a more influential ally – the French government; the 'cruel and unprincipled conduct of [Edward Gibbon] Wakefield' had seemingly made little impression upon Baron Damas. Granville, in his letter to Canning of 31 March, informed him that he had received a decided refusal to his application for assistance, and was 'induced to think that the want of reciprocity will always be urged, as creating an insuperable objection to the delivering up of any British Subject, who [has] offended against the Laws of his own Country'.[36]

Throughout his life Edward Gibbon Wakefield's 'undertakings, both public and private', it was said, 'suffered from his refusal to recognize difficulties patent to any ordinary man'.[37] Now, he was faced with the choice of remaining in France with his children, albeit in exile; or returning to England, in the hope of reclaiming his young wife, together with her father's fortune and influence, and an entrée into public life.

9

A Master Passion is the Love of News

Two days after his arrest in Dover, William Wakefield was borne into Stockport by a coach, named, ironically, *Defiance*. It was a somewhat subdued William, who had left behind in Paris his distraught young wife, exchanging the comforts, pleasures and cultured coterie of the French capital for the cramped and fetid conditions of the New Bailey. Incarcerated in the lock-up on Dungeon's Brow he found himself companion to a sordid assortment of miserable wretches: rogues and vagabonds, swindlers and debtors, cut-purses and poachers. At ten o'clock the following morning, Friday 31 March, William was taken before the magistrates at the Ram's Head, Disley, a small town at the gates of Thomas Legh's estate, some thirteen miles north-east of Macclesfield, on the Derbyshire border. Legh, who had issued the warrant for William's arrest, now sat alongside his fellow magistrates, George William Newton and Salusbury Pryce Humphreys, in the back room of the inn set aside by William Hancock, the landlord. To everyone's surprise the prisoner was a genteel-looking young man of 'a somewhat foreign appearance',[1] apparently not much more than twenty-one years of age. His vulnerability seemed at odds with the charges against him. That he was alone and unsupported and without professional assistance reinforced this impression; but this would not save him from the wrath of Mr Turner.

The arrival of William Turner and his daughter, accompanied by their solicitor Thomas Grimsditch, unnerved the already dispirited and disconsolate William. Defenceless, and indefensible, he could not meet the eyes of the young girl with whom he had disported himself so gaily and in such brotherly fashion but three weeks previously. However, his discomfiture was relieved somewhat by the commotion that accompanied the unexpected entrance of a white-haired old gentleman, who immediately 'begged to apologize to the magistrates for his intrusion'.[2] The sight of his stepmother's aged father, Dr Davies, lifted William's spirits. He was further encouraged by the affirmation of the well-respected headmaster of Macclesfield Grammar School who, while assuring the magistrates that he had not come to interfere with the administration of justice, asserted that he could, from his intimate acquaintance with the family of the prisoner, bear testimony to their respectability, and, if required, offer himself as bail. Only recently had Dr Davies discovered just how intimate was his connection with the Wakefield family – his only daughter Frances had three years earlier become the wife of William's father. Though encouraged by Dr Davies' avowal, the appearance of Ellen, as her written statement was read to her, dismayed William. The vibrant and vocal young woman with whom he had shared that fateful journey seemed now but a chastened child, her small voice heard briefly as she gave her deposition on oath. She reaffirmed her unequivocal denial that she had ever seen William or his brother Edward Gibbon before they had received her at the Albion Hotel in Manchester. While admitting that no force was ever used against her, she nevertheless asserted that she would not have 'consented to accompany Mr Wakefield, or to marry him, had it not been for the artifices practised upon her, and especially the representation of the probable ruin of her father if she refused'.[3]

In support of Ellen's evidence, Thomas Grimsditch then refuted the Wakefield brothers' claim that he, Grimsditch, had been in Carlisle in hiding with Mr Turner on the day of the Gretna marriage, stating that both he and Mr Turner were on that very day attending to business in London. Moreover, he had never met nor spoken to Mr Wakefield in his life before seeing him in Calais on 15 March. William Turner was the last to give evidence, confirming that Ellen was his only child and therefore heir apparent to all his 'real property', testimony which he hoped would bring this case within the statutes which would render the offence capital. As the hearing proceeded, William was forced to confront the magnitude of the crime which he and his brother had committed. Mr Turner's violent accusations culminating in an outburst that William was a villain served to deliver the *coup de grâce*, a charge which, to his credit, the young man accepted with a dignified bow. At this, the magistrates complimented William on the propriety of his demeanour, to which he replied that 'he hoped he did not require to be taught how to behave himself as a gentleman'.[4] The irony of this statement could only have served to further fuel the anger of the already incensed William Turner. Asked whether he had anything to offer in reply to the evidence he had heard, William declined, except to beg that were he to be remanded, he might be brought before them again at the earliest opportunity. The magistrates declined bail, adjourning the hearing to the following Monday, at two o'clock, when it was hoped Elizabeth Daulby, joint proprietress of Ellen's school in Liverpool, would give evidence. When Mr Barratt was summoned to return William to the New Bailey, the magistrates, no doubt impressed by the defendant's demeanour that morning, requested that the deputy constable pay every attention that circumstances allowed to the comfort of his prisoner. Whereupon William thanked the magistrates for their consideration, adding, politically perhaps, that he found himself perfectly satisfied with the accommodation Mr Barratt had provided for him.

While those intimately concerned must have passed a weekend of turmoil and distress, others, not personally involved but deeply interested nevertheless, were busily engaging themselves in the affair's developments – notably the gentlemen of the press and those who would fain see their words in print. One such, William Broderick, the same who had defended the unfortunate Miss Turner in a previous letter to *The Times*, was now determined to 'inculpate parties not hitherto named in the transaction'. Writing to *The Times*, on Saturday 1 April, he stated that William Turner was indebted to him for information he had received which would reveal their involvement in an 'offence in turpidity equal to the blackest in the catalogue of crimes'. Clearly a self-appointed vigilante, Broderick fiercely asserted that 'it is capital felony – and so it ought to be – to steal a black man; and it would be monstrous indeed if the stealing of a white man, in any manner, were considered a venal offence or less in magnitude'. He concluded, 'Mr Turner has not, nor will not leave any stone unturned towards bringing every delinquent to justice'.[5] On the same day, the *Westmorland Gazette* saw fit to ridicule the Turner abduction in this short account:

ANOTHER YOUNG LADY OF 15, STOLEN
One Michael Armstrong has been committed to prison, at York, for stealing a lady, of 15. He took her, however, not from a Boarding-school, but from a Church-yard. The fellow, after all, had more sense than Miss T.'s admirer; he took only the hand of the young lady, whereas Armstrong seized the body. Had Mr W. acted like Michael, perhaps Miss T. would have cast her heart into the bargain.[6]

While William Turner would hardly have taken kindly to such flippant allusions to his daughter's ordeal, there were other suppositions being advanced in the press which he perceived as potentially far more dangerous – notably, one printed by the *Manchester Courier* a week earlier. This newspaper had reprinted an early account of Ellen's ordeal which had first appeared in the *Macclesfield Courier*. In alluding to this extraordinary case, the *Manchester Courier* had referred to it as 'an elopement', intimating at the same time that Ellen may have been party to the deception, and claiming that the official announcement of the marriage in the newspapers supported that assumption. The newspaper had subsequently reported an invasion of their premises by an extremely irate Mr Turner and two friends, possibly Thomas Grimsditch and Robert Turner, demanding the name of the author of this despicable piece.

> The tone and menacing air with which this requisition was preferred were certainly not remarkable for their courtesy and but for the handsome conduct of the gentlemen who accompanied him the enquirer would scarcely have accomplished the object of his visit.

Clearly, while showing some inclination to placate the angry father and ameliorate the family's distress, the paper's proprietors defended their right to protect their author, claiming, 'A person has no more right to walk into our office and demand the names of the authors of articles in our paper than we have to enter a manufacturer's warehouse and insist upon knowing where he got this or that piece of goods'. Furthermore, they reasserted their inability to comprehend how the young lady could have been dragged from Liverpool to Manchester, from Manchester to Gretna Green, and from Gretna Green to Calais, and detained in the custody of her ravisher for the space of about a week, entirely against her own consent, the more especially as we are informed by a Mr Broderick, of Bow Church-yard, London, that she is an acute and intelligent young person.

Though reluctant to give up the offensive, the newspaper sought to safeguard its position by stating that the whole question would no doubt be resolved when Edward Gibbon Wakefield was put on trial, conceding that they believed it to be by no means his first exploit of that kind. Contrary to other reports, they asserted that the runaway marriage was legal under the law of Scotland, which allowed a girl to marry from the age of twelve, although, they concluded, 'this is certainly not the best of Scotch laws'.[7] With this, William Turner had to be content.

As arranged, the examination of William Wakefield continued at two o'clock on Monday 3 April in the Ram's Head, Disley. On this occasion William was represented by an attorney from London, a Mr Harmer, instructed either by his father Edward or his uncle Daniel, a barrister in chambers. To William's relief, Mr Harmer had visited him in the New Bailey after his first appearance before the magistrates. And then there were the witnesses. As if there were not drama enough in this increasingly notorious case, when Miss Elizabeth Daulby and her sister were on their way to Disley, the fore-wheel of their chaise came off on the road between Macclesfield and Stockport, sending it crashing to the ground. Consequently, the horses set off at full speed, galloping out of control and dragging the disabled carriage and its hapless passengers for at least half a mile before striking a post, whereupon the Daulby sisters were released. Astonishingly, they were quite unharmed by their alarming experience. Who knows what the consequences might have been for the prosecution of the Wakefield brothers had the accident proved fatal. Elizabeth Daulby, who was the only witness examined on this occasion, outlined the facts surrounding Ellen's departure from her school. She had had no reason to question the veracity of the letter which requested Ellen's return home; and had been ignorant of the facts of the abduction until she received Margaret Turner's letter. She neither knew nor had heard of either Edward Gibbon or William Wakefield, nor did she believe that they could have seen Ellen in Liverpool. Ellen had made no visits anywhere since her return to school after Christmas, apart from attending church or going out walking with members of her family or friends.

Mr Harmer, while declining to question Miss Daulby, begged to know what course of action the magistrates intended to take. Thomas Grimsditch, who was conducting the case for the prosecution, forcefully submitted that the evidence he had laid before the magistrates fully made out 'the capital offence', and he felt it his duty to call upon them to commit the prisoner for trial on the capital charge. Mr Harmer countered that the offence amounted only to a misdemeanour, as Miss Turner was not heir apparent but only heir presumptive to her father; various contingencies might yet arise to prevent her from inheriting his property, for example, he might still have a son, an event which would prevent her succeeding to the inheritance. After further legal argument, Mr Harmer asked the magistrates to grant William bail; although he did not mean to palliate the case of his client, he contended that any lawyer must know that it was not a felony and therefore a bailable offence.

The *Morning Chronicle*, which had mischievously observed that the examination of William had taken place very appropriately at the '*Ram Inn*', recorded Mr Grimsditch's response to Mr Harmer's submission, claiming that the evidence he had laid before Thomas Legh of Lyme and George William Newton, the presiding magistrates, fully made the offence capital, and he therefore felt it his duty to call upon them to commit the prisoner for trial on that charge. At this point the magistrates left the room and remained for some time in consultation. On their return, the *Morning Chronicle*, unable to resist a further play on words, reported that, Mr Grims-ditch – ('*Grim* Ghosts are howling – Pale death is prowling')[8] was to be disappointed when William was committed for misdemeanour only. However, Mr Harmer was informed that his client would not be granted bail. A warrant of committal to Lancaster Castle was drawn up, and William told that he would be taken there the following morning.

Needless to say, then, as today, the public's desire to know more of the participants in this intriguing drama proved insatiable. William, a presentable youth of medium height, with his mother's fair complexion, was the first on the stage, exciting much interest, apparently of a most favourable kind. He was, it was said, 'a gentlemanly young man', attracting the 'kindest attention from the magistrates as well as from Mr Barratt',[9] his custodian. Moreover, his stature was enhanced by the rumour that he had married the daughter of a baronet only two or three days before his apprehension. Much excitement was engendered by reports that she was related to the poet Percy Bysshe Shelley, and, as the only daughter of Sir John Sidney of Penshurst Place in Kent, would be heir to £8,000 of vested property and a considerable landed estate in the event of her brother dying without issue.

While the young William Wakefield's affairs were increasingly the subject of public curiosity, his father, too, found himself subject to scrutiny. Due to recent events in Reading, where he was a parliamentary candidate on 'the Blue interest', he was now the recipient of publicity, but of a most unwelcome kind. During Edward Wakefield's temporary absence from the constituency, 'virulent' handbills had been distributed throughout the borough, insinuating that he had been a party to 'the gross and revolting deception which is said to have been practised on Miss Turner of Cheshire'.[10] His supporters were most anxious, therefore, that he take steps to disprove the degrading allegations which could injure him not only as a parliamentary candidate, but as a father and a gentleman.

Consequently, upon his return to Reading some 300 gentlemen and a great number of electors assembled to meet him in the White Hart. There, Edward Wakefield was welcomed with resounding cheers, and was soon able to persuade his audience that he had been utterly ignorant of the 'transaction' in question, pledging that he would do everything in his power to give his accusers every opportunity to prove their 'insinuations' – if they could. He demanded that 'the question, with respect to himself in particular, should be most thoroughly investigated, and pledged to entirely cleanse his character which had been so foully assailed, by taking the most strenuous measures to bring his libellers before the constituted tribunals of their country'. While commiserating with William Turner as one who had been 'so cruelly placed by the temporary loss of his daughter', he felt that he could not ignore the extraordinary handbill from the Radical press which purported to be an extract of a letter from 'Mr Turner to a gentleman in Reading'. Edward Wakefield declared politically that he found it hard to believe that a gentleman of Mr Turner's standing, someone who was within days of being invested as High Sheriff of his county, could have been guilty of this 'low and vulgar' onslaught. The handbill claimed that Edward's two sons William and Edward Gibbon had hatched the plot for the abduction at the home of Dr Davies in Macclesfield, who was cited as Edward's future father-in-law. Edward suggested, cogently, that the letter contained in the handbill might well have been a forgery, both clumsy and pointless, for the writer had 'doubtless malice, but [lacked] the wit to enforce it, the depravity of the serpent without its venom or its cunning'.[11] Meanwhile the case was attracting the attention of those more interested in the legal battle than in the combatants, their ammunition the niceties of law; *The Times* carried a letter from a law student who cited the recent repeal of an Elizabethan statute, the consequence of which would mean a person convicted of abduction would face transportation or imprisonment with hard labour for up to seven years.

Alongside his fervent desire to see his daughter's abductors punished was William Turner's determination to ensure that the social disaster which had befallen his beloved child and heir should not in any way detract from either her marriage prospects or her social standing. Indeed, the social implications not only for Ellen but also for himself and his wife Jane could be far reaching. From master of Mill Hill in Blackburn to wealthy industrialist and lately High Sheriff of Cheshire, squire of Shrigley, he had travelled fast and far, and would clearly brook no reversal of his fortunes at the hands of a mere fortune hunter and adventurer. He lost no time instructing his lawyers to instigate a summary process in the Ecclesiastical Court to determine the legality of 'the marriage farce'. In this he was encouraged by the judgment on the validity of the Gretna Green marriage of Sir William Scott: 'marriages on elopement to Gretna Green may be considered valid if the consent of the parties be obtained fairly and without fraud, and the marriage is solemnized according to the forms required by the laws of Scotland.'[12] This precedent, together with emerging details of

Edward Gibbon Wakefield's previous marriage which had come under the spotlight of press scrutiny – the *Morning Chronicle* reporting that he had been 'married to his first wife in very peculiar circumstance'[13] – further encouraged William Turner, who found parallels between the alleged forced union of Eliza Pattle and that of his own daughter. According to newspaper reports, Eliza had been 'a young lady possessing considerable attractions, with a most amiable disposition and handsome fortune',[14] only yielding to Edward Gibbon's entreaties after intense pressure and pursuit. Turner was unlikely to have been impressed by the knowledge that whatever the intent of the wooing of Eliza Pattle, her mother had clearly fallen under the spell of this 'charming adventurer', willingly endorsing the marriage – Edward Gibbon was soon to discover that Ellen's father was to be far less tractable.

William Turner, son of a Lancashire entrepreneur, residing in Blackburn, born in 1776, both the year of the American Revolution and, according to local tradition, the year in which the first piece of calico had been woven in Blackburn, seemed destined to make his fortune in the calico business. His father, Robert Turner, had prospered sufficiently to establish a calico printing works at Mill Hill, which extended along the Darwen valley, a mile southwest of Blackburn, the business to be conducted by his five sons. Thus, in time, both William and his younger brother Robert joined the family firm and at their father's death in 1811 a second large print-works was in operation.

In 1810 William had married his cousin Jane, who at thirty-six was four years his senior. Little more than a year later, their first child Ellen had been born on 12 February 1811. She was closely followed, in June 1812, by Mary Jennet, who died, aged four years and six months, on 17 January 1817, and was buried in the family vault in St John's Church, Blackburn. Although there may have been other pregnancies, Jane Turner's age precluded many more years of childbearing, and Ellen was to be their only surviving child.

It would appear that Mrs Turner did not enjoy good health, although it is difficult to ascertain the exact nature of her ailments; Thomas Grimsditch described her as suffering from an 'attack of paralysis'. In March 1826, a doctor had diagnosed 'a determination of blood to the head',[15] and it is possible that on this occasion she had suffered a mild stroke, although her health had long given her husband cause for concern. In the nineteenth century this condition was popularly known as the 'vapours' or *fabricula*, while later in the century the word neurasthenia was invented to describe an illness characterised by chronic physical and mental exhaustion. Such a condition would obviously be exacerbated by stress such as that Mrs Turner would have experienced at the death of her younger daughter, and to which she was further subjected at the time of Ellen's abduction. However, in view of her age, her symptoms may well have been menopausal. In spite of these difficulties, the marriage of William and Jane appears to have been happy, and in his will William made generous provision for her

> to occupy, use and enjoy my said Mansion House called Shrigley Hall with the gardens, coach houses and stables together with all my furniture therein for and during the term of her natural life and profits of the said estates to pay and allow my said dear wife such annual or other sum or sums of money the Trustees shall think proper and necessary for the support and maintenance of my wife in an establishment at my mansion house, Shrigley, with sufficient money for her to be able to maintain a suitable carriage with two good horses.[16]

Both William and Jane Turner were engaged in charitable works: in 1812, William Turner was one of the fifty-three eminent citizens of Blackburn who met to draw up a resolution for the establishment of the National School, later built in Thunder Alley to promote the education of the infant poor; while Jane Turner is still remembered in Blackburn as the benefactor of almshouses erected at Bank Top in the town in 1834.

By 1818, William Turner's wealth and ambitions were growing. In addition to keeping a house in Parliament Street in London, he had finally acquired a country estate in a prestigious area of Cheshire noted for its abundance of long-established gentry families. Old Shrigley Hall, and its estate of 1700 acres, had been owned by the Downes family for nearly 500 years before it was sold to William Turner for £75,000 by William Downes. The sale was handled by Ryles and Daintree Bank of Macclesfield, who, ironically, were to advance Edward Gibbon's stepmother Frances the money subsequently used to fund the abduction. Shrigley Hall was situated on the edge of the Peak District, in the small village of Pott Shrigley with a population of just over 300, where coal, slate and stone were plentiful, although the appearance of the surrounding countryside was agricultural.

For several years the Turners had lived in the Old Shrigley Hall, enjoying the benefit of the rents from the farm cottages and coal mining, which formed part of the estate. For William Turner, who in the course of one morning could have visited one of the largest mansions in Cheshire, Lyme Hall, seat of Thomas Legh, two and half miles distant, and also Adlington Hall, five miles to the west, it was imperative that he build a suitably impressive mansion to replace the crumbling Old Shrigley Hall. Designed by the architect Thomas Emett the new hall was completed in 1825. Constructed in sandstone, with a porch of towering Ionic columns, it was a large house designed in a neo-classical style, reminiscent of the Wyatts. This 'new modern building, prettily situated on a height', enjoyed spectacular views:

> the scenery of the neighbourhood is magnificent; and the view from the terrace on which the house stands is varied and delightful extending northwardly from the hills of Lancashire, over Bowden Downs, Alderley Edge, and across the bleak expanse of the 'brown Forest', to the heights of Beeston and Broxton, – the scene terminating in the bold perspective of the Clwydian Hills and on a clear day, the town of Manchester could be discerned. The front of the edifice embraces the whole of this view.[17]

If Edward Gibbon Wakefield was to be believed, William Turner had built a fine new house, but not a fine new reputation; in the eyes of his neighbours he remained the Mr Turner who had made his fortune by trade. At Alderley, the home of the Stanleys, cotton magnates from Manchester were known as 'Cottontots', Lady Henrietta Maria complaining that 'they were more annoying as trespassers than the operatives', because 'it was not so easy to handcuff or great dog them'.[18] In his efforts to be 'a country gentleman', William Turner had become the object of jealousy to the old established gentry, and of envy to the many manufacturers of the neighbourhood where he had now settled. They sneered at the 'New Squire', denouncing as bad taste the construction of his new house atop a bleak hillside. Edward Gibbon had defended this decision by wryly observing that William Turner had 'thereby removed himself further from the envy and quite out of the smoke of Macclesfield'.[19] His substitution of the Turner family crest in tin for the ancient weather vane of the village church did little to dampen his neighbours' contempt, simply reinforcing their opinion of Mr Turner as a 'low bred ignorant upstart cursed with purse pride and a most unforgiving and savage temper'.[20] Proof of their abhorrence of the pretentious Mr Turner was a cat, intended as Turner's effigy, which had been gibbeted on his park gate. In fairness to William Turner, these comments from Edward Gibbon had, by his own admission, been gleaned from gossip when he had visited Macclesfield a few days before the abduction, and were set down by him in a statement he gave shortly after his marriage to Ellen Turner. While evidently not reluctant to relay this tittle-tattle, Edward Gibbon nevertheless distanced himself from it, swiftly making the point that 'The Macclesfield School for Scandal and one Sir B. Backbite in particular', found him an unappreciative 'audience for their stale sneers'.[21]

Whether William Turner was aware of the existence of such hostility is doubtful, since there was so much of greater significance at that time to occupy his attention. Although apparently personally unaffected by the downturn in Blackburn's fortunes, nevertheless, only two days after his daughter's abduction he was to learn of the bankruptcy of three calico printers in the town. 'The considerable gloom and despondency felt among the commercial men of the city on account of further failures';[22] the stoning of a market coach by desperate hand-loom weavers displaced by the introduction of machine power; and the presence of a troop of horse to restore order, must have perturbed him. Turner, who was spending much of his time in Blackburn attending to business connected with the death of his brother Thomas six months previously, could not help but be troubled by the events unfolding there, which were possibly instrumental in encouraging his later political ambitions.

It is a measure of the man that despite his business interests and therefore the source of his wealth, rooted as they were in the cotton trade of industrial Blackburn, Turner had, during the course of but six years, achieved sufficient standing in his adopted county for his peers to recommend to the King that he be installed as High Sheriff of Cheshire, a highly prestigious appointment. On 6 February 1826, a month before his daughter's abduction, he was duly sworn in. Upon his appointment the previous year, Mr Daintree had given the public a grand breakfast – no less would be expected of the wealthy William Turner. Although the new Shrigley Hall, a 'noble structure of stone',[23] had been completed, its interior was not yet finished. However, the three principal apartments were fitted up for the breakfast rooms, their floors covered in crimson cloth; the music room at the front of the second storey was appropriated for the exclusive use of the ladies; and, in addition, apartments at the east end of the quadrangle were provided for the tenantry of Shrigley and Lyme Park.

At about nine o'clock in the morning of Saturday 1 April, the guests began to arrive, some of them uninvited. Several hundred sat down to a truly sumptuous repast: pride of place went to a noble baron of beef, beautifully decorated with various heraldic devices, above it the family crest moulded in butter, a lion passant guardant holding in his dexter paw a cross surmounted by elegant bannerets, on which was inscribed the family motto, *Esse quam videri* (Be what you seem), on the reverse the initial *T* with the Union Jack in the corner. Newspapers reported every detail of the incredible banquet: 'every delicacy and novelty that could be procured was there in abundance. The confectionery both in design and execution was equally grateful to the eye and the palate; and jellies were in the greatest variety and of the most exquisite quality.'[24] No expense had been spared. The health of the High Sheriff was proposed by Thomas Legh of Lyme, who, soon after noon, led the parade accompanied by the tenantry of Lyme. Thomas Grimsditch preceded the High Sheriff, who was mounted on an elegantly caparisoned horse. Against the delightful and romantic backdrop of Shrigley, Pott and Bollington, the effect of the cavalcade as it wound its way along its scenic mountain route must have been marvellous, the road from Bollington to Macclesfield, a distance of some two miles, lined by a vast concourse of people. Never before had the inhabitants of Macclesfield witnessed so grand a spectacle. 'Even the distress which [had] been accumulating and pressing upon its almost starving thousands seemed for a moment forgotten and joy and gladness beamed in every countenance where sorrow and despondency had so long predominated.'[25]

For William Turner, this day must have marked the culmination of all his hopes and aspirations, serving not only to assure him of his neighbours' regard, and his acceptance by the wider community, but also to reassure him of their sympathy and support regarding the outrage which had befallen his daughter. The occasion had proved to be an unqualified success; proof that he was indeed worthy of the honour bestowed upon him, and, if Edward Gibbon Wakefield is to be believed, must have 'driven the most bilious of his detractors mad'. Dr Davies, he asserted, had only pledged to join the High Sheriff's procession as he doubted any other 'county gentlemen' would lend their support to William Turner's ceremonial progress to Chester, if only to 'show those people's pitiful jealousy'.[26] Furthermore Edward Gibbon claimed that this gave him the final impetus to marry Ellen Turner, and then provide an escort which would enrage William Turner's supposed detractors. The *Stockport Advertiser*, which had so proudly reported the High Sheriff's illustrious breakfast and procession, was later to challenge *John Bull* over what it described as an

attempted ridicule on our respected High Sheriff . . . adopting the stale trick of repeating the whole of our description marking it pretty particularly with italics and small capitals – a species of wit, which like Lord Burleigh's [William Cecil, first minister of Elizabeth I] significant shake of the head means unutterable things, and may be employed on all occasions, with infinite advantage to the initiated.

The *Advertiser* concluded: 'if the shafts of this ridicule, however, are all as pointless as that which this week were aimed at Mr Turner . . . [then] we would advise the author to try some new mode of obtaining popularity.'[27] Bearing in mind the recent abduction of Turner's daughter, *John Bull*'s snide opening comment, 'We extract the following glowing detail of the hospitalities of Shrigley, whose loveliest ornament, although happily restored to its shady groves, is the only person or thing belonging to Mr Turner not mentioned', is a particularly cruel one. They proceeded to print the *Advertiser*'s account verbatim, adding, 'we are inclined to think the Editor of the paper is either hoaxing or has been hoaxed in the publication, for if it be serious, it is perhaps the most comical affair ever submitted to notice'.[28] This was clearly a flimsily disguised attempt to undermine the newly appointed Sheriff, and could be said to support Edward Gibbon Wakefield's assertion that the 'New Squire' was not without enemies.

On Monday 3 April, at nine o'clock in the morning, preceded by his trumpeters and halberdiers, on horseback, and followed by the carriages of several of his personal friends, William Turner set out in his landau and four for the Welsh border to meet the Judges of Assize on their way from Mold to the Lent Assizes at Chester, the High Sheriff and judges returning at eleven o'clock to attend divine service in the cathedral. There, the main tenet of the sermon given by the Reverend Mawdesley, the High Sheriff's chaplain, that covetousness was the original cause and continued source of every sin which man is liable to commit, and of every evil to which human nature is subject, was something which, in the light of the recent abduction of his daughter, must surely have struck home with the new High Sheriff. The chaplain sternly censured the manufacturers whose speculations he claimed had brought ruin and misery not only upon themselves but also to the operatives in their employ. This rebuke, following close upon the heels of the warm and generous response of the Macclesfield populace, may well have motivated Turner's letter to the Mayor a couple of days later, requesting, in vain, that a special assembly be held during the Assize Week to seek relief for the distressed silk weavers of the county, whose privations were considerable. Clearly, there was reason for concern. Such was the tension and disaffection in Macclesfield that a few months later Sir Walter Scott, who was staying in the town, was advised not to travel at night.

It is surely to William Turner's credit that a time when his role as father would have taken precedence, he maintained a laudable interest in the plight of the Macclesfield weavers. Although William Wakefield was now incarcerated in Lancaster gaol, Edward Gibbon was still in France and could not be apprehended; Turner's wife and daughter were still traumatised by the abduction, and fearful of the outcome of the affair; and ahead of him lay an arduous legal challenge: to secure the annulment of his daughter's marriage and bring the Wakefield brothers to justice.

10

Things and Actions are
What They are . . .

It had been reported in England that no effort had been spared to secure the apprehension of Edward Gibbon Wakefield, the English authorities still being hopeful that the French government would surrender 'the principal in this case of unparalleled abduction'.[1] The French Cabinet, however, had informed the British government that, as the crime of abduction was not a capital felony under French law, they felt unable to intervene. Since the French government appeared to be in no hurry to return Edward Gibbon to England, he, doubtless having no quarrel with this stance, remained in Paris with his two children, safe in the bosom of the beneficent Mrs Bathurst; and there he could stay as no extradition treaty existed between France and Britain. Indeed, he was free to take his children to America, as some friends had urged. Notwithstanding, he declared his intention to return to England and surrender himself to the laws of the country, announcing that he 'did not want to shirk the consequences of a trial'.[2]

Edward Gibbon, who had promised Ellen's uncle Henry Critchley that he would return to England as soon as he had made provision for his children, was to remain true to his word. Whether he would have honoured his promise had it not been for the plight of his younger brother William, who alone had faced the full wrath of Mr Turner and the weight of British justice, is questionable. But there is the distinct possibility that Edward Gibbon, ever the optimist, had no intention of relinquishing his young bride and all that went with her. Experience had taught him that he had never entertained a project which he had not accomplished – three weeks after Ellen had been taken from him in Calais, he made preparations to slip quietly back into England.

Meanwhile, William's attorney Mr Tindall had applied to the Court of the King's Bench for his client to be granted bail. William appeared in the custody of his gaoler Higgin to hear the Attorney General oppose the application on the grounds that even if his offence constituted merely a misdemeanour, it was one of such an aggravated nature that the court ought to pause before admitting the defendant to bail. Consequently, the Lord Chief Justice ordered that William remain in custody until the court had considered the case. The following day, William was granted bail on his own recognisance of £2,000. Frederick John Cuthbert of Grosvenor Square, who owned chalk works in Rochester, entered into a recognisance of £1,500, but the qualification of James Johnson, a cabinet-maker and undertaker of Mary-le-bone to stand bail was denied because he admitted to owing £3 parish taxes; and so William had to remain in custody until a further security of £500 could be obtained. Two days later, Dr Davies journeyed with William to Manchester. Here before Mr Norris, magistrate, he entered into a recognisance for the final £500, whereupon William was liberated, to depart by mail coach for London the following morning.

For the 71-year-old Reverend Dr Davies, respected headmaster of Macclesfield Grammar School, it had been an exhausting and distressing week. Since his appearance at the examination of William Wakefield at Disley, it had transpired that his only child, Frances, might well be implicated in the abduction. Details of her secret marriage to Edward Wakefield, a widower much her senior and father not only of the now notorious William and Edward Gibbon but also of seven other children, began to appear in newspapers. Two days after William's release, the *Macclesfield Courier* of 15 April carried the marriage announcement of Edward Wakefield and Frances Davies, which had been conducted by Bishop Luscombe on 3 August 1823 in the chapel of the British Embassy in Paris. The couple had kept their marriage secret because Frances was either unwilling or afraid to tell her father, the reasons for which can only be ascertained by the evidence of Edward Wakefield's clandestine letters to his secret wife. Writing to her only sixteen days after their wedding, he spoke of his pleasure in their marriage, although initially it had been contracted 'to cure her fickleness'. Their separation now entailed him 'making the greatest earthly sacrifice',[3] particularly in view of Frances' aversion to committing her feelings for her husband to paper as he would have desired, despite their enforced estrangement. Clearly his 'greatest earthly sacrifice' was not enough, for, eighteen months after their marriage she was complaining, 'I am not pleased at not hearing from you', adding that he must send her 'a new riding hat 21½ inches round the head, black – like a gentleman's'.[4] He wrote of her father's 'whim, tyranny and despairing'[5] and suggested one way of winning him over might be to bestow the name of Davies on any children they might have. It is clear from his letters that the couple went to great lengths to prevent knowledge of their marriage reaching Dr Davies:

> I shall expect you at Congleton sooner after eleven as I suppose you will leave Macclesfield as soon as your father goes into school, so do not come down in a gig or any particular way to excite attention at home – there is much less risk at Congleton than at Macclesfield.[6]

Even Edward Wakefield's political ambitions would appear to stem from a need to win over Frances' father, his letter assuring her, 'in all fair probability you will see both me and Edward Gibbon Wakefield members of the next Parliament'. However, he was still hopeful of Brougham exerting his influence on Oman, son of David Ricardo, the economist, who had recently died, to allow him his father's seat for the remainder of the present Parliament; though he confessed, 'I differ from you in thinking that there is a lack of talent in the House, the lawyers never shone as much as Messrs. Brougham, Mackintosh, Weatherall, Denman and Scarlett'.[7] Despite mention of Dr Davies' possible ill-health, it would seem that the reason for their secrecy had more to do with his temper and obduracy than anything else. Neither the health nor temper of this distinguished and scholarly headmaster could have been improved by the astounding revelation that not only had his daughter been secretly married but, in addition, her husband was the father of the two youths who, having previously been involved in runaway matches with heiresses, were now embroiled in yet another marital escapade. Like father, like son would appear a fitting description of the Wakefields' 'fine irregular genius for marriage'.[8]

Edward Gibbon had probably arrived back in Britain early in April, possibly reunited with his brother William, and more than likely had hastily conferred with his uncle Daniel, the barrister, and his father Edward. On 17 April *The Times* reported that Edward Gibbon had caused notice to be served on Thomas Grimsditch, the solicitor for the prosecution, expressing his earnest desire to submit himself to any judicial inquiry and, moreover, declaring that he would attend at any time or place that his accusers might appoint, providing six days' notice had been given to his solicitor Mr Harmer. A week later, the death of his grandfather, Edward, may have provided an opportunity for him to meet not only his father and brothers, but also his grandmother Priscilla. Her grandson's latest exploit, coming hard on the heels of the announcement of her son Edward's secret marriage and the death of her husband, must have caused this elderly lady much anguish. Priscilla also learned that her son had lost his libel action against the *Reading Mercury*, which, he had claimed, 'indirectly and by innuendo imputed to him a participation in the crime of which his two sons [stood] charged'.[9] Edward Wakefield had sworn on oath that he had no prior knowledge of his son's Gretna marriage, although his own affidavit stated that he had seen both William and Edward Gibbon only seven days before they left Macclesfield to carry out the abduction. Furthermore, when Edward Gibbon had written to him on 10 March from Carlisle, 'My dear Father, I write to you instantly after my marriage etc.', it is notable that he did not say whom he had married, nor the time nor circumstance of the ceremony, which suggested his father had no need of this intelligence. That he was able to circulate extensively a public announcement of the marriage and its details, and in a letter to Dr Davies had proclaimed his son's high connections and excellent character as a husband, would appear to contradict his claim.

The fact that the Lord Chief Justice would not allow Edward Wakefield to take his action any further indicated that the *Reading Mercury* had no charge to answer. The newspaper triumphantly pointed out that it considered that a man who aspired to 'the high and responsible situation of a representative of the Electors of Reading must necessarily submit his conduct and pretensions to the public scrutiny and animadversion'; adding, 'if a public journalist is to be subjected to a criminal information for publication on the character alluded to, the liberty of the press will soon become an empty name'.[10]

From London, on 6 May, Edward Gibbon Wakefield circulated his friends with a copy of a statement that he had prepared for his counsel, justifying his abduction of Ellen Turner. It began:

> In the end of February I went to Macclesfield for the purpose of paying a long promised visit to my friend the Reverend Dr Davies. At that time I had heard Mr Turner's name mentioned, but merely in casual conversation about Cheshire people, and I had no more knowledge or thought of his daughter or any of his family than I have of people in the Moon.[11]

It was a telling document: a compelling vindication both of his motives, and the execution of the enterprise to carry off and marry the young heiress; it was also further evidence of his supreme self-assuredness and apparent inability to countenance failure. This statement quickly found its way into the newspapers, accompanied by a letter written by Edward Gibbon to Mr Turner, claiming that he had not wished to make his daughter the object of public discussion. However, in view of the 'ridiculous mortifying paragraphs' which had appeared, for the most part in a newspaper which he supposed was in the control of William Turner's agent and bore 'his stamp of authority', he now felt compelled to correct these misrepresentations by highlighting Ellen's 'amiable character and admirable conduct'.[12] He concluded by assuring Mr Turner that his only concern was for Ellen's welfare and reputation; he sought neither to mitigate Mr Turner's anger nor to escape any punishment which Mr Turner might wish to inflict.

On the morning of Tuesday 16 May, Edward Gibbon Wakefield arrived in Macclesfield where he breakfasted at Percyvale House, the home of Dr Davies, before riding the eight and a half miles to Taxal Lodge, home of George William Newton, who had signed the warrant for his apprehension, and to whom he now surrendered himself. Mr Newton, quite nonplussed by Edward Gibbon's unexpected appearance, asked him to remain in Taxal until Mr Turner's legal advisers could be summoned. The following morning

William Turner and his solicitor arrived to confront Edward Gibbon. The meeting must have been a momentous one: Turner, the vengeful father, struggling to contain his pent-up anger, face to face at last with Edward Gibbon Wakefield, the unrepentant bridegroom. When asked if he had anything to say, Edward Gibbon coolly rejoined, 'Nothing!' At this juncture, Turner's legal adviser William Hopes requested that since his partner Mr Grimsditch was in London, any further examination of Edward Gibbon be delayed until Saturday.

Edward Gibbon was consigned to the custody of Deputy Constable Barratt who, to the marked disapproval of Mr Turner, was instructed to afford his charge every convenience and comfort. Thus, Edward Gibbon was to find himself in the New Bailey which had so recently confined his brother William. From there, on Saturday 20 May, he was taken to the Ram's Head at Disley where he appeared before the two magistrates who had committed his brother William, namely Newton of Taxal and Humphreys of Bramhall. (Thomas Legh was unavailable, being engaged in preparations for the coming election in his parliamentary seat of Newton-in-Makerfield.) After prolonged consultation, the prisoner was called before the magistrates and informed that, owing to the unavoidable absence of a third magistrate, he would be remanded until the following Monday. Clearly, this was not to Edward Gibbon's liking; application was immediately made to Thomas William Tatton of Wythenshawe, asking him to attend that day, Monday; since he was also unavailable, the hearing was postponed until the following day.

At midday on Tuesday 23 May, the proceedings began. It promised to be an uneven battle. On the one side were ranged the forces of Mr Turner: his brother Robert, his brother-in-law Henry Critchley, the formidable Mr Grimsditch, Elizabeth Daulby and Ellen Turner; on the other, Edward Gibbon, his only supporter, the long-suffering yet faithful Dr Davies. Edward Gibbon Wakefield, described by *The Times* as a 'bel-homme',[13] presented every appearance of an 'accused innocent', undaunted and unbowed, seated beside him the white-haired elderly gentleman lending the miscreant a certain air of gravity and respectability. Edward Gibbon, who had recently entered his thirty-first year, looked the perfect gentleman, slender, fair-haired, his elegant dress suggesting a mere touch of dandyism.

It was hard to equate this man with the crime of which he stood accused. Informed that the evidence brought against his brother would be adduced against him, he agreed to its being read without the examination of witnesses.

Ellen then made her entrance accompanied by her father, her uncles Robert and Henry, and dressed in deep mourning for her uncle John who had died three weeks previously. Edward Gibbon, probably to the disappointment of his adversaries, appeared in no way to resemble the scoundrel depicted in the national press; neither did Miss Turner fulfil their expectations of a gauche, somewhat naïve fifteen-year-old schoolgirl, the *Manchester Gazette* conceding,

> her fine form and figure are peculiarly commanding and her manner altogether bespeaks a more than ordinary share of intelligence. Her countenance is somewhat pale but the fine expression of her eye adds considerably to her personal beauty which is heightened by a set of peculiarly white and beautifully formed teeth which ornament a gracefully turned lip.[14]

The Times thought her 'rather tall of her age, her countenance enlivened by two piercing eyes, and teeth a fine contrast to her ruby lips'.[15] Her manners, the *Gazette* noted, 'are those of highly finished lady without the slightest trace of gaucherie, and she seemed to create a very great degree of interest and admiration in all present'.[16] *The Times* concluded, 'there is something so fascinating about her'.[17] During the reading of her evidence, not a single glance was exchanged between Ellen and Edward Gibbon, her eyes cast downwards throughout the whole proceedings. After the evidence had been read, Edward Gibbon declined to make any comment, except to state that the whole of the proceedings met with his approbation. Grimsditch then rose to address the magistrates, calling upon them to commit Edward Gibbon Wakefield for the crime with which he stood charged, arguing that the severity of the offence required that he be refused bail. The room was then cleared, the magistrates remaining in consultation for nearly an hour before informing Edward Gibbon that they intended to commit him under the Act of Henry VII, to Lancaster Castle to await trial. At this announcement, Edward Gibbon, who had hitherto seemed so nonchalant, momentarily appeared agitated, turning visibly pale before quickly regaining his composure and assuming that indifference to the proceedings which he had affected throughout, lolling in his seat, with his hand to his head.

While his opponent was, if only for an instant, discomfited, a triumphant Thomas Grimsditch rose to deliver the final blow, seeking to vindicate himself from some remarks of Edward Gibbon's contained in his statement published in *John Bull*. The magistrate, Humphreys, perhaps displaying some sympathy for the defeated Edward Gibbon, declared the subject irrelevant to the proceedings, observing furthermore that Mr Wakefield must already have had 'enough to oppress his feelings'.[18] Edward Gibbon had pointedly denied placing the statement in *John Bull*, despite the attorney's assertion that his name was attached to it. Grimsditch, however, determined to have the last word, insisted that the statement had appeared. Before leaving the inn in the custody of the constable, Edward Gibbon wrote to his friends, sending a copy of his committal to his solicitor Mr Harmer. For some time afterwards, Ellen watched from the window as Edward Gibbon strolled outside with Dr Davies, but neither wife nor husband acknowledged the existence of the other.

The *Stockport Advertiser* could be depended upon to 'prick the balloons' readily offered up by their competitors:

The usual disgusting trickery has been employed by 'the gentlemen of the press' to excite the sympathy of the public on behalf of this dashing gentleman and the most minute particulars of his behaviour during his examination have been reported as though the fate of empires depended upon the style in which he had lolled on the sofa, or the peculiarly gentleman like manner in which he ever and anon applied himself to his snuff box. The appearance and manners of Miss Turner too have furnished ample materials for the paragraph-makers; and one 'pendulum-like gentleman' who was present at the examination, is truly poetical in her praise . . . nobody but a Cockney could have written such stuff as this. Leaving the bad taste of the thing entirely out of the account we cannot conceive anything more insulting to Miss T and her family than all this rodomontade about her personal appearance; she is a fine tall girl of her age

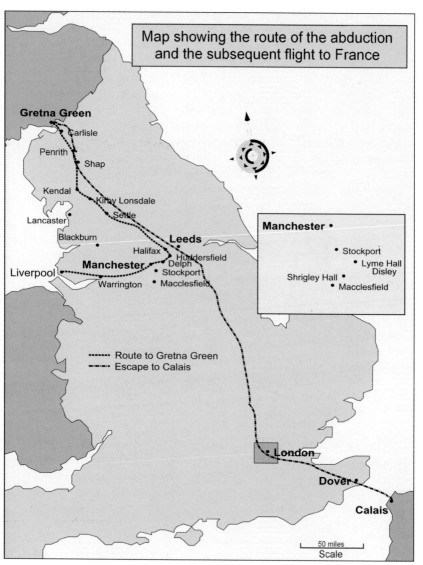

Map showing the route of the abduction. (*John O'Connor*)

Ellen Turner's school-mistress, Miss Elizabeth Daulby of Breck House, Liverpool. Drawing assigned to T. Hargreaves, J.A. Picton's *Memorials of Liverpool*, 1873. (*Courtesy of Liverpool Record Office, Liverpool Libraries*)

The signature of thirteen-year-old Ellen Turner on the fly-leaf of one of her school textbooks. (*By kind permission of Mr and Mrs Stewart; photograph by Audrey Jones*)

Edward Gibbon Wakefield as a young man by an unknown artist. (*By courtesy of the National Portrait Gallery, London*)

Mrs Priscilla Wakefield.

Edward Gibbon Wakefield's grandmother Mrs Priscilla Wakefield, aged sixty-seven. James Thomson after T.C. Wageman, published 1818. (*By courtesy of the National Portrait Gallery, London*)

Edward Gibbon Wakefield's grandparents Edward and Priscilla Wakefield with her sister Catherine Bell, the mother of Elizabeth Fry, by Francis Wheatley, *c.* 1774. (*Norwich Castle Museum and Art Gallery*)

Edward Wakefield, father of Edward Gibbon Wakefield, by George Romney, date unknown. (*Reproduced by kind permission of Sir Humphry Wakefield Bt. of Chillingham Castle; photograph by John O'Connor*)

Eliza Pattle, first wife of Edward Gibbon Wakefield, from a portrait painted by the miniaturist artist William Gwynn, 1812. (*Alexander Turnbull Library, National Library of New Zealand, Te Puna Mātauranga o Aotearoa [Ref: A-087-024]*)

Nina and Edward Jerningham Wakefield, from a portrait by J. Mills in 1822. (*Alexander Turnbull Library, National Library of New Zealand, Te Puna Mā tauranga o Aotearoa [Ref: A-087-023]*)

Gretna Hall, where Edward Gibbon Wakefield and Ellen Turner were married. (*Dumfries and Galloway Libraries, Information and Archives*)

David Lang, the blacksmith priest who married Edward Gibbon Wakefield and Ellen Turner. (*Dumfries and Galloway Libraries, Information and Archives*)

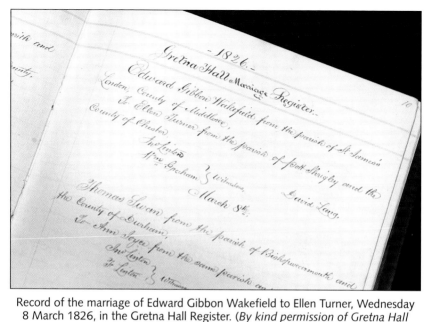

Record of the marriage of Edward Gibbon Wakefield to Ellen Turner, Wednesday 8 March 1826, in the Gretna Hall Register. (*By kind permission of Gretna Hall Blacksmiths, photograph courtesy of* The Times)

The arrival of the judges at Lancaster Assizes in 1833, from an engraving by T. Allom. (*Lancaster City Museums*)

Miss Turner

"Deep were my anguish, thus Compell'd,
To wed with one I ne'er beheld."

Fashion-plate of Ellen Turner, frontispiece of *Une Nouvelle Manière D'Attraper Une Femme*, published in 1826. (*British Library, Tracts 1809–1836*)

Edward Gibbon Wakefield, aged twenty-seven. Engraved by B. Holl from a drawing by A. Wivell, 1823. (*By courtesy of the National Portrait Gallery, London*)

William Wakefield wearing the habiliments of the First Society of Europe, sketched in the court of the King's Bench upon being brought up from Lancaster Castle. After an unknown artist. (*By courtesy of the National Portrait Gallery, London*)

Henry Brougham, who led for the prosecution at the Wakefield trial. (*Mary Evans Picture Library*)

Oil painting of the trial of Edward Gibbon Wakefield in the Shire Hall, Lancaster Castle, March 1827, by an unknown artist. Henry Brougham is pointing at the accused. (*Lancaster Castle, Lancaster City Council; photograph by John O'Connor*)

William Turner's mansion Shrigley Hall, designed by Thomas Emett. A lithograph by W. Gauci from a drawing by Henry Winkles. (*Chester Record Office*)

Lyme Hall, seat of Thomas Legh, engraved by T. Allom, 1837.
(*Lyme Park, National Trust*)

Thomas Legh dressed in Eastern costume, aged twenty-one, by William Bradley, *c.* 1813. (*Lyme Park, National Trust, Newton Collection*)

Miniature of Thomas Legh of Lyme, aged fifty-four by Sir W.C. Ross, 1846. (*Lyme Park, National Trust*)

Oil painting reputed to be of Ellen (Turner) Legh, by Henry Wyatt, 1837. (*By kind permission of the Trustees of the Higher Museums Trust and the Lancashire County Museum Service; photograph by John O'Connor*)

Ellen (Turner) Legh's memorial in the Legh Chapel, St Oswald's Church, Winwick. (*By kind permission of Canon Lewis and the Parochial Church Council, Winwick; photograph by Audrey Jones*)

William Turner's crest on Blackburn almshouses endowed by William and Jane Turner. (*Photograph by Audrey Jones*)

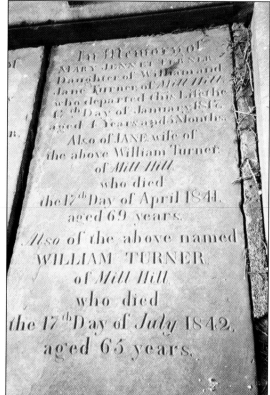

In Memory of
MARY JENNET TURNER
Daughter of William and
Jane Turner of Mill Hill
who departed this Life the
6th Day of January 1817
aged 1 Year and 5 Months.
Also of JANE wife of
the above William Turner
of Mill Hill
who died
the 17th Day of April 1841,
aged 69 years.
Also of the above named
WILLIAM TURNER
of Mill Hill
who died
the 17th Day of July 1842,
aged 65 years.

Turner family graves, St John's Church, Blackburn. (*Photograph by Audrey Jones*)

Edward Jerningham Wakefield in middle age. Painting attributed to William Beetham, *c.* 1855–61. (*Wellington City Council*)

Edward Gibbon Wakefield, aged fifty-four, 1850. Painting by J. Edgil Collins and R. Ansdell. (*Canterbury Museum, Ref: 1871.71.1*)

and we believe that she has sense enough to feel consummate disgust at the bare-faced flattery that is thus heaped upon her, coupled as it is with the similar expressions towards the man from whom she has received such an irreparable injury. While we are on the subject we may just notice that [Edward Gibbon] Wakefield is said to bear a strong resemblance to Sir Walter Scott. We have had as many opportunities perhaps of ascertaining this fact as the individual who makes the assertion but we can assure all parties concerned that resemblance exists nowhere but in the imagination of the writer of the article.[19]

On the very day that Edward Gibbon Wakefield was committed for trial, a debate relating to Gretna Green marriages took place in the General Assembly of the Church of Scotland. Magistrates or borough justices who allowed such marriages to be witnessed in their presence were fiercely criticised, and a committee appointed to inquire into the best means of preventing them. *The Times*, tongue in cheek, commented, 'should this committee succeed fewer post-chaises and four will drive to the north with heiresses and boarding schoolgirls'.[20]

On Thursday morning, Edward Gibbon Wakefield was taken from the New Bailey, Stockport, to begin the journey to Lancaster Castle and gaol. *John Bull* took the opportunity to censure Edward Gibbon for the statement they had recently published, which the paper was now certain had been penned by him:

how greatly does it aggravate the monstrous offence! What must the moral part of the public of England think of the heart of that man, who, after despoiling an affectionate father of his daughter, turns into 'personal ridicule' the affliction of the almost disconsolate parent! Let Mr W ruminate on these matters in the gaol of Lancaster; and let those in this neighbourhood who have 'aided, comforted and abetted'[21] him in the circulation of his infamous memoir, chuckle over the fiendish fun they have ineffectually attempted to create, amidst the execrations of all classes of society.

11

Thro' All the Drama . . .
Women Guide the Plot

Edward Gibbon Wakefield, 'child stealer', was one of an assorted company of miscreants committed variously for murder, assault, theft and machine-breaking and thus remanded in custody at Lancaster Castle on Thursday 25 May. For those brought to trial from all over Lancashire, including Manchester and Liverpool, Lancaster was frequently the last stop; conveyed by carriage up the steep cobbles of Nip Hill, past the Judges' Lodgings, through the sheep fields close to the Lune by the side of St Mary's churchyard, they were taken to face their final moments on the scaffold. Those sentenced to transportation were brought to St George's Quay, 300 yards from the castle, and thence to the port of Liverpool to begin their journey to the prison hulks which would convey them to their destination, the convict colonies of New South Wales or Van Diemen's Land.

Lancaster, situated on the River Lune, was an important port on the border of Cumbria and the Lake District. A bridge of five elliptical arches formed an imposing entrance to well-lit, substantially paved streets, yet the aspect was cheerless, 'the houses being built of freestone, easily susceptible of impression in a climate so humid, soon look dark and gloomy and impart their sombre character of the streets'.[1] The huge gate of the heavily fortified castle, with its two lofty and massive square towers, would have presented a daunting prospect to any prisoner.

A very brief reconnoitre was sufficient for the settlement of any doubts as to the place being a most excellent one for safe detention. All around were high barriers of masonry, and we felt

P.s cottage in front of woods (↓ not shown!)

J Arthur DIXON

POSTCARDS

LOCHINVER VILLAGE
Photography by D. Richardson, Sutherland Tourist Board
PSC 27054

© Published by John Hinde (U.K.) Ltd., Redruth, Cornwall.
Tel: 01209 211111

Sitting on slipway waiting for ferry to take us in to a minibus which we hope will get us to Cape Wrath! - We have visited the only two other capes in the British Isles - Cape Clear in S.W. Ireland and Cape Cornwall so hope we make this one! Hand shaky! cold but sunny & dry. Great day yesterday on Handa Island nature reserve. Much love to you & Sarah

hermine & Bill

Mr & Mrs T M Fisher
126 Newhurst Avenue
Sycamore Chase
Baguley
MANCHESTER
M23 9SA

as completely shut in from the world, as if we were at the bottom of a great well.[2]

However, the regime at Lancaster was fairly relaxed in comparison with other gaols, although the refractory cells were dark and horrid dungeons at the base of the Old Saxon Tower, where prisoners on punishment could languish for three days on a diet of bread and water, the lockup being known as the 'smoothing iron'.[3] There were also two treadmills, primarily for prisoners sentenced to hard labour. Notwithstanding, Lancaster gaol was regarded as one of the best prisons in the country, indeed there were some who reputedly preferred the gaol to the workhouse.

After the Peterloo Massacre of August 1819, the orator Henry Hunt and the Radical Samuel Bamford were taken to Lancaster gaol, which the latter described as a 'capital prison'; his cell, 'as white and sweet as constant application of quicklime could make it'. However, at night, Bamford found that his cell was 'hot and noisome', adding, 'we turned in and I began to feel as if I were being smothered. I now began to feel as if I were closed up in a coffin and not a breath of air above and around me . . . I thought of the black-hole of Calcutta, and concluded that the fate of its sufferers would be mine.'[4]

The *Lancashire Gazette* of 21 September 1818 reported a visit paid to Lancaster gaol by Edward Gibbon's cousin, Elizabeth Fry, the prison reformer. With her brother Joseph Gurney she 'examined every part minutely and expressed much satisfaction on its plan and the cleanliness, order and industry on the men's side of the prison, observing they had seen nothing like it at other prisons'.[5] But eight years later, her cousin Edward Gibbon Wakefield was to encounter different circumstances: the gaol then held 574 prisoners, 115 of whom were awaiting trial, 66 for rioting and machine-breaking; so overcrowded were conditions that some prisoners slept in the debtors' wing and the infirmary.

Shortly after his arrival in Lancaster, Edward Gibbon wrote to his stepmother, Frances Wakefield. He was, he assured her, well lodged and treated in this castle. 'You ought to know how little I care for personal luxuries. Air, exercise, water, privacy and books are all sufficient for any man of common sense and courage.'[6] However, he was soon to discover that prison life was not quite so accommodating as he had at first thought. His cell door would be opened at six o'clock in the morning when prisoners went to wash, those who worked did so until breakfast at half past eight; after breakfast, all had to attend chapel for half an hour and then work until noon; dinner was followed by exercise; and then prisoners worked again until supper. It is evident, however, from Edward Gibbon's letters to his stepmother that he was in some respects a privileged inmate – whether this can be attributed to his personal bearing and standing as a gentleman, or his ability to purchase favours, can only be surmised. James Weatherley, a fellow inmate who particularly remembered Edward Gibbon being brought in, recorded in his *Recollections of Manchester* that 'he was a Gentlemanly looking man who wore a white hat'. He reinforced the suggestion that Edward Gibbon was both well treated and well connected: 'Davies of Macclesfield used to come to see him. We could see him walking in his ward with young Mr Higgin, the Governor's son. From one of our windows I have seen hampers of wine go through our yard to him.'7 At his own request Edward Gibbon had a cell to himself, measuring 24 feet square and a yard, 50 feet long. In the cell was a fire, a table, two chairs and plenty of water. Every evening he was locked up at seven o'clock, but provided with candles. The *Macclesfield Courier* got wind of this: 'he is indulged with separate apartments and his situation made as agreeable as restraint will permit'.8 Edward Gibbon told Frances that he was obliged 'to attend chapel every day; when, however, at my own request, I sit alone, unseen in the condemned pew. (Ominous!)'.9 James Weatherley confirmed this: 'The first Sunday he came to chapel he sat in a pew in the recess. He was so stared at that he had slabs at the front of his pew the following Sunday so that we could not see him.'10

In his next letter he told Frances that much of his time was taken up in preparing his defence, corresponding with lawyers and answering letters from 'named and nameless correspondents': letters of consolation, the law, and love – one an offer of marriage! Nevertheless, Edward Gibbon confessed that without love he would be very unhappy: 'so I have a cat, with one draggle of a kitten, and a root of grass which grows in a hole in a wall, which I watch and nurse as if it were a cutting from the Tree of Life'. Edward Gibbon must have felt keenly his separation from his two children, his family and many good friends, however, Quaker instincts led him to empathise fully with his fellow inmates: he wrote of the 'stout Wigan engineer' unfairly confined for three years; and, with obvious sympathy, of 'the pathetic Irishman, Patrick Blake who expects to be hanged for highway robbery'. Finally, he told her of the magistrates who come to 'stare at me, I compel them, by standing and staring formally with my hat on, to be regularly introduced by the turnkey'.[11] Whatever the exigencies in which he now found himself, Edward Gibbon, as we might expect, was unperturbed; he may have broken the law but the law would not break him. Still assailed by the press, he was outnumbered but not outwitted. The *Bury Gazette* denounced him as 'a miserably weak-minded creature – a nervous fool', and dismissed him as 'a fine hero for a seduction story indeed'. The paper expressed incredulity that he could have composed a statement which reflected the 'perfect coolness', 'self-possession' and 'gay phrases of a clever and thoroughly practised writer'. It scoffed at the notion that Edward Gibbon could possess such talents and accomplishments. However, in confirming that this statement was indubitably the work of Edward Gibbon, *John Bull* consequently conferred on him the glowing tributes the *Gazette* had unwittingly paid their unknown correspondent. It was to *John Bull* that Edward Gibbon in his letter of 12 June swore that he did not wish to appear to seek newspaper notoriety, of which he had 'had enough to satiate the gluttonous lover of it'.[12] In a further letter to the same newspaper he thanked the editor, whom he acknowledged to have been the only one to have abstained from publishing 'the most ridiculous falsehoods respecting me'.[13]

The summer of the Wakefield trial would be remembered in Lancashire and Cheshire for the worst drought for half a century: the hay harvest was almost ruined, many pastures literally scorched and 'the lively verdure of summer exchanged for the dying tints of Autumn'.[14] As the date of the Assizes approached, Lancaster was inundated with lawyers, witnesses, relatives, friends, and curious onlookers. They filled every hotel, inn and lodging house in the town, drawn not only by the very large numbers of those to be tried, but also by the notoriety of the Turner abduction. To the undisguised joy of Grub Street and the 'peekers', commoners and nobility alike, reports circulating in some morning papers during the first week of August that the proceedings against the Wakefields were to be dropped, proved to be false. However, upon reading these mischievous reports some of the ninety-five witnesses subpoenaed by the Wakefields had returned to France, under the impression that their presence would not now be required, and the Wakefields' agent had to resort to the tedious process of serving them all over again. The Attorney General for England, Sir John Copley, Mr John Williams, Mr Sergeant Cross and two others, Mr Starkie and Henry Brougham who had himself, ironically, contracted a hasty Scottish marriage, would lead for the prosecution. The renowned Brougham, nicknamed, significantly, 'Beelzebub', or 'Old Wickedshifts', had first made his name in journalism as a founder of the *Edinburgh Review*, contributing no less than eighty articles to the first twenty issues on the arts, poetry and science. Later, having distinguished himself in politics and the law, he was described by Lord Stuart de Rothesay as the 'cleverest man he had known, but the least steady'.[15] James Scarlett, who it was believed might appear for the prosecution, had obtained a King's licence to become counsel for the prisoners – the hard work of their barrister uncle Daniel obviously not going unrewarded. It was expected that the trial of the Wakefields would occupy at least a whole day. However, there were many legal arguments to be considered: the nature of the indictment; the jurisdiction of the court; and finally the expectation that the relevant Act of Parliament would not recognise the offence as indictable unless force had been used.

On Tuesday 8 August, the High Sheriff of Lancaster, Mr James Penny Machell, met Mr Justice Parke and his fellow justices at the county boundary with Westmoreland, escorting them with due pomp and ceremony to the castle. Inside the Crown Court the Assizes were opened by the reading of the Commission of Assize, which was followed by a civic banquet in honour of the judges.[16] Mr Justice Parke was by all accounts a gentleman of a 'pleasing exterior', cutting 'a goodly figure on the bench' and, seemingly,

upon the best terms with himself; he is continually laughing and smirking – and, will sometimes rather lower the dignity of his situation by a far fetched pun, or a witticism of which few but himself can see the point. He appears very dextrous at unravelling the web of sophistry in which the ingenuity of counsel frequently envelops a bad cause.[17]

Whether Edward Gibbon Wakefield or William Turner be the weaver of the web, Mr Justice Parke, it would seem, might prove their equal. Edward Gibbon wrote to his sister Catherine, 'It is very uncertain when the trial will come on. I will write to you constantly.'

The following day, the judges, accompanied by the High Sheriff, attended divine service at St Mary's Priory, before continuing in stately procession to the Crown Court within the castle. The interior of the court was oak clad, its doors, benches and bars also of solid oak. On the wall behind the judge hung an imposing full-length portrait by James Northcote of George III, the law incarnate, magnificent upon a white horse – it was a *mise en scène* calculated to arouse the profoundest foreboding in the prisoner's breast:

> The court is gloomy, it has a right to be gloomy, it is a hall of agony, from its centre many a poor soul has seemed to cast off peripheries of misery which have impregnated the atmosphere both within and without. There is no court in the Kingdom to which more persons have been sentenced to death than in this Crown Court of Lancashire.[18]

Here, until 1826, it was the custom for prisoners beginning trial to be required to hold up their hand in court so that it could be immediately ascertained whether they had a previous conviction. After a prisoner had been sentenced he or she would be branded before leaving the dock – branded for life as a malefactor, a red-hot iron pressed against the 'brawn of the lumb'. To the judge's left was the Grand Jury bench, elevated above the well of the court, the prisoners, in the dungeons below, confined in the darkness until brought to be tried through a trap door below the dock. At twelve noon Mr Justice Parke, magisterial in grey wig and red gown, entered a courtroom crammed with several hundred spectators, witnesses to the swearing in of the twenty gentlemen of the Grand Jury who would judge whether or not the 233 indictments for these Assizes were valid, and hence the accused had a case to answer. Many of these had been indicted for riot, machine-breaking, highway robbery and an attack on Helmshore Mill, owned by William Turner's cousin of the same name.

Saturday 12 August dawned, and with it the mounting

expectation of the curious spectators. Miss Turner, the reluctant heroine of the piece, entered the courtroom to be sworn in, before withdrawing to tender her evidence in the room of the Grand Jury. She was still in deep mourning for her uncle: dressed in a black dress of bombazine; and, to the chagrin of her audience, the thick veil of her silk-trimmed bonnet concealed most of her features. After giving evidence for almost an hour, Ellen left the court to be greeted by a 'numerous assembly' which had collected outside hoping to catch sight of her as she left. They were to be foiled,

> distracted by a curious stratagem which her friends practised on the occasion. Instead of bringing Miss Turner out by herself, they brought out three young ladies all about her age and dressed like her in every respect, so nobody who had seen her in court, or on the stairs leading to the Grand Jury Room could say which of the four was the identical lady whose abduction had assisted so much interest in the country. They were pursued to their lodgings by a crowd of people all speculating as to which was the real Miss Turner.[19]

There were others with still greater reason to mourn the swift and secret passage of Miss Turner – the 'gentlemen' of the press suffered a disappointment they would have to pass on to their readers, in whose minds the proceedings had excited more interest than any trial for many years past.

On Monday 14 August, Edward Gibbon Wakefield was expected to make his first appearance in court. In consequence, the court became so crowded

> that the very dock to which the prisoners are brought up for arraignment, and the bar at which they are tried, were both filled with gentlemen of the highest respectability. Above sixty counsel congregated themselves round and in front of the table. Such a display of *wigs* was never before seen in the Crown Court. The Grand Jury Box, and the lady's gallery presented the appearance of large beds of lilies, roses and tulips thickly planted, and curiosity sparkled amongst them like the morning dew.[20]

A nice metaphor – the ladies, among them Lady Copley, wife of the Attorney General, having succeeded by who knows what powers of persuasion to attend the trial of Mr Wakefield, were present, we suspect, not so much out of maternal indignation or horror as from a desire to both see and be seen. There was something deliciously appalling, yet fascinating about this affair. In their minds was the conundrum – as yet unresolved – neatly implied by the mischievous *John Bull*: had Miss Turner, 'at any time during her ordeal, explained the real state of the case, the ravisher in the post-chaise would have been laid by the heels in a twinkling'.[21] The 'ravisher' intrigued both the ladies and the press –

> The act of the Wakefields is far from appearing in an odious light
> . . . the same offence, as the ladies mistakenly think, is committed every day, in novels, in comedies, and in real life; and however ill taken by the honoured parent himself, seldom to the great displeasure of the damsel concerned, or to the great scandal of the lookers-on – more especially to such as are of the female sex. . . .[22]

This last was the controversial comment of the *Literary Magnet*. Many a husband must have wondered at his wife's perhaps dubious interest in this outrageous exploit – was it the act or the man that so engaged them?

To the acute disappointment of everybody, particularly the London reporters who were waiting 'charged and full cocked to fire away on their notebooks, while expresses were in readiness to scamper off with the important result to the Metropolis',[23] Mr Justice Parke announced that he would first hear the pleas of the seven prisoners waiting in the dock, charged with breaking and destroying machinery. It was five o'clock in the afternoon before the trial of the power loom weavers was concluded and the counsel flooded into the court as before. Mr Justice Parke, obviously weary after the day's proceedings, seemed to be a little out of humour. Meanwhile, Edward Gibbon, in the 'sweating room', was waiting to be called. Finally motioned to go forward, he descended the steps that led to a long subterranean passage, at the furthest end of which 'the light increased and voices and a confused hum' could be heard. Mounting the steps, he found himself in an oblong box surrounded by iron spikes, in a large crowded chamber lit by numerous lamps and chandeliers. The spectacle was certainly calculated to inspire the prisoner 'with awe and alarm'.[24] As Edward Gibbon Wakefield made his appearance at the bar, all eyes were upon him.

To the palpable annoyance of the husbands, and the delight of their wives, he presented an elegant and handsome figure, sporting a black handkerchief, yellow-toned waistcoat and a dark buttoned-up frock coat. *The Times*, somewhat peevishly, reported the personal appearance of Edward Gibbon Wakefield to be 'not all prepossessing. There is much doggedness and inflexibility in his countenance and none of that *je ne sais quoi* air of gentility which is said to be so irresistible in captivating the fair sex. His brother is a little better looking.'[25] Edward Gibbon's manner was pensive and somewhat melancholy; a poetic figure, his studied nonchalance betrayed but briefly by a stray glance at the spectators. The ladies were disappointed, they yearned for some small sign, some satisfaction – he would not grant it. When Scarlett's lengthy appeal for the case against his client to be discharged was dismissed, he appeared unruffled. Equally, when Mr Justice Parke reluctantly agreed that his trial be postponed on the grounds that 'Edward Gibbon Wakefield had not been upon the present charge against him twenty days before the commencement of the present Assizes', he remained impassive. Edward Gibbon was thus bailed on his own recognisance of £2,000, and on a further two sureties of £1,000 to appear at the next Assizes. His stepmother, Frances Wakefield, was bailed on similar terms. Additionally, Edward Gibbon was bound by the court to keep the peace in respect of Miss Turner and her family.

The gentlemen of the press were quick to inform their readers of the postponement of Edward Gibbon's trial, while assuring them that legal proceedings against his brother would most likely take place a week later, on Monday 21 August. 'Thus the alleged accessory will be tried before the principal, this appears rather like putting the cart before the horse, but it is one of the anomalies in which the genius of our law especially delights.'[26] *The Times* was criticised for giving publicity to the contention that Ellen Turner was to all intents and purposes the wife of Edward Gibbon Wakefield, and readers were warned that if this notorious case was to go unpunished it would serve only to encourage unprincipled fortune hunters; for in similar outrages miscreants would rely on the natural disinclination of parents to bring the wrongs of a daughter before a public tribunal:

> The fellow who endeavours to trick us out of our baser property is looked upon as a despicable thief, and we set him to hard labour, bread and water and imprisonment, without mercy; but he who attempts to steal a child, in order to trick the parents out of a fortune, is looked upon as a delinquent of a superior order.

The crime of the Wakefields was, they claimed, a cold, heartless and premeditated plot perpetrated by a 'family gang'[27] intent on carrying off a girl no more than a child.

By Wednesday 16 August many rioters and machine-breakers had passed through the court. Next came three hours of legal wrangling surrounding the application by William Wakefield's defence to have his trial postponed. Scarlett argued that several questions of great difficulty on point of law were likely to arise as there had been no prosecution under the statute of Philip and Mary for some time, and witnesses, who had been subpoenaed, were now abroad and unlikely to return before the Spring Assizes. Furthermore, William Wakefield did not yet know whether he was to be charged with a felony or a misdemeanour. Despite Scarlett's best endeavours to secure a delay, the Attorney General disagreed with the grounds for postponement. William Wakefield then claimed that an article in the *Macclesfield Courier* was prejudicial to his case (its sole proprietor, it now transpired, was the solicitor for the prosecution, Thomas Grimsditch) and that indeed one of his witnesses had left the country after seeing the newspaper paragraph which stated that the trial would not take place at the present Assizes. The Attorney General, observing that this paragraph had appeared in an obscure evening paper called the *Sun*, intimated that 'it may well have been inserted by the authority of the "Messieurs" Wakefield' or at least with their knowledge.[28] At this point Scarlett and Grimsditch clashed. Grimsditch had imperiously informed him that the defendant's witnesses were in fact all present, and that William Wakefield was ready to stand trial forthwith. Scarlett contemptuously questioned how the solicitor had obtained this information, unless he had some means of knowing the defendant's case even better than the defendant. Thomas Grimditch, with unconcealed displeasure, informed the court that one of the defendants, Edward Thevenot, could not be found in England, although a warrant had been issued for his apprehension in March. Numerous applications to the French government had failed, although it was believed that he was living in Edward Gibbon Wakefield's home at 66 Rue de la Paepinare, Paris. During the greater part of this long exchange Edward Gibbon Wakefield provocatively paraded up and down the castle green, accompanied by his stepmother, Frances Wakefield, and another lady.

At six o'clock that evening the Grand Jury brought in True Bills against Edward Gibbon Wakefield and his co-conspirators: against Edward Gibbon, one for misdemeanour; against William, two, one for misdemeanour, one for conspiracy jointly with Edward Thevenot who had disguised himself in Mr Turner's livery; and one against Frances Wakefield, the stepmother, for unlawfully conspiring to bring about a marriage between her son and Miss Turner. (Despite the declaration by Edward Gibbon's father that he would stand by his wife, Frances, he was not indicted.) Again, the following afternoon Edward Gibbon was observed strolling about the confined yard attached to his 'apartment' in the castle. Again, he was described as 'a genteel looking man'[29] of slender build, dressed in a straw hat, a blue surtout and trousers of the same colour. He was seen to walk briskly the length of the yard before disappearing into the kitchen, emerging with his brother and a fashionably dressed woman upon his arm. He appeared to be reading a letter. After crossing the yard, the trio were observed climbing the stairs to Edward Gibbon's cell. The minutiae of Wakefield's movements, and of those connected with him, no matter how slender the ties, were of a burning interest to the spectators, and to those who would relay their findings to the unfortunates unable to witness for themselves this unfolding drama. The 'reverend blacksmith' from Gretna, who had so irreverently united Mr Wakefield and Miss Turner, had been seen in the town. Dressed in black with top-boots, and presenting the appearance of a country curate, he had naturally attracted much attention; young ladies were particularly anxious to catch sight of him. However, his manners were, apparently, not of the most engaging. Daily, the comic figure of Mr Lang could be seen strutting about the town – hardly seemly behaviour for a country curate. There was universal disappointment at the non-appearance in public of Miss Turner and her family. Even 'Paul Pry' had failed to catch so much as a glimpse of the young lady, though an unprecedented number of reporters from both the London and the provincial broadsheets were in attendance at these Assizes. It was said that the proprietors of the leading morning and evening papers had commissioned stations and relays of horses along the road from Lancaster to London for the sole purpose of conveying the verdict of the Wakefield trial to the metropolis. Then, as today, for the proprietors the whole affair was to prove very expensive, their outlay, it was hoped, soon to be recouped; very large sums of money were expended by the leading London papers intent on obtaining 'an exclusive'. It is believed that the owners of one evening publication promised their reporters £200 if they could convey news of the proceedings respecting the Wakefields to town before the agents of any other journal.

The following Monday 21 August, in anticipation of a postponement of William Wakefield's trial, the crowds, converging on the castle from an early hour summoned by the bell which tolled at quarter past seven, were to be entertained by the execution of five condemned prisoners. This macabre spectacle, so near in both time and place, could scarcely have failed to affect the emotions both of the Wakefields – perpetrators of what the press assured the public was 'an offence so dangerous to the happiness and honour of families'[30] – and of the waiting throng, some of whom, however, were there out of idle curiosity; others simply lusting for a punishment commensurate with so heinous a crime.

Long before the hour appointed for the doors leading to the body of the Crown Court to be opened the terraces were thronged, chiefly with genteelly dressed ladies. Shortly beforehand, a rumour had circulated around the town to the effect that something had happened which might render the proceedings of little interest. 'William Wakefield was off!' 'Off to a certainty'[31] was the general cry; in the event, that proved to be the case. Word had it that late the previous evening those in the confidence of his family intimated 'with very significant gestures' that he would certainly not be tried during these Assizes. But the intimation was considered nothing more than a further instance of that 'impudent swagger'[32] with which the friends of the Wakefields had conducted themselves, and was deemed unworthy of the slightest credit. There was much speculation as to what course might be adopted and it was generally believed that the trial, notwithstanding the absence of the principal actor, would proceed.

At precisely nine o'clock the doors were opened; crowds of ladies succeeded in gaining admittance, but many more were refused entry. They ranged themselves along the benches and in the galleries, a party of 'Quakeresses' even taking their seats in the prisoner's dock! Such was the determination of the ladies that many magistrates were unable to reach the seats generally reserved for them and were seen standing in the crowd. It was only thanks to the kindness of Mr Higgin, the governor of the gaol, that a portion of the court was set aside for reporters.

At half past nine, when Mr Justice Parke had taken his seat on the bench, Mr Hopkins, Clerk of Arraigns, asked if there was anyone present from the prosecution, whereupon Mr Justice Parke ordered that William Wakefield be called on his recognisance. Reynolds, the crier, three times called for him to come forward, but when he failed to do so, Dr Davies and the others who had stood bail for William were ordered to bring him forward or forfeit their recognisance. Mr Dennison of Manchester, William's solicitor, then stated what was by now obvious to everyone – that it seemed his client did not intend to appear. Consequently, Mr Brougham, for the prosecution, was granted permission to apply for a warrant for William's arrest. So terminated the initial proceedings against the Wakefields, Mr Justice Parke's request to those occupying the bar to clear it, as there were 'persons coming' who were 'far more guilty than any of you'.[33] This was greeted by much laughter and so the 'fair Quakeresses rose and left the court, covered with the blushes which so curious a compliment excited'. Some expressed little surprise at William's flight: 'trickery is expected from this family' and 'what is to be the next trick they are to play before the wondering public?'[34] But his friends were quick to defend his actions by explaining that he had put off his trial for the present so that he did not disclose his brother's defence; but how, many wondered, could his defence injure that of his brother, if his brother had any valid defence? If this was the dress rehearsal, what great theatre was in store for actors and audience alike!

12

So Many Men, So Many Opinions,
His Own a Law to Each

For Edward Gibbon Wakefield the postponement promised to buy 'the time which heals all', and a welcome dissipation of the general high dudgeon generated by his case. *The Times* opined, 'Mr [Edward Gibbon] Wakefield has cunning enough to perceive that every delay was in his favour'; Ellen's 'injured and irritated'[1] father might die leaving her open to his renewed attentions; alternatively William Turner might buy him off in exchange for his co-operation in securing an annulment. For William Turner this could only serve to increase the pressure and anxiety: at stake his daughter's future marriage prospects, hence the urgency of an annulment; the pressure of his business interests, especially after the recent deaths of two of his brothers; the exigencies of his role as High Sheriff; and the happiness of his beleaguered daughter and distraught wife – a swelling tide of crushing responsibilities. Reports in the press that Edward Gibbon Wakefield was considering not only a move for a writ of habeas corpus to force Miss Turner to be restored to him, but also a suit in the Ecclesiastical Court for the restoration of his conjugal rights, could only add to his woes.

In the event, there was to be no respite for the poor embattled father. Christmas arrived at Shrigley Hall accompanied by a splendidly bound copy of Ackermann's *Forget Me Not* in a parcel forwarded by post and directed to Miss Turner. Coincidentally, Mr Turner had given his daughter a copy of that very book only a few days earlier. At first sight the book afforded no clues as to the sender, but upon closer examination 'a well executed likeness of Mr Edward Gibbon Wakefield'[2] was discovered on a leaf which also contained a translation from Ariosto. Entitled 'The Praise of Love', the last verse read:

> Let others deem time must unloose
> Love's firmest bonds, decay'd by use,
> Or when those bonds we cherish:
> For me, whatever be my lot,
> I still will love – when I do not,
> Why let me die and perish.

It was reported that the gift rendered Ellen Turner 'highly indignant'. Considering the sentiments expressed in this verse, it is more likely that she was highly flattered. Her proposal to send the book back immediately to Mr Wakefield would, no doubt, be the reaction expected of her by her father. However, Mr Grimsditch advised that it would be wiser to treat the gift as though it had never arrived. The fact that Edward Gibbon had apparently been seen walking in the lanes adjoining the Turner residence at Shrigley might suggest, if one takes a generous view, that his desire to remain wed to the young Ellen rested not solely on his desire to avoid the approaching trial. It is equally possible, of course, that this was Edward Gibbon Wakefield, dissembler *par excellence*.

Early in the new year, on Saturday 10 February 1827, an application was made by counsel in the King's Bench, a division of the High Court, for the Wakefields to be tried by a special jury, who, it was argued, would be less biased than a common jury. However, their counsel Scarlett was anxious not to contradict a popular saying that 'the Common Jurors in Lancashire were the best in England!' He further argued that his clients would stand a better chance of an unprejudiced and impartial trial if their case was heard in Yorkshire, or even Carlisle. Cross, for the prosecution, submitted that the defendants had insufficient grounds for having their case moved, and Scarlett assured the judges that he was confident of William Wakefield's return for his trial to avoid his bail being prejudiced. He concluded by saying that he had 'no need to tell their Lordships that no case had for years excited so strong a feeling as this case had in the county of Lancashire'.[3] Nevertheless, the court refused Scarlett's application and, on the motion of Mr Sergeant Cross, the date for the trial of the Wakefields was set for Wednesday 21 March, when all defendants were ordered to attend.

Twice a year the judges attended the Assizes in Lancaster. The Spring Assizes of 1827 were to be presided over by the fine-sounding Mr Baron Hullock: 'a man in whose countenance you may discover all the qualifications for a dispenser of law and justice.' Regarded as one of the best judges on the Bench, he was not noted for his oratory, but there would be orators aplenty at this trial; his skills were more subtle and suitable for this challenging case. He had, it was said, 'a great aptness for getting at the bottom of a cause; and a facility in detecting its weak points, which renders it almost impossible to deceive him by the most crafty statement – the most ingenious pleading'. Like Mr Justice Parke, he had practised as a barrister for many years on the circuit, and was highly respected both in and out of court; a humane judge, and a patient one, who, when passing sentence of death, 'does it with a feeling that clearly evinces the contention which is struggling in his bosom, between mercy and justice'; seen on these occasions, 'so overcome with emotion that his voice has been choked and the tears have rolled down his cheeks'. The *Macclesfield Courier* of August 1826 paid tribute to Baron Hullock in its series, 'Sketches on the Northern Circuit', with the following verse:

> He, as he clears his rugged passage round,
>   Or delves into the bosom of the ground,
> With all the care of age, the zeal of youth,
>   From its deep burrow oft unearth's the truth,
>
> Conceal'd with care beneath the dark abode,
>   By crafty cunning, or foul lurking fraud,
> And, safely hidden from the eagle sight
>   Of eloquence that takes a higher flight.[4]

It had been decided that Mr Baron Hullock would preside over the Wakefield case in the Shire Court in Lancaster Castle, a civil court used for criminal trials only in exceptional circumstances. [In 1975 it was the venue for the trial of the 'Birmingham Six'.] The Crown Court, which had been used in August 1826, had proved too small, and as the case continued to excite increasing curiosity, it was thought prudent to utilise the Shire Court since it could accommodate several hundred people.

The Shire Court was described by the King of Saxony, who visited it in 1844, as 'one of the handsomest in Europe', the courtroom, 'a noble and spacious hall'.[5] It is a splendid ten-sided chamber. Around the body of the court, rising in tiers, semi-circular stone benches provide extensive seating with excellent viewpoints and perfect acoustics. Over the judges' bench rises an alcove of magnificent tracery, and those seated on the bench look out on to the splendid curved sweep of the semi-circular wall which bounds the court, on which are mounted the many coats of arms of past sheriffs.

At the beginning of March 1827, Mr Baron Hullock left Appelby in Westmorland to travel to Lancaster to open the Assizes. Charles Gibson, the High Sheriff, had made preparations with his friends to escort the judges into town with more than ordinary éclat, nearly thirty carriages accompanying him from his residence at Quernmore Park. However, his lordship, arriving in his travelling carriage at four o'clock in the afternoon, immediately proceeded to open the commission an hour earlier than expected, thereby missing the honours intended him. The following morning the High Sheriff and the usual retinue attended divine service at St Mary's; the preacher was the Reverend Robert Gibson, brother and chaplain of the High Sheriff.

Of the 200 causes entered in the Calendar of the Assizes, reported the *Westmorland Gazette*, 'none are of very peculiar interest, that which attracts public attention shall be laid before our readers'.[6] These included arraignments for horse-stealing, machine-breaking, destruction of power looms, thefts of bacon, a bible, handkerchiefs and silver spoons, and forgery. Indeed, many newspapers had already made arrangements, seeking to present exclusive reports of the trial for the gratification of their customers. The *Sun*, sarcastically assured its readership,

> we are really grieved to be under the necessity [of] throwing cold water not only upon the laudable exertions of our spirited rivals, but upon the growing impatience of our fair readers, by informing them in due time that there will be no trial at all – as Mr Turner *will* not appear *against* Mr Wakefield. This is *turning round to some purpose*, but what a lame and impotent conclusion![7]

The trial of the indictments against Edward Gibbon Wakefield and his brother William was then fixed for Thursday 22 March. Once again the town gave way to chaos, displaying 'a continual excitement and bustle'[8] in the grip of this Wakefield hysteria. By Sunday 18 March, Mr Turner and his family had not yet arrived in Lancaster, preferring to remain at Shrigley Hall where the Daulby sisters had joined them. They were expected to occupy the house they had rented at the foot of the castle on Wednesday. The Wakefield party had already taken up their old quarters near the Assembly Rooms. Accommodation had been provided for the prosecution witnesses, the principals being Mr Newton, Mr Humphreys and Mr Sutton, Cheshire magistrates, and Robert Turner and Henry Critchley. Mr Grimsditch, attorney for the prosecution, had been in Lancaster for a week giving instructions to the prosecution counsel. None of the defendants' witnesses had yet arrived, although accommodation had been secured for them. Dr Davies had also been in the town all week and one of the more flamboyant characters in this affair, the 'far-famed Gretna parson'[9] was expected to arrive that day – but those who met the coach were to be disappointed. On Tuesday, public patience was rewarded by the first appearance of Mr Edward Gibbon Wakefield, followed by the arrival at six o'clock in the evening of Ellen Turner in her father's carriage – 'rumour is as busy as ever and a thousand improbable stories are in constant circulation', rejoiced *The Times*.[10]

For want of proper news, the *Westmorland Gazette* advanced the cynical opinion that interest in the trial was waning and that in the end nobody but the lawyers would rejoice that it had ever begun; that is, with the exception of the witnesses, who were 'thus enabled to while away their time at the shrine of weakness and folly'. Lang, the Gretna blacksmith, was targeted as one who 'may exult because his business is to quarter upon the madness of one caprice or another'.[11] The *Sun* heaped more insults upon this unfortunate fellow, claiming that he was 'as usual getting drunk with the bold brandy'[12] at his lodgings on the Preston Road. Under fire from all sides, the old 'reverend' no longer ventured out, having been severely pelted by a mob of mischievous boys who had recognised him in the street.

Delay came from an unexpected quarter: Scarlett, Edward

Gibbon's leading counsel, who had previously appeared in excellent health, was suddenly taken with a severe cold, and had become extremely hoarse, this rendering him almost inaudible at the end of a long day in court on Wednesday 21st. That evening he was forced to send a message to Mr Baron Hullock confirming that he was indisposed, and consequently Hullock postponed the opening of the Wakefield trial until Friday. The still jaundiced *Westmorland Gazette* remarked that some of the parties were beginning to flag, pontificating: 'no wonder when we consider the severe inroads that must already be made upon their purses.'[13]

For true aficionados of the Wakefield saga, had they kept watch outside the lodgings near the Assembly Rooms they would have been rewarded. Late that night William was visited by a party of the posse comitatus with a writ for a debt of 500 shillings owed to a Preston tradesman. Waxing lyrical, the *Morning Chronicle* described their enterprise:

> Watchful and active as cats they espied their prey and although cunning as a fox they scented him to his retreat . . . After a parley of some continuance the door was opened and the officer communicated his errand which turned out to be not only a writ of execution . . . A question was then raised, 'that the defendant could not be taken', he being under recognisances to appear to take his trial. This caused some alarm to the officer, but still not so much as to induce him to abandon his captive.

The stalwart departed with his prisoner, leaving the Wakefield assembly bloodied but unbowed, 'not singing the Hundredth Psalm but drinking champagne like hearty food fellows although not well met'.[14]

The following morning dawned on a castle under siege: an infinite number of 'Wakefield watchers' massing in its precincts. The *Sun*'s correspondent, one of the few privy to knowledge of the trial's postponement, watched with amusement as the crowds jostled each other at the doors of the Shire Hall, knowing they were to be disappointed. However, there was to be some consolation for the impatient multitude, a tantalising side-show to the event, as one member or another of the Wakefield family, dressed in the most

fashionable style, obligingly promenaded the streets. An added sop
was the sight of Mr Edward Gibbon Wakefield himself, as he strolled
to the top of Castle Hill, a route which, incidentally, took him
directly past the residence of Mr Turner at least twenty times a day
– a fitting prologue perhaps, for the denouement which was to be
played out.

13

He that Takes Woman is Surely Undone

Early on the morning of the trial, Friday 23 March, a splendid travelling barouche arrived at the King's Arms tavern, carrying a younger brother of the Wakefield family. To the amusement of the crowd, he was accompanied by a flamboyant group of foreigners, some of them sporting most 'formidable mustachios'.[1] These, it was assumed, were the witnesses whose absence at the last Assizes had formed the principal ground of postponement. The Shire Hall, like the Globe Theatre, its motley audience now pressing about this high drama, was surely a backdrop worthy of the Bard himself. Paul Bloomfield compared the trial to a Shakespeare play: 'The trial of the Wakefields had something for everybody. There were knotty points for lawyers, comic exchanges for those who wanted a laugh, delicate situations for those who liked that kind of thing; there was romance for the sentimental, suspense for anyone with a sense of the dramatic.'[2] The hour appointed for the trial to begin was nine o'clock, but when Baron Hullock took his seat on the bench an hour earlier, the court was already crowded to excess. Despite the best endeavours of many to secure admittance only the press had been assured of their seats, especially selected by the Keeper of the Gaol, Mr Higgin. Throughout the drawn-out proceedings of the Wakefield case, he had displayed a marked eagerness to please the reporters of the London and provincial newspapers, perhaps for not altogether altruistic reasons.

First on stage was William Turner, Ellen's father, looking most determined, clearly a man of substance and resolve. Accompanied by his solicitors, '*Grim* ghosts are howling' Grimsditch and his partner William Hopes, he took his seat beside Sergeant Cross, counsel for the prosecution. The audience's appetite was whetted, a modest murmur of anticipation arose, only to be drowned almost immediately by the buzz of excitement emanating from the predominantly ladies' section of the court. Bonnets were shown to best advantage and gloved hands fluttered as Edward Gibbon Wakefield, the popular villain of the piece, made his entrance. Flanked as he was by his father Edward, his uncle Daniel the Chancery barrister and his eminent defence lawyers, a round of applause would not have seemed out of place. To a discerning onlooker, however, this trial, held in the Shire Court rather than the Crown Court, would have constituted a travesty. In the Crown Court, a procession of murderers, machine-breakers, thieves and horse-stealers, the severity of whose crimes rendered them liable to the heaviest sentences, would be dealt with in peremptory fashion, almost always without any representation. Yet here in the Shire Court this masquerade was attended by the most distinguished advocates: for the defence James Scarlett, the most famous 'verdict getter'[3] of his day; and Messrs Coltman, Parke and Pattison, all three future High Court judges; and leading for the prosecution the eminent Henry Brougham, supported by Messrs Starkie, Williams and Sergeant Cross. A future Whig Chancellor, Brougham was renowned for his defence of Queen Caroline at her 'trial' in the House of Lords six years previously. He was certainly well acquainted with both Edward Gibbon's father and his uncle, Daniel Wakefield.

A special jury was duly sworn in: an interesting assortment of merchants, three of them from Manchester and four from Liverpool – most surely to the satisfaction of Mr Turner. The judge, Baron Hullock, then ordered the defendants to be called on their recognisance; whereupon it transpired that William Wakefield was not present. When Mr Pattison reminded the judge that William had been arrested on Wednesday evening in a civil action for debt, Baron Hullock ordered that he attend forthwith. Consequently, he was brought into court in the custody of Mr Higgin, the gaoler. Thevenot, Edward Gibbon's servant, was still abroad and, much to the disappointment of the spectators, the enigmatic Frances Wakefield, stepmother and 'contriver of this wicked enterprise',[4] though indicted, was not bound to appear.

All eyes were now on the two brothers, the leading lady having yet to make her debut. The representatives of the law launched into their carefully prepared briefs: Mr Starkie did not disappoint, reading the indictment in fine bombastic style; and Sergeant Cross, leading for the prosecution, his arguments carefully considered, quoting statute and precedent, outlined the cases of Lucy Ramsey and Swendsen, observing chillingly that the perpetrators had suffered the ultimate penalty. A palpable shudder passed through the courtroom as he explained that had the Wakefield brothers committed the offence on English soil, they would surely have been condemned to an ignominious death. However, he added with undisguised disappointment, under a recent statute, Sir James Mackintosh's Act, 1 George IV, theirs was no longer a capital offence – the Wakefields need not fear the noose. Furthermore, their crime had been committed in Scotland, a separate kingdom under municipal law, for which the penalty was five years imprisonment and a fine at the discretion of the court.

Well aware that the character, appearance and disposition of Ellen would play a strong part in the Wakefields' defence, with commendable foresight Cross carefully prepared his audience for the supposed ingénue. During the past year Ellen had been painstakingly reconstructed by the creative accounts of a Fleet Street ever ready to fill the imaginations of their avid readers – and their own pockets. Judiciously he paved the way for the deconstructed Ellen, someone who, as the evidence would reveal, had never been the naïve, untutored schoolgirl of Shrigley. Cross was at pains to emphasise that Ellen was only fifteen years and one month at the time of her abduction, patently anxious to prepare the court for her maturity and composure, which, he asserted, were due to her reaching the age of sixteen, the age at which 'persons of both sexes do grow very fast to maturity'. But, a year ago, he assured them, she had been 'a delicate child'.[5] Describing the abduction and ensuing events, Cross painted a picture of enacted pantomime. He outlined the machinations of a plot verging on the ludicrous, one concocted by the coterie in Paris of whom Frances Wakefield was a prominent member, and detailed the involvement of her friend and accomplice Mrs Bathurst, who had busied herself in the escapade both before and after its execution.

The first witness for the prosecution, Mr Turner, his strength that of the injured father, the solid, affluent master of Shrigley, was, nevertheless, somewhat shaken by the guileful Scarlett, who gently wrested from him confirmation that the Cheshire squires had visited Shrigley only *after* his prestigious appointment as Sheriff, implying – as asserted by Edward Gibbon in his published statement – that William Turner was not highly regarded. Ellen's school teacher Miss Elizabeth Daulby was called next. Ill-health at the time of her cross-examination may well have occasioned her to be led unwittingly into the trap of declaring Ellen a clever, quick-witted girl, not, as Scarlett would suggest, one to be effortlessly led down a path she did not wish to tread. Brougham, a tall, angular man, jerking to his feet, 'like a gigantic marionette',[6] swiftly countered Scarlett, eliciting from Elizabeth Daulby evidence of the openness of her young charge, her trusting and child-like nature – one who could fall easily into the trap set by a practised Lothario.

Despite the non-appearance of Frances Wakefield, stepmother of the accused, 'directress of the plot',[7] she was to play a significant role in the trial. Exactly of an age with her stepson Edward Gibbon and, like him, having lost her mother when young, she had been brought up by her father; a rather privileged upbringing owing to his standing in the community as educator of the children of the chief families of Cheshire. A regular visitor to Paris, it is probable that it was there that she had first encountered Edward Gibbon's father, Edward, whom she had married secretly at the British Embassy when she was twenty-seven. Prior to Christmas 1825, she had persuaded her unsuspecting father to visit the French capital, where he most probably first met Edward Gibbon and William Wakefield who were domiciled there; members of the coterie, 'The First Society in Europe'. There, Frances, no doubt having a great deal of time on her hands, enjoyed the idle gossip and speculation of her female counterparts: a Mademoiselle Blanc, and, in particular, her great friend, ally and partner in prittle-prattle, Mrs Phyllida Bathurst. In her evidence, Anne Brocklehurst of Macclesfield stated that Frances often went to Paris; and had purchased several items for her during her Christmas visit of 1825. She testified that on the return of Dr Davies and his daughter from France at the beginning of February 1826, Frances had expressed a wish to visit Shrigley. As she was not acquainted with the Turners she had asked Mrs Brocklehurst to accompany her and effect an introduction. This was accomplished, Frances meeting not only Mrs Turner but also her sister Mrs Critchley. Apparently disappointed to learn that Ellen had already returned to school, Frances had declared, perhaps ironically, that she looked forward to making the young lady's acquaintance before very long.

Thomas Grimsditch, who it transpired had known Frances Wakefield for some years, told the court that he had met her at the beginning of March 1826, but could not remember whether it was Wednesday the 1st or Thursday the 2nd. His testimony was a damning one for Frances Wakefield, clearly implying her deliberate and largely successful attempt to obtain information from him regarding the forthcoming whereabouts and intentions of William Turner. On his way to see Frances, in response to a message, he had encountered her on horseback in the street, accompanied by the two Wakefield brothers whom he had never met before and who did not speak. She had told him that she and her two friends had been to Shrigley and Lyme, commenting that she had not seen William Turner while out riding. He had informed her that Mr Turner had been away from home lately because of the death of his elder brother at Blackburn, but that he had now returned to Shrigley, though he was soon to leave for London.

Even more damaging was the evidence of Robert Bagshaw of Brocklehurst Bankers of Macclesfield, who remembered being summoned by Frances on 5 March to arrange a substantial loan of between £150 and £160, on the pretext of settling an account for her cousin, John Davies. As far as he could recall, this consisted of a £50 Bank of England note, a bank post-bill for £60, the rest in £5 and £10 notes. During the course of the transaction two men had entered, one definitely Edward Gibbon Wakefield, the other possibly William. He remembered Edward Gibbon jokingly asking Frances whether she was signing a will when she signed for the notes. Although denying that this money had been used for the abduction, she had admitted lending Edward Gibbon some as he only had French bills. However, William Carr the coach-maker from Manchester, who had supplied Edward Gibbon with the green barouche used in the abduction, testified that he had been paid by him on 6 March with a £60 bank post-bill. There was a contradictory response to this testimony: on the one hand, the audience entertained and appalled by Frances Wakefield's female betrayal, on the other, barely disguised disappointment at the non-appearance of the guilty party.

However, their spirits were soon to be raised, their sensibilities suitably engaged, by the appearance of the heroine of this 'tale of anguish, deceit and violation of the domestic hearth'.[8] Miss Turner was duly called, the crowd bristling audibly with expectation as, led by her father, she entered the court by the side door to the left of the judge and was directed to the box set aside for the crier. *The Times* described her as a 'pretty, genteel girl';[9] evidently the audience held her to be much more than this. She wore, as befitted the gravity of the occasion, a plain black silk dress, but her leghorn bonnet, trimmed with scarlet ribbon, framed a face which the *Guardian* described as 'very pleasing, her complexion good, and the expression of her lips particularly beautiful. Her figure was particularly and deservedly admired.' She was, the article continued, 'a young lady of very interesting and prepossessing appearance' – the audience was vindicated. Despite the ordeal of her abduction, and the trial to which she was now subjected, she looked 'extremely well'.[10] Raised to the heights of expectation, there was a visible deflation in the courtroom when Scarlett rose to request that Ellen might leave the court for a short time, whereupon she was led out by her father. Scarlett then submitted that as Miss Turner was in fact the wife of Edward Gibbon Wakefield, she could not be examined as a witness against him. A lengthy exposition ensued in which Scarlett sought to prove that Ellen was legally married; that, as in law a wife could not bear witness against her husband, he would prove the legality of the marriage; that no force had been used in effecting it, nor had there been any intimidation. At this, Baron Hullock declared that he would hear the evidence of Miss Turner, and then that for the defence, after which he would reach a decision. He added, that if necessary the jury would be instructed to disregard the defence's evidence.

Ensconced before the ladies' box directly opposite the jury, Ellen's manner, when asked to stand, was unexpectedly easy and graceful for one in such a tense situation. With admirable coolness, and a distinct voice, she outlined the facts of the abduction, asserting that, in agreeing to the marriage her overriding desire had been to save her father from financial ruin. Throughout her testimony, Edward Gibbon Wakefield, who was sitting within only a yard or two of Ellen, kept his eyes fixed resolutely on hers; she looking straight past him to the jury, never permitting her eyes to meet his, nor betraying the least agitation. Submitting to a brief cross-examination by Scarlett, Ellen agreed that the wedding ring had been too large, and another bought for her in Calais; that she did believe herself to be Edward Gibbon Wakefield's lawful wife until informed to the contrary in Calais by Grimsditch and her uncle Critchley; and that she had used the name of Wakefield when writing to her mother from Calais. Throughout her examination Ellen 'behaved with great propriety and composure notwith-standing the intense curiosity with which she was viewed by so large an assembly'.[11]

After Henry Critchley had been questioned by Brougham, Scarlett opened for the defence by commenting on the 'studious panegyric'[12] made by Sergeant Cross in his address, concerning the elevation to the Lord Chancellorship of Lord Copley who had led for the prosecution in the aborted Wakefield trial of the previous August. He speculated as to whether or not the former Attorney General would serve independent of the political parties, confirming the criticism of him that he was wont to use the Bench as a political platform, for which, it transpired, he was later heavily criticised by both Parliament and the press. Scarlett admitted that Edward Gibbon Wakefield owned the 'transaction' to be wrong and unjustifiable. However, he accused Mr Turner of seeking vengeance rather than justice by including Frances Wakefield in the prosecution, maintaining that, by the same token, any six persons in Macclesfield could have been indicted on the same testimony. One such could have been Mrs Brocklehurst who had taken Frances Wakefield to Shrigley, her only offence having been to call on Mrs Turner at a season when persons were expected to be full of gaiety at a time when the High Sheriff was about to give a public breakfast. Furthermore, he questioned whether it had been a crime to call on a lady and ask after her daughter – a natural politeness, he posited – the female sex ever being desirous of participating in innocent amusements of that sort. 'It is not necessary', he suggested, 'to resort to the supposition that this lady was introduced there with any intention to defraud them of their child or their property.' True, she had admitted to lending money to her stepson, but from this it could in no way be inferred that she had lent it to him for the express purpose of funding the abduction. This unjustified indictment had inflicted upon his client 'a degree of punishment more severe than any Mr Turner could wish to inflict upon her.'[13] Scarlett contended that he had not asked Ellen many questions because he had been so instructed by Edward Gibbon, disingenuously drawing the attention of the jury particularly to her appearance, 'undoubtedly very captivating'; and to the evidence given by Miss Daulby, that she was 'a very clever girl of quick apprehension and sagacity and undoubtedly of considerable talents', which, he submitted, had been confirmed by what the jury had seen and heard of her that day. He went on to argue that Ellen had married of her own free will, and it was his intention to prove that the marriage was legal both under the law of Scotland and England. Although it was a crime under statute to force a girl below the age of sixteen to marry against her will, one girl of sixteen was very different from another. He intended to show that the marriage was legal, and that 'the lady, when she set out from Manchester with which she was well acquainted, knew that the horses' heads were turned towards the Oldham Road, and not the Macclesfield Road'.[14]

There followed a succession of post-boys, waiters, landladies and landlords; and even Monsieur Augustus Quillac, in whose hotel the couple had stayed in Calais, stating through an interpreter that he had known Edward Gibbon Wakefield for some years. All confirmed Scarlett's contention, testifying to the marked gaiety and warmth emanating from the wedding party and the evident happiness of Ellen; assuredly reliving for the wedded couple the circumstances leading up to the ceremony and the brief honeymoon period which was brought to such a dramatic and unhappy conclusion for them both; and highlighting the marked change which appeared to have been made at the moment of Ellen's uncles' arrival at Calais. The only voices of dissent were those of Sarah Holmes, landlady of the Bush Inn, Carlisle, who noted Ellen's dejected appearance, and a 'respectable lady' who described the 'young creature' as a 'picture of despair'.[15] In contrast, by the time they had reached Gretna she was described as seemingly perfectly happy, indeed Frances Linton, daughter of the landlord of Gretna Hall, testified that Ellen sat on [Edward Gibbon] Wakefield's knee as they awaited the arrival of the blacksmith priest who was to marry them.

Had the attention of the audience wavered, or the Fleet Street couriers been left loitering at this point in the proceedings, the farcical appearance of the 'celebrity of Gretna Green', the 'veteran minister of bliss',[16] David Lang, would certainly have provided a welcome interlude. In his own eyes he was undoubtedly the star of the proceedings and he rose to the occasion with quixotic zeal. Ironically, it was also to be his swan song, since he was to meet an untimely and unprepossessing end, falling victim to a chill as he returned to Gretna from the trial. An elderly man of at least seventy-five years, he was, to all appearances, a vulgar fellow, dressed in a black coat and velvet waistcoat with breeches of the same colour, and a shining pair of top boots; the ensemble topped by a hat of deliberate clerical fashion. On entering the witness box he looked around with the kind of stare from which 'it might be inferred that he considered himself the most important personage in that court',[17] leaning forward towards Mr Parke, counsel for the defence, 'with a ludicrous expression of gravity upon his features', and accompanying every answer with 'a knitting of his wrinkled brow and significant nodding of his head, which gave peculiar lie to his quaintness of phraseology'.[18] On several occasions he had the court convulsed with laughter. Brougham countered the considerable presence of Lang with his own particular brand of theatre, entering into the dramatic exchange with that 'certain glare in his eyes', a mischievous excitability its most obvious expression. 'Were he a horse', Bagehot had written, 'nobody would buy him, with that eye nobody would buy him.'[19] Brougham, in derisory fashion, cross-examined the blacksmith, who having 'forged the chains of so many fugitive supplicants . . . was a disciple of Vulcan',[20] dismissing and discrediting him with a number of well-aimed salvos. Alluding to his qualifications, he culminated by flourishing a copy of the marriage certificate, a printed register, at the top of which was a rudely executed wood-cut, apparently of the royal arms.

This comic interlude concluded, the defence called Duncan McNeil, the sheriff-depute of Perthshire who, having been present in court throughout, stated that he had heard nothing which in his opinion would suggest the marriage was illegal, and therefore the proceedings at Gretna were all that were needed to constitute a marriage. Brougham, establishing that McNeil had served only eleven years at the bar, questioned his competence to pronounce on

tirred the world to arms' may not be deemed
If not visited by the strong arm of the law,
ciety would be in perpetual fear and danger of
peace and happiness broken in upon by any
might suppose that he would enhance his worldly
alliance with a wealthy family. That the plan of
was well laid and ingeniously and promptly
will deny — the handy work of an adroit yet
racter, struggling to maintain his dashing course of
ost unjustifiable — most villainous — and most
ans. Had the scheme blown up at Manchester,
ps it ought to have done, the fellows (all three)
een transported for life at the next Assizes and the
d have been rid of a pest.

tribute to Edward Gibbon's intellect was followed
her complimentary reference to his victim:

umstance of Ellen raising no alarm at Manchester,
ng presumption that either her intellect is not of the
lity, or that she inherits a mind tinctured with levity
s. In thus hazarding an opinion, let it be understood
into account her tender years, notwithstanding this,
tate powerfully against all that we heard in Court
nfiding nature, her ingenuousness of indisposition,
An ingenuous indisposition is most commonly void
deceit, yet generally possessing a strength of mind
ment to watch and guard against those qualities in
then becomes of her sagacity? If she had possessed
talent (for we question the very term as applied to a
he have been deluded, from day to day, by the weak
deceitful villain? Could she not rather have told her
ears – her distress at an Inn on the road, and such is
unceremonious nature of John Bull, that she would
afe under his sheltering and protective arm; and
efield and Thevenot might have thought themselves
had got off without a severe drubbing, consenting to
eir prize. Such is our view of the case, but we leave
abler minds and for the benefit of lawyers.[27]

the validity of such marriages. For his part, Scarlett parried with a hypothesis: If a lady, though originally obtained by fraud and deception, was subsequently shown to have made a long journey in apparent contentment, pleasure, satisfaction and joy, without the least restraint, finally freely and openly consenting to a marriage, would the jury have any doubts as to it being a good marriage?

A watercolour by an unknown artist and now hanging in the Barristers' Robing Room at Lancaster Castle, shows Brougham, with thrusting jaw and pointing finger, surrounded by some twenty-two counsel and attorneys crowded on to the fine oak benches in the body of the court. Delivering his closing speech in a voice 'ranging from thunder to dramatic whispers',[21] he looked directly across the court at Edward Gibbon, and declared that there could not be the slightest pretence that a marriage conducted by a drunken pedlar, at an alehouse, before a post-boy, was a marriage according to the form of the Church of Scotland.

The most prodigious of stage-managers could not have engineered what was to follow: the heat and pressure in the court, like the proceedings, had become intense, when at about three o'clock 'considerable alarm prevailed in the town, in consequence of a shock having been felt which it was imagined was an earthquake'.[22] It appeared to strike in all directions, being felt at Shap, some twenty-eight miles from Lancaster. At Ulverston, the sand was hurled into the air in heavy showers and 'men and horses were overthrown in several places of that dangerous tract of sand, which these poor people cross daily with peat etc to earn something about 2s 6d'.[23] The journal responsible for the metaphorical reference to Lang's 'Vulcan' connections must have been tempted to attribute this to the heaven's protest at Brougham's proclamation, particularly considering that the windows of his residence, Brougham Hall, had been shattered. Not until the arrival of the Ulverston coach the following evening did it become clear that the cause of the upheaval had been an explosion on a cargo ship carrying cotton and gunpowder, which caught fire and was scuttled near Piel Castle on the Lancashire coast.

Judge Baron Hullock, having heard the submissions as to the legality of the marriage, pronounced that although he was not satisfied in his own mind that it had been a legal marriage, nevertheless, he was prepared to admit Miss Turner's evidence.

Scarlett then concluded his case for the defence by saying that with respect to Frances Wakefield he did not think it necessary to offer any evidence although, if required, he had witnesses available. Sergeant Cross then addressed the court, arguing that during the last five hours they had been totally carried away from the real question in the case: the taking of a young female from the custody of her instructors with the intention of marrying her to one of the culprits. He attributed Ellen's undeniable good spirits throughout the adventure to her conviction that she was serving her family. Had the defendants, he contended, who took possession of Ellen by means of forgery, obtained a bale of goods by the same means, they would have been transported as swindlers long ago. Once again he cited Frances Wakefield as the 'suggester and contriver' of the plot, asserting that it could never have been executed without her assistance; for the Wakefield brothers, residing as they did in Paris, would never have known of the existence of Mr Turner or his daughter:

> Miss Davies visits them at Paris, she marries their father and conceals that marriage for three years, and during all that time has been, I am sorry to say, practising duplicity towards her father and her friends and acquaintances until the marriage was discovered. She must from that course of life have been pretty well practised in the habits of dissimulation. Far from condemning the abduction, she corresponds secretly on the subject with two of her confederates only several days after the final commission of the crime.[24]

Cross concluded the case for the prosecution by advising the jury that the fate of all three defendants was in their hands, maintaining that it was impossible to entertain a doubt with regard to the Wakefield brothers, the only area of doubt remaining relating to their stepmother, Frances.

The facts of this astonishing 'tale of real life, which far surpassed everything . . . ever met with in imaginary history'[25] had taken but one day to examine. By early evening, Baron Hullock had begun his summing up in his customary mild and measured fashion. Addressing the jury, he made it plain that although there was little question as to the guilt of the Wakefield brothers, in the case of

The *Kaleidoscope*, self-styled the *Literary and Scientific Mirror, 'Utile Dulci'* of 3 April 1827, informed its readers that it would forward to its agents extra copies of the journal the following Saturday, when, it added smugly, documents in its possession, which had not yet appeared in any public journals, would be published. 'The conduct of [Edward Gibbon] Wakefield', the paper pronounced, was 'unlike that of most other criminals'; moreover it could 'discover no redeeming feature to palliate its atrocity'.

His sole motive was of the most sordid and vulgar description. In order to possess himself of the fortune of a mere girl, whom he had never seen, he did not scruple to employ falsehood, fraud, forgery, cruelty and the vilest hypocrisy, in feigning a passion he could not have entertained, unless the young lady, like the fabled Princess Rezia in the Persian Tales, possesses the power of instantaneously depriving of their wits all who had the temerity to contemplate her charms.

We heartily congratulate the public upon the conviction of Wakefield and his swindling associates, at the Lancaster Assizes. Never was a more correct verdict pronounced in any court; never was the guilt of a culprit more unequivocally proved – as mean, foul and heartless a transaction as we ever had occasion to record – this cold-blooded profligate adventurer, the anguish which the parents of Miss Turner must have endured greatly aggravates an offence, which, had the young lady been an orphan, would have been sufficiently heinous. Suppose that Mr Turner had in his possession a favourite dog, and that one of his neighbours, regardless of the commandment which enjoins us neither to covet other people's goods, nor to steal had, by artful means, enticed the animal from his home, and endeavoured to obtain its affections while he detained it under his own roof: – we would ask whether that circumstance would have altered the character of the transaction, and whether the fellow would not still have been a dog stealer, and liable to be punished as such, notwithstanding his pleas that the animal remained with him of his own free will.

It is interesting to examine this proposition, made with the greatest confidence and clearly anticipating universal assent: the comparison of Miss Turner to a favourite dog brings home the position of the young daughter in this affair – she, like the dog, regarded as Mr Turner's possession, her affections that of an animal, and her desires and free will circumscribed like those of a family pet. Grandly, the *Kaleidoscope* posed the question: 'If any thief, who thus possessed himself of Mr Turner's dog, would be compelled to give it up, ought a swindler to be permitted to retain possession of Mr Turner's daughter, who had been kidnapped and trepanned into a marriage of a very doubtful character?' The journal also contended that had Ellen been an orphan, the crime would have been 'sufficiently heinous', but the anguish that her parents must have endured 'greatly aggravates the offence'. At no time is any serious consideration given to the hopes, aspirations and natural feelings of the girl herself. Pressing on with their character assassination of Edward Gibbon, they sealed his fate:

we forbear to speculate upon the nature of the punishment with which Wakefield may be visited; but if it be, as we presume, imprisonment, he may, in his cage, to banish ennui sing the song of his great predecessor, Captain Macheath:

Man may escape rape or gun;
Nay, some have outliv'd the doctor's pill;
But he that TAKES WOMAN is surely undone.[28]

Assuredly convinced by their own argument, the journal commended Mr Turner for the 'good work' he had already 'so meritoriously commenced' by applying for a divorce. Trusting that the 'disgraceful ceremony' would be annulled either by ordinary law or, if necessary, by a special Act of Parliament, they added, 'we confidently hope that Miss Turner, not Mrs Wakefield, will soon be restored to her friends, *sans tache et sans reproche* [without stain or blame].' In fact, to the surprise of many, Frances Wakefield was also soon to be 'restored to her friends': it appeared that William Turner had, 'in a manner and with a forbearance in the highest degree credible to his injured feelings, intimated his intentions of not pressing for the judgement of the court against the female defendant'.[29] He was reported to believe the verdict of the court alone to have been sufficiently humiliating, and a severe punishment for Frances Wakefield. The *Atlas* was scathing about 'the undue commiseration' afforded her, judging that she was not 'a legitimate object of pity' and indeed that her sex, which it believed had procured her 'exemption from the sentence of the law', merely served to aggravate 'the turpitude of her conduct . . . the idea of a woman plotting against an innocent girl detestable'. Furthermore, they accused, 'the levity with which she alludes to the affair in her letters, is perfectly in the slang style: and she seems in every way worthy of the name Wakefield, which she has since assumed'.[30]

At a hearing of the Court of the King's Bench at the end of April, the Attorney General agreed that Frances Wakefield had 'suffered much in consequence of the verdict given against her'.[31] Brougham, appearing for Mr Turner, informed the court that he had not yet had time to consult with his client, and it might well be that on meeting with Mr Turner the case against Frances Wakefield could be deemed to be nolle prosequi [the plaintiff undertakes not to continue], thus terminating any further proceedings against her. In the event, Mr Turner was unwilling to sanction the added punishment of incarceration. Thereafter, for reasons which are not clear, there was to be an estrangement between Frances Wakefield and her stepson, Edward Gibbon. According to his great-granddaughter, Frances' 'affection and sympathy were apparently swamped by her bitterness at his disgrace and by her natural resentment against him for the precipitate folly which had implicated her as well as himself in unpleasant consequences'.[32] This affair had undoubtedly ruined her social prospects and destroyed her husband's chance of being selected as parliamentary candidate for Reading. Moreover, her father, loyal both to his daughter and to the Wakefield brothers, had clearly been traumatised by the case, which may well have contributed in some part to his death the following year. Nevertheless, in retrospect, it is difficult to understand why Frances should have taken this attitude in view of what seems to have been the significant role she had played from the outset in the instigation of the whole escapade – her husband's reference to her 'fickle' nature coming pertinently to mind.

Meanwhile, as he languished in Lancaster gaol, Edward Gibbon Wakefield's thoughts had turned to the possible repercussions for his family, and in particular his children, Nina and Edward

Jerningham. Mindful of them, he had entered a plea for mitigation in which he stated that the legal proceedings had cost him £6,000 – Scarlett's services not having come cheap. Edward Gibbon had been forced to raise money at a very high rate of interest, and compelled to find a further sum by the sale of a reversionary life interest of £1,500 a year. Should he have needed to raise yet more funds, it would have entailed sacrificing the interests of his children under the terms of their mother's marriage settlement. For him, a heavy fine would 'amount to perpetual imprisonment',[33] for he knew full well that debtors remained in prison until their debts were discharged. He therefore begged that he be spared a fine. The *Sunday Times*, joining its brothers in print in pursuit of their 'pound of flesh', looked forward to a summary process in the Ecclesiastical Court, 'to annihilate the mockery of the marriage, when [Edward Gibbon] Wakefield had pounced on her like a Corsair, who makes a descent from his vessel, or the Tartar, who tears a Georgian maid from the arms of her weeping parents'.[34]

On Monday 14 May, the Wakefield brothers were duly brought from Lancaster to London to attend the Court of the King's Bench at Westminster where they both swore affidavits. No sooner was the court opened than, just as in Lancaster, it was filled to excess; public curiosity yet unassuaged, the galleries overflowed with both men and women. For the ladies, sight of the brothers had been worth the wait. Standing shoulder to shoulder they looked pale but composed. Edward Gibbon wore a blue surtout with a black velvet collar, his face set, his eyes blue and piercing, as so often described by his observers; his younger brother William, clad in a blue dress coat, also with a collar of velvet, looked both exposed and vulnerable. There was about William a certain air reflected in his eyes; the more fanciful of the ladies whispering behind gloved hands of his enforced estrangement from his own recently acquired bride.

As the indictments and evidence from their Lancaster trial were read out, William betrayed no anxiety, his thoughts apparently elsewhere; Edward Gibbon, although ostensibly composed, sought perhaps to conceal his anguish, occupying himself for most of the time in reading a book which was lying on the clerk's desk. Eventually, addressing the court at great length from a written paper he held in his hand, he dwelt on the hardship of his confinement in Lancaster. Further, he claimed that since his arrival in London the previous day he had been 'precluded from consulting efficiently with any professional adviser', adding that in consequence he had been subjected to 'positive suffering', having been obliged to become 'his own advocate'. While making it clear that he would not be so presumptuous as to explain the 'peculiar reasons which had induced him to take so dangerous a course',[35] Edward Gibbon stressed that he did not wish to plead mitigation on the grounds of the usual sentences passed for similar offences. He sought rather a sentence commensurate with his conviction, for he feared that counsel would attempt to obtain a punishment 'unusually severe, and founded, not upon the conviction, but upon other circumstances'. He contended that he had been denied the opportunity to refute the charge against him, not because of 'any difficulties arising out of the facts' but by 'careful management of those who made the charge'. Patently he flattered the court, stating that it was well known for its dispensation of justice and not vengeance. While owning that his offence was 'grave' and deserved a 'corresponding punishment', Edward Gibbon charged the prosecuting counsel, Sergeant Cross, with being either ignorant of the statute which had repealed the penalty of capital punishment for abduction or of having intentionally made 'a wil-ful mis-statement' to the jury at Lancaster, dramatically claiming that had the Wakefield brothers committed their offence in England they might well have faced execution. This, he contended, had been 'for the purpose of distracting, without any conceivable object, the harassed feelings of a man who already had enough to bear'.[36] Moreover, wounded by what he referred to as the 'cruelty and depravity of the defence resorted to at the trial', he trusted that their lordships would be mindful of it.

He proceeded to draw their attention to the similarity between his case and that of *The King* v. *Bowditch and others* where eight or nine defendants had been convicted of a conspiracy to carry away a young lady of the age of sixteen by force to procure her marriage with one of them against her will. Like Ellen Turner, the victim had been a 'person of good condition, and entitled to a large fortune in her own right';[37] furthermore she had been a total stranger to the man to whom she was to have been married. Edward Gibbon claimed that the evidence on which the defendants in the Bowditch case were convicted was tainted by perjury, proposing that there was a strong resemblance between that case and his own. In mitigation, Edward Gibbon reminded the judges that he was abroad when the charge of felony was first preferred against him and, despite the urging of his friends to escape to America, he had voluntarily returned to England and surrendered himself to Mr Newton, the Cheshire magistrate.

Clearly, in a bid to exonerate William he owned that he had always possessed over the mind of his brother a 'remarkable and almost unlimited influence'; moreover his younger brother had 'always been accustomed to consult him on matters of interest and to follow his course and suggestions, whenever they offered as much on subjects of importance as in the merest trifles'.[38] He maintained that his brother had only taken part in the abduction at his request, although unfortunately William had earlier made it clear in his deposition that he had wished to be close to his brother at that time because Edward Gibbon was negotiating, on his behalf, a marriage settlement with his prospective father-in-law, Sir John Sidney. Ironically, as a direct result of the transaction out of which these indictments had arisen, no settlement whatsoever had been made on the marriage of William and his wife, therefore he was totally dependent for his support, and that of his wife and child, upon such allowance as his father and father-in-law thought fit to bestow. Significantly, and no doubt in view of the forthcoming annulment proceedings, throughout the whole of his address Edward Gibbon took every opportunity to refer to Ellen Turner as his wife.

Mr John Williams, for the prosecution, responded to Edward Gibbon by reiterating the indictment, namely, that Edward Gibbon Wakefield had practised 'sundry stratagems and artifices, and false pretences' to possess Miss Turner and that it was his object not only to obtain all that belonged to her father but also to take from the Turners their 'support and ornament – the comfort and delight of the declining age of her parents – the daughter herself'. Pressing for punishment against such an offender as Edward Gibbon, Williams said that he was reminded of 'a celebrated declaration of a great orator of antiquity [Cicero] – *Hoc in negotio illa me res consolatur Judices, quod haec quae videtur esse accusatio mea non tam accusatio, quam defensio est existimanda?*' [In this business, that which consoles me, Judges, is that this which seems to be my accusation should be considered not so much an accusation as a defence.][39] And he expressed astonishment that Edward Gibbon Wakefield should have invited the court to consider the parallels between his case and that of Bowditch and his co-conspirators.

After further lengthy, and to many, convoluted legal argument, Mr Justice Bayley finally delivered judgment: while acknowledging that William was younger than Edward Gibbon, he pointed out that despite his obvious affection for his brother he was still of an age to be fully aware of his culpability, and of the disgrace on himself and all his family which would surely ensue, notwithstanding 'the destruction of the prospects and, ruin of the comforts of those individuals against whom his scheme was directed'.[40] Passing sentence, Mr Justice Bayley, while taking into consideration the time Edward Gibbon Wakefield had already served in Lancaster gaol, ordered him to be imprisoned in 'His Majesty's Gaol of Newgate for the space of three years', and William Wakefield to 'be imprisoned in His Majesty's Gaol of Lancaster for the same space'.

Thus, observed Collier in his introduction to the *Art of Colonisation*, 'did the gates of a prison close on two of the ablest, most enterprising and, with all their faults, noblest men of that generation'.[41]

14

The Man Hath Penance Done, and Penance More Will Do

The 'gay philanderer, the careless, irresponsible boy, the reckless seeker of adventure',[1] was dead: Edward Gibbon Wakefield's incarceration in the infamous Newgate gaol was to provide the 'sobering influence of a great catastrophe' needed to 'submerge his lighter attributes and bring his nobler faculties to the surface'.[2]

Newgate stood on the north side of the Thames:

> the solid masses of its granite walls were strong enough to resist artillery, unbroken by door or casement, save those low and narrow slits in the centre, iron-bound and mounted as they are – frown down upon the great arteries of London, as the Bastille formerly did upon the Rue St Antoine. The situation and surrounding objects also help to make it striking: standing in the very centre of the city, in the shadow of the national church [St Paul's Cathedral], dividing the two life streams which run along towards Holborn and the Strand.[3]

This 'English Bastille', deriving its name from the gate of which it once formed a part, was used as a prison for persons of rank as early as 1218, but was rebuilt some two centuries later by the executors of the famous Lord Mayor of London, Sir Richard Whittington whose statue, complete with cat, stood in a niche until the time of the great fire of London in 1666. The old prison, 'an accumulation of misery and inconvenience',[4] was pulled down, and then rebuilt between 1778 and 1780. However, in the year of its completion, a mob under the leadership of Lord George Gordon was

156

responsible for the destruction of the whole interior by fire, and the setting free of the prisoners. Soon afterwards it was repaired, the front consisting of a rustic wall, broken at intervals by grated windows and niches, partially filled with statues.

There were others, both the famous and infamous, who had preceded Edward Gibbon into Newgate: Daniel Defoe in 1703; Lord George Gordon who ironically died there of gaol fever in 1793; Thistlewood, leader of the Cato Street Conspiracy of 1820, upon whom Charles Dickens was to base the character of Barnaby Rudge, who was executed in the open space outside Newgate, a common body-snatcher having been hired for twenty guineas to cut off his head. In 1799, the brother-in-law of Francis Place had also been confined in Newgate after being sentenced to death for highway robbery. Place, once the close friend of Edward Wakefield and frequently censorious of his son Edward Gibbon, had been instrumental in having his brother-in-law's death sentence commuted to transportation.

Edward Gibbon's time in Lancaster gaol, though irksome, had in no way prepared him for the grim oppressiveness of Newgate. Admitted through its enormous grated and iron-guarded doors, he entered into a dark and dismal stone-vaulted lobby, guarded by men of 'stern aspect'.

Dispersed about the yard were groups of savage looking men of every age. While gazing in astonishment on the scene before us, the clanking of irons was heard; three or four unhappy but desperate looking individuals made their appearance. The *tout ensemble* was now complete, nothing was wanting. We had now before our eyes, vice and its dreadful consequences. When I contemplated the fettered limbs, sunken eyes and sallow dirty complexions of the prisoners . . . here we had an opportunity of beholding the effects of religion without morality. . . . Having waited some time in this delectable situation, we were ushered into the office, and measured with as much precision as though we had been candidates for the situation of full privates in the Horse Guards . . . our beds consisted of some excellent door mats and some horse rugs. Raw meat and vegetables were excluded as rigorously as our sex from an eastern seraglio.[5]

The secretary's office was armed and ornamented with short muskets surmounted by bayonets ready for use in case of resistance or rebellion by prisoners. Each door was unlocked to let him pass, then shut instantly, the key turned upon him. Marched through narrow passages Edward Gibbon Wakefield was conducted to his cell, a room some 24 feet square, adjoining an exercise yard 50 feet long. From the outset, he appears to have been granted special privileges, but though considerably more comfortably accommodated than most of his wretched companions, Edward Gibbon could not have been spared the disagreeable and disquieting thoughts which now assailed him. Foremost in his mind must have been the unhappy situation of his brother William, whose young wife Emily had given birth to a daughter during their remand in Lancaster; his guilt surely compounded when news of her death reached him in August. The *Gentleman's Magazine*, no doubt echoing the thoughts of many, had sympathetically observed, 'this accomplished and beautiful young lady has fallen victim to a broken heart. She has left one infant daughter, six months old.'[6] Fortunately, Edward Gibbon's thoughts were soon to be diverted to the arrangements for the care and education of his own two children, Nina and Edward Jerningham. Almost nine and six years old respectively, they had been brought from Paris to the home of his only sister, Catherine, and her husband the Reverend Charles Torlesse. The couple lived at Stoke-by-Nayland, some ten miles from Ipswich, close to their great-grandmother Priscilla's home. Now, rooms were to be obtained near Newgate for them to live with their governess, Mrs Matthews.

After the death of their mother, their aunt had often looked after them during their father's absences, a letter to her giving careful instructions for Nina's welfare and education and written as early as January 1822 illustrating his great love for his daughter, who had filled the terrible void created by her mother's death. Asking his sister to prepare the children for a journey, he not only gave details of which clothes should be packed for his five-year-old daughter, but also issued explicit directions for the nurse as to how the child was to be dressed.

Let her have the best as well as common clothes, a sufficiency of strong and thin shoes and let some of the latter be of silk or jane with sandal like strings to tie crosswise round her uncles [sic] teach the nurse how to tie them and how to put on and *adjust* her clothes neatly and prettily. This may be done by half a dozen dressings and undressings and they will be a good trial of my soul's patience, a virtue which she must practise against her will very often before it becomes habitual. Let her have combs and rollers and pomatum in short everything that her hair requires.

In these letters can be detected early signs of the delicate state of Nina's health. He instructs his sister to prepare doses of the calomel which his daughter had been accustomed to take as precaution against 'one of her violent attacks'; emphasising that Reeve her nurse must be given a long and careful lecture about Nina's health, knowing that 'so much is to be preserved by watching her extraordinary little stomach'. Furthermore, he insisted that Reeve be given 'most positive instructions about what she [was] to eat and drink and about regularity in hours in all matters'. Conscious also of Nina's educational and social needs, he asked his sister to prepare Nina's books for her studies, and her workbox, including her knitting apparatus and anything else which would amuse or employ her. Clearly, Edward Gibbon was confident of his sister's good influence upon his daughter, trusting that from her Nina would 'learn virtuous principles and happy inclinations'. At the conclusion of one of his letters he wrote, portentously, 'She is a dear little soul and I love her so much that I am sure almost that I shall be deprived of her. If that were to happen, goodbye to my philosophy. I should think even worse than I do now of this incongruous, contradictory, mottled world.' There is, however, a notable absence of reference to his eighteen-month-old son; at the end of a long letter devoted to the care of Nina, he added just a couple of sentences alluding to Edward Jerningham. 'I long to see Master Edward for my pride is alarmed at the possibility of his legs being crooked by injudicious walking etc.' Significantly he added, 'I shall love him bye and bye, I suppose, as much as I do his sister.'[7]

Whenever separated from Nina, Edward Gibbon continued to maintain close touch with her progress. In December 1824, he had chided his sister Catherine for not writing more frequently to apprise him of her progress. Although evidently not sharing his sister's religious beliefs, he nevertheless wished 'his chicks' to imbibe some religious impressions, while maintaining that he had 'a sort of conscience', one he would like his children to have. There was a genuine fatherliness in his involvement in his children's upbringing, a kind of participation not always evident among his contemporaries. He wrote to his daughter, telling her that he was very, very glad to learn that she 'is good in the tub'[8] and hoped that she would remain so because he would be very sorry to have to quarrel with her any more about washing. He was delighted to hear that Nina had learned many French words and was now able to put a map of England together.

While Edward Gibbon's energies were engaged in ensuring his children's welfare, William Turner was devoting himself to securing his daughter's future. Only three days after Edward Gibbon had entered Newgate, on 17 May the Lord Chancellor presented a petition to the bar of the House of Lords to grant leave to William Turner to bring a bill to annul his daughter's marriage. *The Times*, maintaining its moral high ground, wished Mr Turner every success: 'late as it may come, to soothe the spirits of his literally heart-broken wife and also at last the reward for that undaunted perseverance shown by him'.[9] At the same time the Earl of Eldon, who had first encountered Mr Wakefield on the occasion of his first 'irregular marriage' eleven years previously, presented a petition from Edward Gibbon Wakefield, praying permission to be heard at their Lordships' bar to allow him to reply to Mr Turner's petition. With the Earl of Shaftesbury, the Tory evangelical, in the chair, a motion to bring in a bill to annul and declare void the alleged marriage was carried. At what was to be a virtual re-run of the Wakefield trial, the second reading of the bill was heard on Wednesday 30 May. Public interest in the case had shown no signs of abating. The sale of the transcript of the trial at Lancaster, bound and published by John Murray, and the publication of a satirical essay, *Une Nouvelle Manière D'Attrapper une Femme, A Bold Strike for A Wife*, complete with a fashion plate representation of Ellen Turner, served to maintain the impetus in this long-running saga. Consequently, a large crowd was expected for the hearing, and similar preparations were made as those for the trial of Queen Caroline six years previously: the Palace Yard before the House of Lords had been railed off with timber palisades and a large number of constables were on duty to repel the anticipated great crowds that collected outside the doors, repeatedly attempting to force an entrance. Not immune to this universal attack of *arrectis auribus*, the Peers were evidently subject to the same curiosity, and attended the house in great numbers. However, 'Members of the Press were not admitted until their lordships had heard prayers'.[10]

At half past ten in the morning, Sergeant Cross and Brougham, who had both prosecuted for William Turner at the Wakefield trial, attended below the bar. Here Brougham brought to the cause of the sixteen-year-old Ellen all the grandiose rhetoric he had employed in the defence of Queen Caroline. Edward Gibbon Wakefield, attended by the deputy-keeper of Newgate, listened carefully as Mr Adam opened the case, recapitulating the whole of the 'transactions connected with this extraordinary affair',[11] and most of the witnesses who had given evidence at the trial repeated their testimonies. To be so central to the avid interest of so many in this House of Lords must surely have been a daunting prospect for one so young and inexperienced; the presence of her audacious kidnapper, though gentle husband, compounding her discomfort. The 'most anxious curiosity was evinced to obtain a glimpse of her face', not least that of Edward Gibbon Wakefield, for whom this could well be the last occasion on which he would see his bride. An isolated figure, he sat pressed upon by the body of noble inquisitors, while Ellen, in contrast and leaning on the arm of a gentleman, was closed around by her aunt Critchley and three other ladies stationed behind her. Wearing a plain cottage bonnet tied close under the chin and a plain black silk gown, she was described by *The Times* as 'rather above the middle size, a good figure, with large dark eyes and what is generally called a pleasing face, her appearance modest and unassuming'.[12] Her composure suggested an underlying strength, an intimation of rather more self-possession than might have been expected of one in her trying situation. Nevertheless, although generally her evidence was delivered without hesitation, there were moments when she appeared to falter, as if affected by recollection of the circumstances. Her observers must surely have speculated as to the innermost thoughts and feelings of this sixteen-year-old. Despite the artifice of this strange wedlock and judging by the evidence of witnesses, there was every reason to suppose that the wedding of this couple was a marriage of minds and feelings – if nothing else. The implacable Mr Turner had invested the considerable sum of £10,000 [some £500,000 today] in attempting to secure the release of his daughter from the arms of this man who had hunted 'his unhappy victim like the base tool of Appius demanding the centurion's daughter'.[13] Her father's plans for Ellen were hedged around by ambitions equally determined as those of his younger adversary, and possibly no less altruistic. Asked to choose between the contenders, there can be no certainty as to whom she would have preferred – had she been allowed that choice. She left the court followed by Edward Gibbon's unfaltering gaze.

Though proud and dignified, of slender build, in blue frock coat, black silk trousers and black silk neck cloth, he cut a lonely, empty figure. In the ensuing silence which hushed the low murmurs, Edward Gibbon was called to the bar. He offered no opposition to the bill. He spoke strongly to the effect that, as he had previously been acquitted on the count of using force, he should be granted the opportunity of challenging the statements made against him for the purpose of attaining the annulment. Without hearing his statement, he contended, it was impossible for their lordships to have true knowledge of the facts of the 'transaction'. He claimed that he had already spent £3,000 in bringing witnesses to Lancaster; it was of the greatest importance that he be allowed time to arrange for their attendance at this third 'trial', in the certain knowledge that their evidence would prove, beyond all reasonable doubt, that his wife had married him from motives of love, and from no other motives whatsoever.

His was, perhaps inevitably, a lost cause. The Lord Chancellor dismissed Edward Gibbon's pleas that he had not been able to call witnesses, saying that despite being served with a copy of the bill ten days ago, Edward Gibbon had not taken a single step to procure the attendance of a single witness. Furthermore, he had been present when the witnesses for the bill were examined, and although invited to do so, had never ventured to put even one question to them. To cheers of 'Hear, Hear' he contended that Edward Gibbon had obtained consent to the marriage by the 'most atrocious fraud'.[14] After support for this position from the Earl of Eldon, Lord Holland and the Marquis of Lansdown, the bill was then read for the second time, and ordered to be committed the following day. Seven days later, on 6 June, the bill declaring void Miss Turner's pretended marriage was read for the third time, and given the Royal assent on Thursday 14 June 1827 – the 'marriage' had lasted fifteen months.

The success of William Turner's arduous endeavours to 'rescue his child from infamy' was greeted with general satisfaction and approbation. One admirer, William Harwood Folliott of Chester, was moved to write to *John Bull*, proposing generously that William Turner should be created a baronet by the King.

The deep impression made on the House of Lords, in the case of Mr Turner, and believing the country from John O'Groats to Land's End sympathize with William Turner Esq of Shrigley Park, in this County for the anxiety, trouble and enormous experience he has suffered by the abduction of his amiable and affectionate daughter, induce me to now address you. He is a gentleman of great respectability, and large fortune; and when he served the office of High Sheriff of the County here, last year, made the most elegant display of his tenants etc. in honour his Majesty I have ever witnessed, and being well aware that the most respectable noblemen and gentry of the kingdom have access to your truly loyal and patriotic paper, I take leave to recommend, thorough the medium thereof, that His Majesty would be graciously pleased to create Mr Turner a baronet, failing his male issue, being an only child, the title to descend to the future husband of Miss Turner and their male issue, as a small recompense for what Mr Turner has suffered in conducting this interesting trial with so much perseverance, and in which parents who have daughters, entitled to large fortunes are deeply interested.[15]

John Bull's tongue-in-cheek response was that they 'had not yet arrived at a station where they could presume to advise His Majesty' and, while conceding that the King could have no 'more loyal subject in his dominions than their correspondent', confessed that they 'did not entirely recognize the claims of Mr Turner to the elevation Mr Folliott suggested'. More circumspect members of the public would no doubt have agreed with them.

Soon afterwards, Ellen passed through Macclesfield and

Bollington on her way home to Shrigley from London. By now, accustomed to public scrutiny and comment, and that not always favourable, she would have been heartened by the overwhelming warmth and solicitude of those who had assembled to greet her return home. 'The bells of Shrigley Church rang merrily, flags were displayed in various directions and the crowds . . . evinced their exultation by loud and hearty cheering.' When William Turner returned the following Thursday from the capital, he too was 'hailed with every demonstration of joy and respect by the local inhabitants'. If rumour was to be believed, William Turner had reason to celebrate not only the rescue of his daughter from a sham marriage, but also the distinct possibility that he would soon be giving her hand in marriage to Thomas Legh, the representative of a most ancient family in the county, with the probable reversion of a fortune of at least £600,000 – the estates of the 'high contracting parties'[16] adjoining each other.

In their final vitriolic attack on the character of the 'odious' Edward Gibbon Wakefield, the *Macclesfield Courier* accused him of seeking to degrade and debase that which he could not have. 'Her person is not in my power, her fortunes are beyond my greedy grasp; but I will avenge myself for these disappointments by tainting her reputation; if I may not enjoy her property, I will at least mar her prospects.'[17] In fact her prospects were far from marred – and there were those more intimately acquainted with the wayward Edward Gibbon who would have thought him rather to have applauded her good fortune.

15

Men at Some Time are Masters of their Fates

Ellen's prospective bridegroom was indeed Thomas Legh of Lyme, who 'like a knight of old thus came to the lady's rescue'.[1] Descended from Piers Legh, who had been granted the manor of Lyme Handley by Richard II in 1398, he had succeeded his father, Thomas Peter Legh, when only four years of age. Colonel Peter Legh, of the 3rd Lancashire Light Dragoons, a regiment he had raised for the defence of the country during the war with France, had died aged forty-four in August 1797. He had never married, and therefore settled the Lyme estate, the barony of Newton and most of his property on his elder natural son Thomas, the remainder on his other natural son, William.

In 1812, after completing his studies at Oxford, Thomas, then aged twenty and a friend of Lord Byron, left to visit the East, rapidly becoming an accomplished archaeologist. From the islands of the Aegean he sailed to Alexandria and thence up the Nile, claiming to be the first Western traveller to reach the Nubian capital of Ibrim. Afterwards he published a *Narrative of a Journey in Egypt and the Country Beyond the Cataracts*, which one newspaper recommended 'should be read by everyone in whose breast the mention of the river Nile produces something approaching to a convulsive throb'.[2] The book drew early attention to the slave trade as it then existed in Egypt, where 'miserable beings . . . were crowded together in enclosures like the sheep pens of Smithfield, the consequences of which may be more readily conceived than described'.[3] Legh carried out the first survey of Petra and on his return published accounts of his visits to the crocodile mummy pits at Armabdi. He brought home to Lyme three Greek stelae, which he placed in the library.

In 1815, England was startled by news that following his escape from Elba Napoleon was leading a large army towards Belgium. On his way home, Thomas Legh stayed in Brussels where the final confrontation was expected to take place. There, when the battle began at Waterloo, he was accepted as a volunteer to carry despatches to the outposts. After the British victory he wrote from St Denis, on 4 July:

> We are *only* five miles from Paris into which impregnable city we march tomorrow myself not as a stupid tourist but as a mighty warrior . . . you are perhaps aware that Frenchmen never stood very high in my estimation. They are now lower than the nearest reptile that crawls . . . one day doing all in their power to assist Napoleon to cut your throat, on the next sticking a piece of white rag in their hats and would, if you would allow them, lick the dust from your shoes. . . . Fancy Old Long Nose . . . being at the gates of Paris without one single shot having been fired.[4]

By 1815, Thomas Legh had formed an attachment to a married woman, Louisa Lloyd of Aston Hall, Shrewsbury, and it was to her that he had sent the letter from St Denis. Five months before, he had written to her from Naples: 'I ought to have brought you by main force. Basically this is the most charming, the most beautiful, the most delightful . . . do come, if you do not I shall throw myself down the crater of Vesuvius in despair.'[5] Yet, despite his romantic declarations he was to confess this view of marriage to her: 'The arrangements of the married state I have invariably found to be strange, yes indeed very strange. The more I hear the more I learn the more I *fear*.'[6] Significantly, it was to be a further thirteen years before he overcame his dread.

Thomas Legh showed no inclination to follow his father into the army, evidently preferring to serve his country in a different way. Thus, in 1816, having reached his majority, he was returned as their Member of Parliament by the freeholders of Newton. Nearby at Haydock, some 15 miles east of Liverpool, he owned an estate of some 413 acres, which included a large farm, parks, nurseries and a school. In 1823, when George Stephenson was visiting the area in order to inspect the likely route of the proposed Liverpool to Manchester Railway, Legh overheard a conversation concerning the project, and as a consequence invited him to breakfast. Subsequently, he engaged the famous engineer to lay a railway track from his Haydock Collieries to the Sankey Canal. Although his home on the estate, Haydock Lodge, had been rebuilt towards the end of the eighteenth century, it had ceased to be a residence by 1806 and after 1826 was used as barracks for troops. Thomas Legh thus possessed two principal residences, one in London and the other the family seat, Lyme Hall, near Disley. Regarded by some as grander than the palaces of many continental princes, it stood aloof, the wild moorland of the Peak District surrounding the house on all sides in a setting described by one eighteenth-century traveller as 'bleak, moorish and unfruitful'.[7] It was, however, set out with formal gardens and boasted a fine deer-park of medieval origin, an

> extensive park, well stocked with deer which are famous for taking the water when driven by the keeper. The soil appears to suit these animals as the venison is of a superior flavour. On top of an eminence in the Park is a building called Lyme cage, a very conspicuous object visible from the county around.[8]

After returning from the Far East, Thomas Legh had carried out various alterations and improvements to the house, commissioning Lewis Wyatt who remodelled the east side, adding a grand new dining-room and designing the tower above the south front.

No record exists of the initial meeting of Ellen Turner and Thomas Legh, although he would surely have called upon her family when they first took up residence at Shrigley. There can be no doubt that he had supported the appointment of William Turner to the post of High Sheriff of Cheshire, playing an important part in the celebrations for his inauguration, and indeed leading his grand parade. Two days later, as a magistrate at the committal proceedings of William Wakefield at Disley, he was present when Ellen gave a good account of herself. Throughout her trials and tribulations of the preceding fifteen months, he would have witnessed her growing maturity, and may well have been impressed by her manner of dealing with events as they unfolded and close scrutiny of the press and public in general. Nevertheless, although tricked into marriage by a scoundrel, and subsequently released from its bonds by an Act of Parliament, there would still be many who would deem this luckless girl unfit for marriage to a man of quality and social standing. Thomas Legh apparently had no such qualms. Perhaps his own illegitimacy, and his early life of travel, which had undoubtedly broadened his horizons, had some bearing on his attitude. Meanwhile, the resolute William Turner would almost certainly have been hard at work persuading the eligible Mr Legh of the benefits of a union with his daughter, and the consequent conjoining of their two estates. Thus, six months after the annulment of her marriage to Edward Gibbon Wakefield, the wedding of Ellen Turner and Thomas Legh took place at ten o'clock on the morning of Monday 14 January 1828, in the ancient church of St Peter, mother church of the parish of Prestbury, which served both Lyme and Shrigley. The vicar, John Rowlls Browne, who had but one week earlier presided over the marriage of Thomas Legh's sister Maria to Robert Dalzell, a barrister, declared Ellen and Thomas man and wife – the bride almost seventeen years of age and her bridegroom thirty-five. The *Macclesfield Courier* reported,

The marriage was solemnized in the presence of the two families, who arrived in the village in four carriages. Although the day appointed for the nuptials was not generally known, a large concourse of people had assembled to witness the ceremony, who appeared to take much interest in the happy union. The youthful and lovely bride was elegantly but plainly attired in an Esterhazy silk dress, with white hat and veil, and looked remarkably well. . . .[9]

After the ceremony, accompanied by their friends the bridal party returned to Shrigley, where, the *Manchester Gazette* informs us,

they partook of a collation provided for the occasion and the happy pair afterwards returned to the ancient and splendid seat of the Leghs of Lyme, where they will probably remain until parliamentary duties require Mr Legh's personal appearance in London. During the day bells were rung at all the different churches in the immediate vicinity of Lyme Park and at Disley . . . and a plentiful and substantial dinner given to the numerous tenantry of Mr Legh residing in that part of the country.[10]

Just as the bells of Disley and Newton and their adjacent villages rang out and cannon were fired, so too the bells at Blackburn parish church 'struck off a merry peal', where

> The people employed at the extensive print-works at Mill Hill and Ewood, near this town, of the firm of Robert Turner and Co were indulged in half a day's holyday [sic]. In addition to this, two fat beasts and twelve sheep were slaughtered. . . . At Ewood one sheep was roasted whole, and another was boiled entire in a large copper used for other purposes, on the premises.[11]

Very little is known of the married life of Ellen and Thomas Legh. Suffice to say that within a space of twenty-two months this young woman had metamorphosed from schoolgirl through 'pretended' wife of an adventurer and very public figure to mistress of Lyme, with all the attendant responsibilities of the wife of an eminent and respected Cheshire gentleman, magistrate, Member of Parliament and landowner. There would be many anxious to see and be seen at the Legh residence, not least those for whom Ellen remained an object of curiosity. Only one month after her wedding, the newspapers had carried an account of a trial in Dublin of members of the Richards' family who had taken a young man from his school, with the intent of forcing him to marry their daughter, Ellen, against the consent of his father. They reported that the Court of the King's Bench, Dublin, 'was unusually crowded, the interest being as great as that excited by the case of Miss Turner'.[12] Two years after her abduction, it would seem that Ellen Legh could not escape her notoriety. The proximity of her mother and aunt Critchley might well have lent her some comfort, but the fragility of her mother's health may have limited the support she could offer her daughter.

The *Stockport Advertiser* of 11 April 1828 gives an insight into the social responsibilities Ellen would have to discharge in her new role. The Grand Fancy Dress Ball held on 8 April for the benefit of the Stockport Dispensary and House of Recovery was one such occasion. In company with Mrs Egerton of Tatton Park, Mrs Vernon of Poynton Park, Mrs Humphreys of Bramhall Hall and thirteen other wives of the gentry, she was a both patroness and benefactor of the event, donating, like her husband, ten guineas to the cause. However, the Leghs were not present on this occasion, perhaps due to the fact that Ellen was in the early stages of pregnancy; or they might well have been in London at their house in Berkeley Square, should Thomas have been engaged in business in the capital.

Few descriptions of Thomas Legh are to be found, for unlike Edward Gibbon Wakefield he had not been subjected to the scrutiny of the nation's press. In his obituary he was described as having 'a commanding figure and a noble presence', his countenance 'eminently handsome and dignified, with a genial expression'.[13] The rather exotic portrait of him which adorns the staircase of Lyme Hall suggests that there was much of the romantic in him, as one might already suspect. The portrait, painted by William Bradley, depicts him in Arabian dress standing beside a spirited black stallion, his arm resting in gentle restraint upon its back. There is an easy grace in his stance; his eyes intelligent, his features fine; perhaps not noticeably handsome, but arresting – a man with all the qualities that Ellen would require to restore the equilibrium of her life. These qualities were soon to be tested: ten months after their marriage, she was delivered of their first child, a son, stillborn. Happily, by the following June Ellen would be pregnant again.

It is likely that news of Ellen's new marriage would have reached Newgate, since Edward Gibbon was well acquainted with those living close to the Leghs. In view of the regard he had for his former bride, almost certainly still strong, he would probably have wished for her a happy and fruitful life. No one knew better than he the capacity of one's children to heal life's hurts and fill the empty hours. Initially, at least, the proximity of his daughter and son, his dedication to their education and the wholehearted support of his family evidently restored his resilience, strengthening his determination to bring back some meaning to his life. His exposure to such privations and distress combined with the painful reflection enforced by his incarceration released from within him those hitherto dormant hereditary influences which would soon turn his attentions to the needs of those poor creatures with whom he now shared the cruel confines of Newgate. He arranged for his children, Nina and Edward

Jerningham, to be brought in daily. Writing to his grandmother, Priscilla, in February 1828, he assured her,

> My confinement is in some respects very advantageous to them, as I have nothing to do but to attend to their education, which is proceeding to my heart's content. Their progress during the last six months surprises even me, who am bound to think my own children prodigies. . . . Both my children are learning to draw, and are as fond of it as I used to be when I scrawled upon everything in your Tottenham house.

His daughter Nina now sustained him. 'She is a little old woman in good sense', he told Priscilla and 'has the tenderest heart in the world.' To add to his comfort, and the ease of his conscience, during the long months of close confinement he had begun to warm to his son. Proudly he wrote, 'he is of an aspiring nature, considering that he is only seven years old'. He wished to be 'a general or a prime-minister or something of that kind'.[14]

But his sister, Catherine, who had always shared his concerns about Nina and Edward Jerningham, was unhappy that her niece and nephew were daily subjected to the unhealthy atmosphere and influence of the environment and inmates of Newgate. Consequently, his brother-in-law, the Reverend Charles Torlesse, visited the prison with the intention of advising Edward Gibbon to send Nina, who was a delicate child, abroad. However, so impressed was he by the obvious affection between father and daughter that he shied from his task. 'His silence did him honour,' wrote Edward Gibbon, hoping that Charles would not be blamed for the 'fruitlessness of his journey. . . . If anyone were to ask me for my teeth or half my limbs, I might perhaps part with them – but my daughter. Who could have put it into their heads?'[15] Nevertheless, as a letter to his sister Catherine demonstrated, he agonised over what might be in Nina's best interests. Informing his sister that he would be set at liberty on 14 May 1830, but not a day sooner, he wrote that by then Nina would be well advanced into her thirteenth year, and consequently he lived 'upon thorns', knowing that he was 'not giving Nina a fair chance', and he was 'quite occupied in guarding her from evil, instead of actively promoting her good'. He owned that Nina now had need of a 'virtuous and amiable woman to whom such a charge would be agreeable'. However, in view of his previous experience of trying to obtain the services of such a 'person of principle and excellent habits', he knew that it would not be easy, bearing in mind 'that the hypocrites pass for the most perfect'. He confessed, 'I have set my face against all professed governesses, knowing from experience that "governess and hypocrite" are synonymous terms'.[16]

Edward Gibbon had other nagging concerns, particularly the continuing estrangement between himself and his stepmother and 'co-conspirator', Frances Wakefield, who would shortly give birth to her first child, a daughter, to be named after Frances, her own mother. Fearful of antagonising her further, he asked his grandmother to write to his stepmother, requesting a painting of his children which hung in her father's house, 'which was an excellent likeness', 'well executed by an artist in Paris' and 'by which she can set no store'. Although saddened by the breakdown in the friendship with Frances and its effect upon his relationship with his father, Edward Gibbon was heartened by his growing affection for his uncle Daniel, who had befriended him in his hour of need:

His disinterested, generous and most friendly, I may say more than paternal conduct in all my late troubles is far above my praise. I shall be grateful to him as long as I live, and afterwards, if we remember this world in the next. I never, I am sorry to say, gave him any cause to wish me well. Yet when I was in need he chose to become my friend; he risked much for himself, and nothing could check his generous ardour, not even the earnest persuasion of some who, whilst I flourished, could never do enough for me. I rejoice to add that he has not suffered by his kindness to me. On the contrary, having lost nothing he has gained the good opinion of many who before regarded him with indifference.[17]

Daniel Wakefield became an eminent barrister and QC, sharing the sanguine and enterprising temper of his brother and nephew. Sadly, when he died in 1846, he was penniless owing to his benevolence, having frequently been known to refuse fees from needy clients.

Mrs Fry, who in her role as philanthropist had been a regular visitor to Newgate, and, indeed, instrumental in effecting some basic reforms, visited Edward Gibbon in February 1828, no doubt taking the opportunity to extend her reforming zeal to her wayward cousin. It is open to question whether he would have welcomed her visit, or for that matter benefited from it – 'not everyone was grateful for her ministrations, or rather the manner in which they were carried out',[18] nor for the condescension with which she addressed them. For his part, although busily occupied with the task of educating his children and in receiving visits from family members who continued to rally around him, corresponding regularly and sending gifts of fruit, flowers and books, Edward Gibbon could not distance himself from the plight of his fellow inmates. According to Paul Bloomfield, he behaved like 'a one-man Royal Commission appointed to investigate the British penal system from within' and 'Mr Wontner, the Newgate Keeper must be put down as one of the procession of men of all degrees from anonymous catspaws to Cabinet Ministers who at some time or other came under Edward Gibbon's spell – who were drawn by his magnetism. It was not long before he had the run of the place.'[19] A note from Edward Gibbon to Wontner, dated 4 May 1830, appears to confirm this impression; addressed to the keeper's office, Edward Gibbon instructed, 'in case the gentleman should call again, will you be so good as to let me see him'.[20] So conscious did he become of the horrors and tragedies suffered by the majority of prisoners that Edward Gibbon's instinct to make the world a better place moved him to take up the cause of the underdog. In true Quaker tradition, his grandmother, his father, his cousin Elizabeth Fry had all displayed the family's utilitarian, philanthropic and altruistic tendencies. His cousin-in-law Sir Thomas Fowell Buxton, Wilberforce's successor as 'leader of the Saints' in the campaign to abolish slavery had campaigned against the death penalty, but whereas they had all worked from the outside, he was working from within. His great-granddaughter, Irma O'Connor, believed that his experiences within Newgate 'stirred his heart to a flame of compassionate tenderness, a tenderness which all his life afterwards was to make him correspondingly merciless in his condemnation of long standing evils'.[21]

Not for the first time did his personal magnetism and ability to communicate enable him to pursue his intent: to rescue common man from the cycle of deprivation, corruption, summary justice, and inhumane and inequitable retribution. Although Peel's Acts of 1823 had abolished the death sentence for some hundred offences, there were still more than a hundred capital crimes on the statute books. However, between 1825 and 1831, out of the 85,257 convicted for criminal offences in England and Wales no less than 9,316 attracted the death penalty, while no more than 410 were executed. During the period of Edward Gibbon's internment, one, George Warner was executed for coining in July 1827; Mary Wittenbach for poisoning her husband, in September 1827; and Esther Hibner, for the murder of her apprentice, in March 1829. Another Captain Montgomery, a forger befriended by Edward Gibbon, was informed that he would hang, despite the willingness of the Bank of England that the sentence be commuted; in the event, he escaped the noose by taking poison the night before. Montgomery left a letter for Edward Gibbon which was read at his inquest and subsequently appeared in the newspapers: 'but for the pressure of your hand, last Saturday evening would have ended the dreadful tragedy. God bless you! May you find such a friend as your heart deserves.'[22] The public's response to the newspaper's account of this tragic case might have been the spur to Edward Gibbon's penning of his numerous observations on the sufferings of his fellow inmates. *The Condemned Sermon* was to invade the consciousness of its many readers with unprecedented effect. Describing the scene in Sunday morning's chapel, it began,

> Some tremble, and sigh or weep – some swagger to their places, tossing their heads, smiling, nodding to their friends, and pretending to glory in the distinction of their danger, others appear stupefied, creeping into the pew.[23]

One of these was a youth of about eighteen years, convicted of stealing goods worth more than £5 from a house, beside him a burglar, a sheep-stealer and a clergyman convicted of forgery. Edward Gibbon described the service:

> They sing the Morning Hymn, which of course reminds the condemned of their prospect for to-morrow morning. Eight o'clock tomorrow morning is to be their last moment. They come to the burial service. The youth, who, alone of those for whom it is intended, is both able and willing to read, is from

want of practice, at a loss to find the place in his prayer book. The ordinary observes him, looks to the sheriffs, and says aloud, 'the Service for the Dead'. The youth's hands tremble as they hold the book upside down. The burglar is heard to mutter an angry oath. The sheep-stealer smiles, and extending his arms upwards, looks with a glad expression to the roof of the chapel. The forger has never moved . . . following the sermon in which the ordinary talks of crimes and punishment, widows, helpless orphans and contrite hearts, the dying men become dreadfully agitated . . . the young stealer . . . no longer has the least pretence to bravery . . . the hardened burglar moves not . . . but his face is of an ashy paleness; and, if you look carefully, you may see blood trickling from his lip. . . . The poor sheep-stealer is in a frenzy. . . . Meanwhile the clergyman, still bent into the form of sleeping dog, struggles violent[ly]. . . . Suddenly he utters a short, sharp scream, and all is still. . . . This exhibition lasts for some minutes, and then the congregation disperses; the condemned returning to the cells; the forger carried by the turnkeys; the youth sobbing aloud convulsively . . . the burglar muttering curses and savage expressions of defiance; whilst the poor sheep-stealer shakes hands with the turnkeys, whistles merrily, and points upwards with madness in his looks.[24]

The *Spectator*, whose editor Robert Rintoul, 'a large browed, gentle-mannered man, who must never be spoken to upon a Friday',[25] was to become a life-long friend, praised Edward Gibbon Wakefield's efforts, declaring 'A voice has . . . risen from amidst the very centre of crime, misery and wretchedness. A strange offence against society threw an enlightened reasoner, an active inquirer, an acute observer, into the place which is, as it were, the nucleus of metropolitan crime.'[26]

But Edward Gibbon also had his detractors; the *Quarterly Review* published his account of a young prisoner who had been condemned to death. The youth had managed to elude the turnkeys and had climbed up a pipe in the hope of escaping, but had fallen on to the pavement below, seriously injuring his legs. Edward Gibbon had questioned why the surgeon had dressed his wounds 'with the same care as if surgical skill could have preserved the use of those limbs for years', adding that when he was carried to the scaffold, 'blood flowed from these wounds evoking pity from the onlookers, one of whom said they would like to see the Home Secretary treated in the same way'.[27] This, the *Review* argued, grossly misrepresented the incident, alleging that Edward Gibbon wished only to raise prejudice against the just severity of the law. He, they continued, had told the story with 'the colouring' of his imagination, and, the journalist evidently missing the irony of the situation, declared that it would have been inhumane not to have treated the poor convict. Furthermore, the incident had nothing do with the justice or injustice of capital punishment.

Taking up his pen once more, Edward Gibbon attacked the social conditions which led to the punishment of young children also confined in Newgate; mostly these were boys, frequently seduced and exploited by the 'Fagins' of the metropolis. His observations and notes, published in 1831 and entitled *Punishment of Death in the Metropolis*, outlined the inadequacy both of the prevention and detection of criminal offences, and the futility of the existing system of punishment as a deterrent. The *Athenaeum* acknowledged,

> Out of evil comes good, for to Mr [Edward Gibbon] Wakefield's three years' imprisonment in Newgate we are indebted for this judicious, sensible and serviceable publication. Mr Wakefield has laboured wisely and diligently to atone for the wrongs he committed, and every good man will be content to forget that he ever erred.[28]

It was, however, Edward Gibbon's other product of his time in Newgate, *A Letter from Sydney, the Principal Town of Australasia*, which would prove to be of the most lasting significance, not only for its author, but for the course of future colonial development. Possibly for the first time in his hitherto largely feckless life, Newgate had provided him with the opportunity to call upon his innate empathy to serve his luckless companions; and it was this experience perhaps which also led to his original and discerning approach to a form of colonisation which would result in greater fortune for those seeking a better life. Although published in book form in 1829, under the editorship of Robert Gouger, a Radical who wrote on colonial matters and had corresponded with Edward Gibbon in Newgate, *A Letter from Sydney* first appeared as a series of eleven letters in the *Morning Chronicle* during August, September and October of that year. Purporting to be from a settler in Sydney, New South Wales, to a friend in England, the letters described his futile attempts to survive without sufficient labour to help him manage his vast grant of land. In much the same way that his grandmother Priscilla had adopted the persona of an Indian chief in her book, *Excursions in North America*, published a quarter of a century earlier, and later an imaginary journey, *Family Tour through the British Empire*, Edward Gibbon similarly described, with incredible accuracy, a country which he had never visited. True, he had read widely on the subject of transportation and migration, 'I had occasion . . . to read with care every book concerning New South Wales and Van Diemen's Land as well as long series of newspapers published in those colonies, and was struck by the phenomenon of scarcity of labour which was associated with foundation of new colonies'.[29] Imprisonment had afforded him ample opportunity to talk to those sentenced to transportation, some of whom admitted that they had resorted to crime in the hope of attracting such a sentence. Previously such convicts were used to provide labour in the new settlements, two newly founded colonies, New South Wales (1788) and Van Dieman's Land (1803) receiving regular quotas of convicts each year.

After 1815, in the period following the end of the Napoleonic Wars, emigration to the New World increased. The combined effect of the Corn Laws, great agricultural changes, unemployment, the burden on the poor law rates, conditions in the factories and new manufacturing towns, and a growing population conspired to force the government and overburdened parishes to seek a new solution for the redundant and destitute. Most emigrants went to North America, emigration to Canada increased, the disasters of the new colony founded in Western Australia supplying Edward Gibbon with his most telling arguments. His *Letter from Sydney* provided a coherent blueprint, a system for colonisation: he recommended that people of all classes should be encouraged to emigrate; that both the practice of transporting convicts and using slaves should cease; land should be sold and not granted; and a tax levied to assist young people of both sexes to emigrate, thus ensuring a plentiful supply of labour, with opportunity for hardworking labourers eventually to acquire land. Most importantly, he believed that colonies should become self-governing at the earliest possible opportunity, thus rendering them

> happy in a most intimate connection with their mother country; and the American War of Independence would no longer be a favourite theme in the still dependent colonies of Britain. Mutual dependence would prevent oppression on the one part, and on the other a wish for independence; reciprocity of interest would occasion mutual good will; there would no longer be injurious distinctions, or malignant jealousies, or vulgar hatred between British subjects, wherever born; and Britain would become the centre of the most extensive, the most civilized, and, above all, the happiest empire in the world.[30]

Edward Gibbon Wakefield's concept would be vindicated; his inherent humanitarianism pointing him, along with four of his brothers, in a direction that would determine the rest of their lives.

16

All Tragedies are Finished by a Death

'How time flies,' remarked *John Bull* upon Edward Gibbon Wakefield's release from Newgate on 14 May 1830, 'a somewhat trite observation', it continued; 'to everybody, except Mr [Edward Gibbon] Wakefield himself, it does not appear half three years since the offence was committed, which he has at length expiated.'[1] For his brother William, released from Lancaster gaol at the same time, the period of imprisonment must have proved lengthy and painful as he reflected on the early demise of his young wife, deprived of even a few weeks of marriage; and as a consequence of his folly, his enforced separation from their young daughter. If only he had heeded the advice of his grandmother fifteen years earlier, 'pray be careful to go only into shallow water, where no mischief can happen'.[2] Unable to face life in England, and leaving his three-year-old daughter Emily in the care of relatives, William immediately left to join the British Legion, to fight in the Carlist Wars in Spain. Meanwhile, his brothers had gone their separate ways: Arthur serving in the Royal Navy; Daniel a member of the bar, practising in London; Felix, who had trained as an engineer, living in Blois, France, with his father Edward who had moved there with Frances; and Howard serving in the Bengal Army, where he would remain for thirty years. Priscilla, his younger sister, was also in India helping to educate Hindu girls in a Calcutta school. Edward Gibbon, with money left from the life interest on the Pattle estate, had taken up residence with his children and servants at Green's Hotel in Lincoln's Inn Fields. Thirteen-year-old Nina and her ten-year-old brother shared a governess until Edward Jerningham was sent to Bruce Castle in Tottenham, a progressive school which had been founded by the 'Penny Post' man Rowland Hill.

After a short rest at the home of his cousin John Head in Carr Street, Ipswich, where his now ailing 79-year-old grandmother had lived since her husband's death, Edward Gibbon had taken a house in London. There he established himself with his children, a governess and housekeeper, regularly visiting his sister Catherine at the vicarage in Stoke-by-Nayland. Since the vicarage could not accommodate his six dogs, he rented a cottage close by where they were cared for by Felix, a French boy. There in the company of his hounds and beagles he spent many hours walking in the countryside, contemplating his future. Like his father, who had been discredited after the fiasco at Reading, he could no longer aspire to a parliamentary career; however, he was embraced by the Radicals who accepted him regardless of the stigma of his conviction.

With most men, conviction of so base and mercenary an offence as Edward Gibbon Wakefield had committed, and a lengthened companionship with felons, would have been a bar to their ever mixing with reputable society, but it was not so in his case. On the contrary, strangely enough, it made his fortune in every sense, and became the stepping-stone to employment and consideration that he might otherwise never have obtained.[3]

Philosophic radicals readily joined him in forming the Colonisation Society, the foundation of which was a direct result of the failure of the British government's Swan River Colony in Western Australia. The Society was established in order to promote emigration to Australasia based on the principles that Edward Gibbon had advocated in his *Letter from Sydney*, 'the little leaven destined to leaven the whole lump'.[4] The pamphlet, *A Statement of the Principles and Objects of a Proposed National Society for the Cure and Prevention of Pauperism by means of Systematic Colonisation* set out their theories. Among the dozen or so founder members was a young and brilliant MP, Charles Buller, with whom Edward Gibbon would later work in Canada; and John Stuart Mill, the son of his father's friend James Mill. Together they petitioned the government to adopt Wakefield's 'System'. In January 1831 they were rewarded when regulations embodying the concept of 'sufficient price', were applied by the government which was now determined to abolish the system of free grants of land in New South Wales, originally settled by convicts and in Cape Colony in South Africa. Although Edward Gibbon was renowned for having 'wrought principally by the pen and tongue',[5] he readily acknowledged the importance of others.

> Whatever the people of Canada and of the English settlements in Australia may gain by the check which has been put upon official jobbing in the disposal of waste land . . . for this great improvement they are . . . immediately obliged to Lord Howick . . . to the leading members of the Colonisation Society, and more especially to Mr Robert Gouger, the secretary of the Society, whose efforts to procure the adoption of its whole plan have been unceasing for several years.[6]

Robert Rintoul, who had praised Edward Gibbon's work on *Punishment of Death*, continued to lend his support, the *Spectator* rapidly becoming the main voice in all matters relating to the colonies.

Edward Gibbon had left Newgate at a time of great change both at home and abroad: in France a counter-revolution had brought Louis Philippe to the throne, and there were uprisings in both Belgium and Italy. On 26 June 1830, just a month after Edward Gibbon's release, George IV had died, to be succeeded by William IV. In November, after more or less forty-six years of Tory rule, the Whigs came into power under Lord Grey who succeeded the victor of Waterloo, the Duke of Wellington. The stage was thus set for reform. The year had begun with strikes and the revival of agitation for parliamentary reform: in Birmingham, the Tory economist Thomas Attwood, whose daughter would later marry Edward Gibbon's brother Daniel, had founded a political union for such a purpose; Cobbett was championing the cause of universal suffrage; and agricultural England was troubled. Affected by the consequences of the Corn Laws, the Poor Laws and market depression, a labour uprising broke out in Kent which spread north towards Lincoln, and in the west to Somerset and Gloucestershire. Between August and December, gangs of agricultural labourers, sometimes as many as a thousand strong, moved about the countryside demanding higher wages, the abolition of tithes, and no reduction in the poor relief. They vented their anger and desperation by breaking threshing machines and firing ricks – actions known as the Swing Riots, attributed by the perpetrators to 'Captain Swing', the name used on letters and in pamphlets in which the labourers publicised their demands.

Edward Gibbon had undoubtedly witnessed such events when staying with his sister and brother-in-law in their Sussex parsonage: his niece Frances recalled that at that time common land was enclosed and 'the labourer was practically a pauper all through his life, wages ran from 7s to 9s a week, and the hours were from sunrise to sunset. Sheep stealing was a common event.'[7] She remembered her father, the Reverend Charles Torlesse, going to the top of his church tower every night to watch the fires. In a pamphlet, *Swing Unmasked – The Causes of Rural Incendiarism*, Edward Gibbon portrayed the 'prowling serf hugging the tinder-box that makes him terrible',[8] lending his support to their cause with splendid eloquence:

A Swing fire has taken place; what a commotion ensues in the parish! Is it credible that the pauper should not view with satisfaction the flurried steps and pale face of the rector, the assumed air of indifference, not half concealing the uneasiness of my lord who owns the soil on which the stacks were burnt, and the violent rage of the neighbouring squire, mixed with nervous indications . . . a new scale of wages becomes the topic of his parish, and is probably adopted, after an understanding between the landlords, clergymen and tenants that rent and tithes shall be reduced in proportion as wages are raised. When his family ask for bread, they receive it, and at noon there is an unusual smell of bacon about the cottage. He has now firing enough to dry his clothes, which, before the stack was burnt, he used to put on of a morning as wet as when he had taken them off at night. Moreover his rustic vanity is gratified by reading in the county paper a minute account of the deed he has done . . . when he returns home, thinking of what he has also read in that paper, as coming from the lips of a Parliament man, about 'the urgent necessity of some permanent improvement in the condition of the poor,' he becomes fonder than usual of his wife, and kinder to his children. . . . He has burnt a stack, and his heart (it has just been discovered that paupers have hearts), lately so poor and pinched, is now swelling with the strange pleasure of hope.[9]

In the parliamentary election, reformers took many of the county seats, including Brougham, who had prosecuted the Wakefield brothers three years previously and was soon to become Lord Chancellor. The opening, on Wednesday 15 September, of the first passenger railway in the world, between Liverpool and Manchester, heralded the birth of a transport revolution. Undoubtedly, Thomas Legh and his wife Ellen would have been present on this historic occasion. Only three weeks previously, Thomas Legh had journeyed on the railway as part of a rehearsal for the opening of this great national work. The procession of locomotives and carriages, a 'splendid and interesting ceremony',[10] was attended by many dignitaries, among them the Duke of Wellington, Sir Robert Peel, a Russian prince and the actress Fanny Kemble. Unfortunately, the occasion was to be marred by the first death associated with this mode of transport: that of the MP for Liverpool, William Huskisson, President of the Board of Trade, who had been at the Colonial Office during the first two years of Edward Gibbon's imprisonment.

Having successfully given birth to a daughter, Ellen Jane, on 20 February, Ellen was now once again pregnant, her third pregnancy in two and a half years of marriage. A portrait, thought to be of her, painted in 1837 by Henry Wyatt, a local artist who had exhibited at the Royal Academy, depicts a comely young woman with dark luxuriant hair framing large, brown, intelligent eyes: not a conventional beauty, but a handsome woman, her face lit by humour; a woman at one with herself, displaying a composure and contentment beyond her years. A fashion plate of Ellen on the frontispiece of the satirical essay, *Une Nouvelle Manière D'Attrapper une Femme*, published in the year of the Wakefield trial, mirrors many of these features: her remarkable arched brows, large arresting eyes and strong face. Her appearance in Wyatt's portrait may give some credence to J.C. Lockhart's description of her in *Manchester Notes and Queries*,[11] of 27 November 1866, belying Ellen's vulnerable appearance, of which so much was made during the trial. She was, he maintained, a 'fine, big, romping girl, very womanly for her youthful years'. He claimed that two or three days before her wedding to Thomas Legh she was following an elderly, demure female relative down the hall staircase, when she nearly frightened the life out of her by leaping down the last three or four stairs.

Ellen may well have sat for Wyatt's portrait during the latter months of her third pregnancy; that bloom associated with pregnancy seems to pervade the painting, though she must have been acutely aware that childbirth was a dangerous and painful ordeal. During the nineteenth century, childbirth was hazardous for both mother and child; for the mother puerperal fever or septicaemia, haemorrhage and thrombosis were common. Moreover, practices surrounding delivery had changed little over the centuries. Charles White, the Manchester surgeon who founded the Manchester Royal Infirmary, contended that the reason so many post-partum women were liable to putrid fevers was due to the bad fashions and customs they observed. He was highly critical of the tightness of the stays and petticoat bindings, and the weight of the pockets and petticoats that Ellen and her contemporaries wore:

much mischief was caused by binding the belly too tight which pressed upon a womb already enlarged by the foetus and its membranes, so strongly against the lower intestines, as to prevent the descent and exclusion of the excrements . . . which is farther increased by a sedentary, inactive life and improper diet.

Those in Ellen's privileged situation were usually attended during labour by a number of friends. Delivery took place in a small room with a large fire, 'which together with her own pains, throw her into profuse sweats; by the heat of the champer, and the breath of so many people, the whole air is rendered foul, and unfit for respiration'. The situation was even worse following delivery:

she is covered up close in bed, with additional cloaths [sic], the curtains are drawn round the bed, and pinned together, every crevice in the windows and door is stopped close, not excepting even the key hole, the windows are guarded not only with shutters and curtains, but even blankets, the more effectually to exclude fresh air, and the good woman is not suffered to put her arm, or even her nose out of bed, for fear of catching cold.

The woman would be confined to bed in a horizontal position for many days, which, White maintained, together with the heat and stuffiness of the bedroom, discouraged the over-distended abdominal muscles from quickly recovering their tone and, more damagingly, prevented them from expelling the 'contents of the abdomen, which lodging in the intestines many days become quite putrid'. He theorised on the causes of the dreadful onset of sepsis: the mother might be damaged during delivery, either by the doctor's hand or his instruments, or by the forcible removal of the placenta, which might bring on inflammation of the womb. A few days after delivery the doomed woman was subjected to shivering fits, and more 'cloaths are heaped upon her'. Eventually she developed a continuous fever, nausea and vomiting. He paints a fearful picture of an all too common scenario:

> the stools are sometimes very copious and frequent, and so exceedingly putrid as to be offensive all over the house . . . accompanied with swelling, pain, and soreness in the belly, and with pains in the head . . . with a cough and difficulty of breathing . . . the face is flushed, the urine is generally very highly coloured and as the disorder advances the patient complains of great anxiety . . . attended with . . . lowness of spirits lassitude and great debility . . . convulsions come on . . . and death, which happens sometimes sooner, sometimes later closes the scene.[12]

Women sometimes died within twenty-four hours of giving birth; more often they experienced days of pain and fear before finally succumbing.

On Monday 17 January 1831, nineteen-year-old Ellen suffered this fate after giving birth to a stillborn son, and, in all probability, was subjected to some aspects of Charles White's dire description of childbirth. The circumstances of her death are not recorded, but she died at her husband's London house in Berkeley Square, possibly attended by Charles Higham, general practitioner, of Davies Street, Berkeley Square. For her husband Thomas, left with their only child, eleven-month-old Ellen Jane, the death of his young wife must have been hard to bear; for her parents, William and Jane Turner, the loss must have been doubly painful, coming as it did on the fourteenth anniversary of the death of their younger daughter, Mary Jennet. Ellen's death was announced in the newspapers. On Sunday 23 January 1831, *Bell's Life in London* reported: 'Mrs Legh, the lady of T. Legh, Esq. MP. Died last week. This was the lady about whom so much interest was excited four years since, in consequence of her abduction by Mr Wakefield.'[13] Even in death Ellen was not divorced from the notoriety of her abduction, or her abductor Edward Gibbon Wakefield.

And so, five years after her abduction, this nineteen-year-old one-time schoolgirl, twice wife, thrice mother, was laid in her lead-lined coffin, her second stillborn son in the crook of her arm. Accompanied by a small party of undertakers, led by the featherman and drawn by four horses, their black ostrich plumes signalling their solemn task, Ellen's hearse made its slow progress north in the bitter cold; the sombre procession halting at turnpikes, stopping every twenty miles for refreshment, and resting overnight. On the morning of 27 January Ellen's funeral procession left Newton. The Legh tenants, 110 in number, wearing hatbands and gloves, rode two abreast, followed closely by six plumed mules and then the hearse, drawn by six black horses. Two mourning coaches preceded the carriages of her husband, Thomas Legh; her father, William Turner; her uncle, Henry Critchley; and those of Mr Orford and J. Wilson Patten MP. Six other carriages, two chaises and eight gigs completed the cortège. A heavy fall of snow, accompanied by a sharp frost, severely hampered their progress as the hearse, bearing mother and son, was hauled up the steep, snow-covered hill to the church.

Finally, Ellen's coffin, clad in crimson velvet and richly ornamented, its pall supported by six clergymen, was borne into St Oswald's Church, Winwick; above the portal was a hatchment bearing the Legh coat of arms. There, within the fourteenth-century Legh chapel, Ellen and her infant son were laid to rest.

A Sort of Natural Canonisation

In the year following his daughter's death William Turner was to realise a long-standing ambition. He became one of the first Members of Parliament to represent Blackburn, the town having been enfranchised under the terms of the 1832 Reform Act. As a Whig, he was to serve with Sir William Feilden, a Tory, for nine years; both cotton magnates, they appear to have been elected due to their local connections. Master of Mill Hill, squire of Shrigley and no stranger to obstacles, Turner tackled his new enterprise with gusto:

> a bombshell, offering himself to the 'free and independent electors' of both parties. . . . To him must be awarded the palm of being the first to deluge the borough with drink. On his arrival in Blackburn, being a great employer of labour, and the Turner family being highly popular with the working classes, a large crowd collected. . . . Barrels of beer were then rolled into the yard of our ancient Parish Church, the ends were knocked out, and the people debauched with drink, and that over the very graves which contained the ashes of their forefathers.[1]

A reformer, he advocated shortening the duration of Parliament, vote by ballot, the removal of monopolies, and the abolition of the death penalty in all cases except murder; ironically aligning himself on the last issue with his former adversary, Edward Gibbon Wakefield. He supported the move to repeal the Corn Laws – 'Plump for Turner – Mr Turner will vote for Cheap Bread . . . is himself a friend of the Poor . . . both Mr Turner and his brother are Manufacturers and Merchants and do their utmost to promote the interest of the whole trading community',[2] so claimed Turner's election handbill. Not surprisingly, the Anti-Corn Law League was supported by the cotton manufacturers whose interests were served by cheaper raw material and large markets for their goods. When the cost of bread rose, it led to unrest and agitation for higher wages.

William Turner was to hold his seat until 1841. During what was to be his final campaign his opponents granted him no quarter, nicknaming him 'William Fickle . . . whose trade is that of a *Turner* in general . . . in his rooms a considerable assortment of first rate *Spoons* ready to stir up anything. Should a *Ladle* be wanted, he can supply one as big as a warming pan.'[3] They derided his acts of charity, mocking his placard with its assertions that he was '*a real Friend to the Poor*', and while conceding that he may have done something to improve the 'Clergyman's stipend at Shrigley', slyly commented he must surely regret the report that 'a former Clergyman's Wife was obliged to fall on her very knees before the late Mrs Turner, interceding for some little allowance for the *necessaries* of life'.[4]

Consequently, on 1 July 1841, the ageing William Turner was defeated by his younger opponent, John Hornby, by only a single vote, which led to such disorder that the mob had to be dispersed by the military. Devastated, William Turner petitioned for a recount, which was duly tried by a Committee of the House of Commons. Commencing on Wednesday 20 April 1842, the hearing lasted seven days, and confirmed Hornby's election. This news was greeted with dismay by Turner's supporters in Blackburn, who responded with yet another attack on the Old Bull Inn, with the cry 'Turner for ever!' Once again the military were summoned and the Riot Act read before the mob eventually dispersed. Three months later William Turner died at Mill Hill, on 17 July, his death, 'according to popular belief',[5] accelerated by disappointment. He was interred in the family vault in St John's churchyard, Blackburn, next to his wife Jane who had died the previous year on 17 April 1841, aged sixty-nine. Two years before his death, William Turner had willed the Shrigley estates to his granddaughter Ellen Jane Legh, who since her mother's death had been raised by her father at Lyme.

Left with his year-old daughter after the death of his wife,

Thomas Legh had other concerns: Newton, part of his Haycock estate, had lost its right to representation under the 1832 Parliamentary Reform Act; and disturbances had taken place in the coal districts close to Haydock Lodge, resulting in an application to the magistrates for a military force to regain control. Haydock Lodge had subsequently become the headquarters of the 43rd Regiment with four companies and a detachment of cavalry. Meanwhile he had maintained his association with the Liverpool to Manchester Railway, selling property to the company, and negotiating deals with several others.

In 1843, twelve years after Ellen's death, Thomas Legh married Maud Lowther, daughter of George Lowther of Hampton Hall, Somerset. By this time, his daughter, Ellen Jane, had reached the age of thirteen. Perhaps mindful of her mother's experience with Edward Gibbon Wakefield, on 18 April 1844 Thomas Legh applied to have his daughter made a ward of court

> with the view not merely of protecting her to some extent from being the object of fortune hunters but of enabling her if it shall be necessary at any future time to call the Trustees to account for the management of and investment of the property in which she is interested under the Will.[6]

Although Ellen Jane would not inherit Lyme or the Haydock estates, since they would have to pass to a male heir, she would shortly inherit the Shrigley estates under the terms of her grandfather's will. In addition, matters had been so arranged that if her father had no more children, she would inherit £20,000 on his death. Thomas Legh died on 8 May 1857 and was buried at Disley, to be succeeded by his nephew, William John Legh.

After her father's second marriage, and following her grandfather's death in 1842, Ellen Jane would appear to have spent much of her time at Shrigley Hall. This arrangement seems to have suited her stepmother Maud, who, recently married, might well have resented the presence of this young woman at Lyme. Ironically, Ellen Jane was soon to be closely connected with her stepmother, for at the age of seventeen she would marry Maud's brother, the 33-year-old Reverend Brabazon Lowther, who had arrived in Disley in 1845, upon his appointment as curate to Disley

Church, a living in the gift of the Legh family. The outcome of this union was rather strange, resulting as it did in the young Ellen Jane becoming not only Maud's stepdaughter, but also her sister-in-law, and in consequence of that, her father's sister-in-law. It was not a prestigious marriage for the daughter of Thomas Legh, although it must have suited not only the Reverend Brabazon Lowther very well, marrying the heiress of Shrigley, but also his sister Maud, who perhaps was not unhappy at the departure of the teenage daughter of her husband's first marriage. Ellen Jane may well have enjoyed the undivided attention of her father for the thirteen years prior to the arrival of his new wife, who four years later was still childless and the stepmother of a teenager – a strong-willed young woman. In any event, Ellen Jane's departure from Lyme signalled, it would seem, the removal of any trace of her mother, or indeed herself: no letters, no portraits, no likenesses of any kind, nor any reminder of their existence were to remain there.

Though Ellen's existence might have been erased prematurely from the annals of Lyme, through her abductor Edward Gibbon Wakefield it was to live on indefinitely. His catastrophic encounter with the young Ellen Turner had proved a major turning point. Dr Garnett, writing some thirty years after his death, maintained that there were in fact

two Wakefields, one of whom was suddenly obliterated by catastrophe which destroyed the careless man of fashion, ready out of pure idleness and irresponsible spirits for any mischief, and left the powerful will and the unequal gift of personal fascination concentrated on the intense purpose of rehabilitating the fallen man in the opinion of society.[7]

Indeed, in 1831, the very year of Ellen's death and within only a year of completing his term of imprisonment, the effects of Edward Gibbon's ideas had already begun to take root, fertilised by the burgeoning enthusiasm for progress and reform of the new Whig administration. Most notable was the publication of his treatise on capital punishment, *Punishment of Death in the Metropolis*, which was influential in the movement to invoke capital punishment for murder only. Edward Gibbon's father, like his son, could not resist the urge to influence events, returning from Blois in France during

May the following year to join those supporting the Reform Bill. Among these were his former friends Francis Place and Robert Rintoul, editor of the *Spectator* and so staunch a supporter of his son. Amidst the agitation for reform, Edward Wakefield made an impassioned speech in Saville House, Leicester Square, railing against Queen Adelaide, 'the German frau',[8] who lived in constant fear of revolution and who, it was believed, was unduly influencing the King. Further, he denounced as 'reverend hypocrites'[9] the Tory bishops who had opposed the bill. Finally the bill was passed on 4 June, sweeping away the rotten and nomination boroughs, instituting a uniform test for voters. Three months later, on 12 September, the remarkable Priscilla Wakefield died aged eighty-one, happy in the knowledge that her constant faith in the inherent goodness of both her son Edward and favourite grandson Edward Gibbon had been affirmed.

Edward Gibbon now became more actively involved as a 'parliamentary engineer'[10] rather than a participant in government affairs; he worked through his many respected friends and associates, including Charles Buller, Thomas Attwood, Robert Rintoul and Sir William Molesworth. His book *England and America*, published in two volumes in 1833, and favourably received by the press, was written

to lay before Americans a sketch of the political condition of England, and before the English an explanation of some of the peculiarities of the social state of America; secondly, to point out the means of removing those causes which are productive of great evil to both countries.

In his opening chapter of the first volume, Edward Gibbon began by painting a very agreeable picture of life in England.

An American citizen passing time in England, 'finds the roads in every direction far better than any he has seen before'. In the towns, the houses are so well built, the shops have such a display of rich goods . . . even the smallest towns appear like sections of a wealthy capital. . . . The inhabitants of London obtain a greater quantity of things necessary, useful or agreeable, to man, than the inhabitants of any other city in the world.

To maintain this, Edward Gibbon believed there should be a just distribution and division of employment, whereby capital and labour would be wisely combined to produce wealth; for if there was to be a separation, it would lead to misery for the majority. He then balanced this picture with a description of its extreme: the misery of the poor and the consequent prevalence of gin shops and the fate of many pauper children at the hands of those who had taken them off the parish, 'you may half starve them, beat them, torture them, nothing short of killing them with perfect security'.[11] In the second volume, examining the reasons for slavery in America, he concluded that the lack of labour caused its early colonists to resort to using slaves, which led to the evils of the slave trade. Once again he presented the principles he believed were necessary for the successful establishment of a colony – the provision of land in proportion to people, and land sold at a price sufficient to prevent labourers from being landowners too soon, thus depleting a much-needed workforce.

The following year, 1834, the South Australian Act was passed legislating for the establishment of a new colony, despite Edward Gibbon's earlier fear that the bill might have been thrown out by the Lords. Ironically, it was the support of the Duke of Wellington, whom Edward Gibbon had described in *England and America* as 'ignorant and even illiterate', which ensured its passage.[12] Bloomfield wrote that such was Edward Gibbon's gratitude that for a time he stopped referring to the Duke as 'old Woodenhead'! Edward Gibbon's younger brother Felix, who had a married a young French girl, Marie Bailey, had already left England to take up a tract of land in Tasmania; while Daniel cherished hopes of obtaining an appointment as a judge in the new colony. After serving in Spain, William had fought in Portugal and, since peace had now been restored there, had returned home to his daughter in England, having perhaps purged some of his guilt and grief. He had been created a Knight of the Order of the Tower and Sword, having acquitted himself with considerable distinction in the service of Queen Donna Maria. Unlike his brother Edward Gibbon, William's life now lacked direction; he had returned from the wars penniless and without prospects; his future, it would seem, like that of his brothers, also lay in the direction of Australia. Fired by her father's fervour and her uncles' ambitions, Nina, not yet seventeen, had also taken up the cause, writing to her aunt Catherine in August, urging her to persuade uncle Charles to give up his meagre stipend as a country vicar

> and turn South Australian for then I think Papa might be persuaded to go and then what a nice party we should make flying from straightened means and anxiety for your children in future, to plenty, large profits for yourself, and easy happy prospects for all your family. Have you read Papa's, *England and America*, the third chapter especially? If not, get it, read that part carefully, and then reflect on the happy opening formed by a new colony for a man of small fortune and a large family. Then get a book called *South Australia*, compiled and edited by Papa, in it you will find full information on every point connected with the colony. The first expedition of settlers sails in the second week of next October the next one probably not until next June; so you will have time to think about it. Tell Uncle Charles to read the chapter in the little book, *Inducements to Emigration*.[13]

Demonstrating that in force of character she was her father's daughter, she concluded,

> I wish I were at Stoke, for I am sure I could persuade him, and then if I succeeded, we should have nearly the whole family of us joined together in South Australia, for I take it for granted that if you went, Papa would too, with both his chickens.[14]

The following month, on hearing that the Attwoods might be contemplating emigration to South Australia, she wrote to her young friend Rosabel Attwood, whose sister Angela would marry her uncle Daniel in 1835, saying that she was trying hard to persuade her father to do the same thing. She dreamed of this new land and how she and her friend might spend their time in their new home, enthusing, 'if "Victoria" is built on the shores of Port Lincoln, we can have regattas in the large harbour and donkey excursions to Sleaford Mere on the Louth Hills'. Even the voyage was viewed as an adventure: 'As for our occupations and amusements on board ship [these] will be manifold, and as neither you nor I mean to be sea-sick, we shall make ourselves comfortable

. . . we will all sail together, singing merrily, "the deep, deep sea"!'[15]

Tragically, Nina was never to realise her dreams; by the end of October, barely a month later, she had been diagnosed with a 'mortal complaint of the lungs'.[16] Edward Gibbon Wakefield confided to Mrs Attwood that Nina had been reduced to a skeleton, and that her physician Dr Cheyne had advised him to take her to either Spain or Portugal in the hope that it might prolong her life. Nina was dying from consumption. On 25 November her father wrote to his sister Catherine, informing her of their impending journey to Portugal.

> As you cannot expect any but a bad account of Nina, you will be glad to hear that she is about to take the only chance that remains. We sail this day from Spithead in a Portuguese frigate (with the best accommodation and a doctor on board) not quite what Nina had envisaged but she is delighted at the prospect of the voyage.[17]

He expected the voyage to take five days, sadly reporting that he had 'next to no hope' because Nina was 'greatly reduced' and her cough was very bad. Yet, he continued, 'the doctors still declare that the lung is not incurably affected and the change may do wonders for her'. Hoping to save his son Edward Jerningham from the pain of knowledge of Nina's condition, he had told him that he needed to travel to Lisbon on urgent business. In Lisbon, Edward Gibbon hired a Portuguese peasant girl, Leocadia de Oliveria, to help him nurse his sick daughter. Within a few a weeks Catherine received a letter from Lisbon.

> I make an effort to write to you for the purpose of warning you of a misfortune which now seems inevitable. Poor Nina is alive, but that is all I can say. She suffers hardly any pain, but sinks gradually, I attend from hour to hour. The next packet will probably take an account of her death. I write by this one, doubting whether I shall be able to write when all is over.[18]

On 12 February 1835, Nina died, aged seventeen years and two months, two years younger than Ellen and three years younger than her mother Eliza, on their deaths. It was two months before her father could bring himself to write to his sister, and he never again spoke of the three women he had lost. The letter, which he finally wrote to Catherine on 14 April, told her that Nina had only become aware of the seriousness of her condition on the last day of her life when she had asked him to give Catherine a lock of her hair. In her final hours she had spoken of her aunt frequently and, he told her, 'made for you a little packet of her hair',[19] which he would send to her when he felt able to open the box in which it was contained. Nina, he told her, 'had become my friend and partner in every thought and object of interest . . . you cannot estimate my loss'. Those who had felt that Edward Gibbon should have paid the ultimate penalty for his transgression would surely now be satisfied. For Edward Gibbon this was a fate worse than death: 'The vulgar notion of death has no terrors for me; but I feel more than half dead myself, having lost her for whom alone, of late years I have lived.'[20]

It is not surprising that Edward Gibbon felt the loss of his daughter so keenly, so alike were they, sharing the 'same vivid imagination, the same intensity of affection, the same fondness for animals, the same capacity for soaring hope and sanguine expectation, the same spirit of adventure and the same keen sense of fun'.[21] If Eliza in death had metaphorically taken his son with her, Nina was to return him. For Edward Gibbon resolved that henceforth his son would live with him. Thus on Edward Gibbon's return to England, Edward Jerningham moved into his father's London house, later attending King's College. There they were joined by the young Portuguese girl, Leocadia, whom, at Nina's request, he sent to a school for young ladies at Twickenham, continuing to provide for her until she eventually emigrated to New Zealand, where she became the wife of a colonist.

Striving to overcome his overwhelming grief, Edward Gibbon immersed himself in a new enterprise, the colonisation of New Zealand, his absence from London having weakened his grasp of South Australian affairs. He also put himself forward as the Radical candidate for Birmingham, connected as he was with its retiring MP Thomas Attwood, the father-in-law of his brother Daniel. In this venture he was encouraged by the support of Sir William Molesworth, who had referred to him in the House of Commons as 'my friend'. After ascertaining that Molesworth himself had no intention of contesting the seat, Edward Gibbon issued his address to the electors of Birmingham, on 8 December, stating that he had 'been continually engaged with one subject in particular . . . the means of preventing Distress . . . of securing a state of Prosperity' and that he would rejoice to see the 'People obtain Universal Suffrage, Vote by Ballot and Annual Elections'. Further, he was of the belief that the House of Commons was not truly representative of the people. He referred to the two matters which, he declared, engaged his closest attention: 'first the reform of our criminal law, more especially as regards the punishments of death and transportation, and secondly the means which our government possesses of abolishing negro slavery in those countries where it is now extending more rapidly than ever'.[22] Despite his initial enthusiasm, Edward Gibbon did not pursue the candidature, for reasons which are not clear. The year closed with the establishment of the colony South Australia, formally proclaimed on 28 December.

His attentions then turned again to New Zealand.

Very near to Australia there is a country which all testimony concurs in describing as the fittest country in the world for colonization [sic]; as the most beautiful country, with the finest climate and the most productive soil, I mean New Zealand. . . . New Zealand does not belong to the British Crown . . . but Englishmen are beginning to colonize New Zealand.[23]

Inspired by his zeal, the New Zealand Association was formed in 1837, the year of Queen Victoria's accession, amalgamating with two other groups in 1838 to form a company to establish a settlement in New Zealand, which would colonise the country according to the Wakefield 'system' and application was made for a charter from the British government. The Association employed agents in fifty-two cities and towns, who used pamphlets to persuade men and women to emigrate under the Wakefield 'system', and were given a commission of £2 for every couple enrolled. Edward Gibbon and the Association were, however, vigorously attacked by the Church Missionary Society, who believed the project would ruin the Maori people; The Times also attacked them:

we can conceive that such an association may be identified with no other ideas than those of fortune-hunting and a fraudulent circumvention of savage chiefs; but in the gorgeous fancy of Mr Edward Gibbon Wakefield and the minor magicians by whose wand it has sprung into existence. . . . That his talents are to be unnapkinned as Governor of the proposed colony . . . just before setting sail he is to be knighted by . . . the Queen . . . that Sir Gibbon shall have a government-house, with a handsome conservatory, a garden and pleasure-grounds . . . that his Excellency must keep a dignified table, with a retinue, plate, and cellar to correspond . . . and a retiring pension – all this is only a vague outline of the agreeable adjuncts (subordinate of course to the higher objects of religion and philanthropy) which induce Governor Wakefield to sacrifice his home comforts for the sake of the New Zealand population.[24]

In May 1838, Edward Gibbon made his first visit to Canada as unofficial adviser to George Lambton, 1st Earl of Durham, Governor General and Lord High Commissioner, whose chief secretary was Charles Buller, in his capacity as enthusiast of long standing in matters of colonial settlement. Edward Jerningham, a skilled linguist who spoke six languages, now proving a 'youth of more ability than conduct',[25] accompanied his father to Canada, where Edward Gibbon's encouragement and ideas influenced Durham's writing of his *Report on the Affairs of British North America* which advocated the union of Upper and Lower Canada under a single legislature. It was here that news reached Edward Gibbon Wakefield that the evidence he had submitted to the Select Committee on transportation had helped effect their recommendation that the practice should cease. It would seem that Edward Gibbon had now regained much of his former vitality and enthusiasm for this current interest, strengthened by the growing relationship with his son. Together they had begun to assume a telling influence on Canadian society. At a 'magnetising soirée' at the house of Charles Buller, father and son appear to have 'produced sleep, real or assumed upon several women present'.[26] This does not appear to have been an isolated incident. At another evening party, 'he had mesmerized a young lady, but was struck with horror on finding that he could not revive her. He jumped into a cab and went in search of his friend Dr Ellliotson. After some hours' search Elliotson was found, and they returned in company, and Dr Elliotson succeeded in reviving the lady.'[27]

Following the failure of the private bill introduced in Parliament on behalf of the New Zealand Association by committee member Francis Baring in June 1838, the following year the Association was reconstituted as the New Zealand Company. Refused a charter, the Company responded by sending a party out to New Zealand, led by William Wakefield, with the intention of buying land from the Maoris as a future site for settlement. They left Plymouth on 12 May, on the *Tory* and were seen off by Edward Gibbon Wakefield, who had hurriedly travelled from London by post-chaise when rumours had reached him that the government intended to delay the voyage. On board was the nineteen-year-old Edward Jerningham, who had joined the expedition with the blessing of his father. The *Tory*, armed with eight guns, was captained by Edmund Chaffers, former Master of Darwin's *Beagle*, and carried various goods for the purpose of barter with the Maoris: muskets, tomahawks, pocket-knives, red cotton night caps, umbrellas, blankets, pencils and tobacco. On 24 September 1839, the ship arrived at Port Nicholson at the southern tip of the North Island. Some six months later the pioneers of the *Tory* were joined by more emigrants who arrived on six ships in January and March 1840. Many of these were retired army and naval officers, professional men, lawyers, doctors, gentlemen and amateur farmers, and land speculators attracted by the opportunity to buy land in what would eventually become the site of a town for only £1 an acre. This first settlement, Wellington, was named after the redoubtable Duke. Although William Wakefield's party had left without the blessing of the British government, the Company's activities doubtless hastened the British annexation of New Zealand, which may well have forestalled a similar initiative by the French.

Edward Gibbon, again in Canada four years later, was to return to London, news having reached him of the death of his brother Arthur, a bachelor, who was killed on 17 June 1843 by Maori chief Rangiaheata, in what became known as the Wairau Massacre. Arthur had left England for New Zealand two years previously, after twenty-five years' distinguished service in the Navy. Having established the settlement of Nelson, on the northern tip of the South Island, he was slaughtered alongside nineteen other Englishmen in a dispute over land, at a site fifty-five miles east of Nelson.

On Friday 15 August 1846, Edward Gibbon Wakefield, now aged fifty, unexpectedly suffered a stroke while at his hairdresser's in the Strand. He was taken to the home of his secretary Charles Allom in Hart Street, Bloomsbury, where he remained in a very serious condition for several weeks. Nursed by Mrs Allom he was attended by two of London's most eminent physicians, Dr Tod, of King's College, and Dr Marshall Hall, who were fearful for his recovery. In a letter to his aunt Catherine, three days after his father's stroke, Edward Jerningham wrote,

> The only chance for my father is perfect tranquillity for some days . . . he had a repetition of his attack of Friday – which tho' not so severe lasted longer. It was determined to bleed him a little; and he had two leeches on each temple – This has done him, I think some good.[28]

Two days later he wrote to Catherine again, telling her that his father had certainly benefited from the treatment recommended by Dr Tod, of quinine and the continuing application of ice to his head as well as blisters behind the ear, and mustard poultices on his back and stomach. Furthermore, Dr Tod had been anxious to reassure the family that, in spite of the gravity of the situation, he had 'not the slightest doubt but that . . . with care and perfect quiet he will recover'.[29] A week after his father's stroke, Edward Jerningham was able to report to Catherine that Dr Tod had visited at ten in the morning and was quite pleased with his patient's progress consequently deeming it unnecessary to make a second visit that day. Edward Jerningham outlined his devotion to his father in a later letter to Catherine:

> I again spent last night by my father's bedside. . . . At 11 I went home for a bathe and a sleep – I have been back here about half an hour, and find that he has been eating chops, chicken and ale at intervals, with great relish and no unpleasant results. . . . His whole appearance is changed – He looks cheerful and animated . . . and always ends with 'Write to Catherine'.[30]

However, her nephew warned her that she still would not be allowed to visit him for some days. Eventually Edward Gibbon was to recover sufficiently to begin a tour of England, at a relaxed pace. In case he suffered another attack, he always carried with him a card which read, 'Do not bleed me', believing that his eventual recovery was due to the intervention of Charles Allom, who had forbidden Edward Gibbon's doctors to continue bleeding him. In the autumn he went to Malvern to take the water cure at Dr Wilson's hydropathic establishment. It was in Malvern that the foundations for the establishment of a Church of England settlement at Canterbury, New Zealand, were laid, when Edward Gibbon invited the Anglo-Irishman John Robert Godley, an admirer of his colonisation theories, to join him. By early December, Edward Gibbon had left Malvern to settle for six months at Warwick Lodge in Reigate, where he would be able to enjoy the company of his Talbot hounds and beagles.

In June 1848, Edward Gibbon retired to the Château Mabille on the heights above Boulogne, close to Calais, the scene of the abduction débâcle. There he was joined by his younger brother Felix, who had returned from Tasmania after sixteen years. Alone with his children, separated from his wife, and now penniless, he had accepted the hospitality of his brother. Although he had failed in his farming enterprise in Tasmania, Felix, an expert naturalist, was later to publish a well-known treatise on horticulture, *The Gardener's Chronicle for New Zealand*. Shortly after the return of his brother, Edward Gibbon learned that a survey had been completed in the South Island on land acquired from the New Zealand Company as a suitable site for the proposed Canterbury settlement, news that stimulated his interest in the enterprise.

During his six months' stay in France, Edward Gibbon's continuing frailty meant he was only able to work for four or five hours a day.

My health, instead of improving, has got worse lately, and will probable never mend. . . . I cannot disobey the doctor's injunction to stay at home and be quiet, with effects that remind me of a bird trying to fly with a broken wing, and knocking itself to pieces in the vain exertion.[31]

Nevertheless he managed to complete his book *The Art of Colonisation* on Christmas Eve, his secretary Charles Allom crossing the Channel that evening on the *Albion*, and delivering it to Rintoul on Christmas Day.

Meanwhile, Edward Gibbon's father, who had been visiting Catherine in Stoke-by-Nayland, had finalised his report on Ireland in the aftermath of the famine. To his son William he had confided that he intended to present it to Lord Lansdowne, clearly flattering himself that it might lead to an appointment in Ireland. He had assured William that his stepmother and stepsisters were well, 'Fanny and the girls are fine and are at Sutton Oak', and that William's old parrot was still alive. His brother Edward Gibbon, he told him, was much occupied with the Church of England colony in New Zealand. He roundly praised their brother Felix, declaring, 'his talent, information and activity astonish me . . . his scientific knowledge of natural History and Botany seem remarkable'. Finally he told William that he had bought a brood of Italian greyhound puppies for Emily, who had joined her father in New Zealand the year before: 'If they arrive alive, they will go out by the next ship'; concluding, 'a letter from you is a *great comfort* to your old father'.[32] Sadly there would be no more letters from William, who had paid so dearly for his loyal service to his much admired brother Edward Gibbon; on 15 September 1848 he was struck by apoplexy, dying four days later. Following his death on 19 September, Sir George Grey, the Governor of the North Island, wrote,

> I have been in constant communication with Colonel Wakefield upon a great variety of subjects connected with the interests of New Zealand, and have found not only that he possessed abilities of a very high order, but that his whole attention and thoughts were directed to the single subject of the advancement of the interests of this country.

William seemed to have atoned for his part in the carrying away of Ellen Turner, and such events seemed long forgotten. By all accounts, his funeral procession was quite remarkable. Dr Garnett later observed, 'William was as much the hand of the New Zealand Company as Edward Gibbon was its brain'.[33] William's daughter,

Emily, who had so tragically lost her mother when her father was in Lancaster gaol, had married Edward Stafford, who later became Prime Minister of New Zealand.

On 13 November 1849, almost a year after Edward Gibbon had resigned from the New Zealand Company, the Canterbury Association was finally granted its charter. In March 1850, John Godley and his family arrived at Port Lyttlelton, the future harbour of the proposed Canterbury settlement. Meanwhile Edward Gibbon's brother Felix, 'Felix Van Diemen',[34] was involved in a publicity drive to attract emigrants to Canterbury, as was Edward Gibbon's son Edward Jerningham (the latter recording in his diary how, during one of his visits to England, he had attended Derby Day with the novelist William Thackeray). Although assisted passages were available for labourers, pamphlets were distributed and public meetings organised to attract those desiring to emigrate who were in a position to purchase land and to offer them advice:

A new colony is a bad place for a single man. To be single is contrary to the nature of a new colony, where the laws of society are labour, peace, domestic life, increase and multiply. . . . Whatever may be the rank and capital of the young colonist – whether a nobleman's son worth £10,000 or a labourer – let him be married for the sake of economy as well as peace and comfort.[35]

Separate banquets were held for those emigrating to the Church of England Settlement on the South Island – at Blackwall for the gentry and at Gravesend for the labourers – Edward Gibbon observing, 'the very smell of pitch will help to give reality to what most people still consider a pretty dream'.[36] Sailing on four ships, 792 'pilgrims', roughly a quarter gentry and a quarter children, left Plymouth on 7 and 8 September 1850. Due to Edward Gibbon's endeavours the numbers of those settling in New Zealand had increased, since 1839, from 2,000 to 22,000 souls.

Finally, by 1853, Edward Gibbon Wakefield had determined to join them. Since 1848 his brother Daniel had been Attorney General of the North Island, while his son Edward Jerningham, his nephew Charley Torlesse and his niece Emily were all making new lives for themselves there. Edward Gibbon had spent the past three years of his life in England, at Reigate, in a cottage in the garden of the White Hart Inn, caring for some of Felix's children and surrounded by his many dogs. Here he received numerous visitors – thirty-six MPs during one weekend alone. Clearly his parliamentary influence was undiminished, but now he regarded his work in England as at an end. When he left London for Plymouth on 29 September, friends and family congregated to bid him farewell. Among these was Frances Wakefield, the stepmother from whom, somewhat inexplicably, he had been so long estranged, but who had been persuaded by his former 'nurse', Mrs Allom, to wish him farewell. So overcome was he by her presence that Edward Gibbon, who had not seen Frances for twenty-six years, knelt down before her and begged forgiveness. His sister Catherine and brother-in-law Charles Torlesse accompanied him to Plymouth, Catherine, not only to say her farewells to her favourite brother, but also to her second son, Henry, who was bound for New Zealand with his uncle. Their voyage on the *Minerva* was delayed for almost a fortnight by gales and storms.

Meanwhile Charles Torlesse had to return to Stoke, but Catherine, faithful to the end, stayed with her brother. At six o'clock in the morning of 12 October, Edward Gibbon took his beloved dogs, Henslow, named after a friend he met at Malvern, Sewell, Bogey, Spring and Violet for an hour's walk to the breakwater before embarking on the *Minerva*. They were to accompany him to New Zealand along with a bull and a heifer. Edward Gibbon knew he would never see his sister, his father or the shores of his homeland again; indeed, he had already referred to this 'eternal severance'[37] in a letter to a friend before his departure. His sister was never to leave Stoke, and their father died the following year on 18 May at Knightsbridge; his wife, Frances, his son's co-conspirator, outliving her husband by fourteen years, to die in Blois on 12 May 1868. They were buried together with Dr Davies, the father whom during the early years of her secret marriage she had kept at such a distance now joining her for eternity. Their raised tomb is situated in the north-western corner of the graveyard of St Peter's Church, Prestbury, where ironically, Ellen Turner had married Thomas Legh.

The sixteen-week voyage was evidently not without its hardships: while Edward Gibbon, who occupied two cabins near the poop, enjoyed the comfort of a 'double-action bed,' the brainchild of a poor and struggling inventor, a Mr Brown of Leadenhall Street, and was unaffected by seasickness, his animals were not so fortunate: despite his ministrations, 'Bogey . . . on landing . . . was like a rake in a bag'.[38] The *Minerva* reached Lyttelton, on the South Island, on 2 February 1853. Deservedly perhaps, for Edward Gibbon this first sight of New Zealand seemed like the 'Promised Land', both countryside and climate far exceeding his expectations: the horses and cattle appearing like 'animals fed for the Smithfield Show; the women appearing ten years younger'.[39] In a letter to Robert Rintoul he wrote, 'All the Creole children are plump and ruddy . . . and you know how I examine the children and dogs wherever I may be'.[40] After visiting Canterbury, he is said to have remarked jovially, 'I could have fancied myself in England, except for the hard-working industry of the upper classes and luxurious independence of the common people . . . I get on famously with the unwashed.'[41]

Edward Gibbon Wakefield arrived in Wellington on 9 March 1853, in the midst of a storm which prevented him from disembarking. Here, finding the climate beneficial to his health, Edward Gibbon was to spend the remainder of his life, although it is evident in a letter written the following month to Robert Rintoul's wife, Henrietta, that initially he had qualms about the future, 'I have no friendship here. Not one person sympathizes with my fears and hopes . . . what I would but give for a few days in London.'[42] He would, however, soon immerse himself in the politics of the day, elected both to the Provincial Council and the General Assembly; his social consciousness and enthusiasm for reform were not yet spent. Soon he was in conflict with the Governor George Grey over his cheap land policy and delay in implementing the constitution in accordance with the terms of the Act of 1852. Grey's intransigence over these issues had led to the resignation of Edward Gibbon's brother Daniel as Attorney General, following the latter's unsuccessful attempts to persuade Grey to establish the constitution on a proper footing.

Perhaps it was this, allied to his disappointment in the progress of his adoptive country, a land in which he had invested so much of his hopes and energies, which after only eighteen months, conspired to induce in him both a physical and mental breakdown. Consequently, Edward Gibbon was to spend the last seven years of his life in virtual seclusion. Edward Jerningham wrote of his father's breakdown to his aunt Catherine.

> About the first week in December last he attended a meeting of his constituents . . . and spoke with great earnestness and vigour for five hours consecutively in a densely crowded room . . . he drove home in an open chaise, nine miles in the face of a cold, south-easterly gale, at two o'clock in the morning. Although he began to feel ill, he accepted an invitation a day or two afterwards to dine with members of an Odd-fellows' Lodge in this town, and sat in a hot room with an open window at his back. The next day he was attacked with rheumatic fever, and suffered acute pain. . . . For a long time he would let no one know how ill he was, and would see no one. But he then wrote to me at Canterbury, asking me to come to him.[43]

He was frequently unwell, nervous and despondent, dwelling on the past, and for long periods seeing no visitors, neither reading nor writing letters, attended by a manservant, Wilhelm Schmidt, a sailor from the *Minerva*, whom he had befriended. 'It was the oddest melancholy contrast to the sociable whirl in which he had always moved':[44] the 'fair Quakeresses' who had thrilled to the sight of their handsome, wayward, multifaceted and gifted 'brother' in the courtroom at Lancaster, would surely have been saddened to witness this transformation.

After retiring as a judge, his brother Daniel, with his wife Angela and daughter Alice, had moved into Edward Gibbon's house on the Tinakori Road, and, when Daniel died on 8 January 1858, Edward Gibbon continued to care for both his widow and daughter. Alice later recalled that her uncle was the most charming man she had ever encountered: 'I feel convinced that I have never met any man with the power that Edward Gibbon Wakefield had, and I have never come across anyone who cared for young people and the improvement in the way that he did.'[45] Towards the end of his life, Edward Gibbon apparently thought often of his mother, even suggesting that his niece, who reminded him of her, should name her parrot Susan, after her; but he never mentioned Eliza or Nina: perhaps the memory of their loss was too painful even then.

Edward Gibbon Wakefield died on 16 May 1862, aged

sixty-six years, at his son's house in Wellington Terrace, Wellington. During the night he had woken Wilhelm, who slept in his room, with the words, 'William this is death'.[46] Alice described how her uncle held her hand tightly, but could not speak, although he had struggled to do so when his son entered the room. The cause of death was recorded as 'natural decay'. The following day, the undertaker, Charles Mills, placed Edward Gibbon's corpse in its coffin. He was buried two days later in Wellington, capital city of the colony he founded, beside two of his brothers, William and Daniel:

> . . . his grave above the city roar
> Not forty rods from Parliament . . .[47]

In its obituary of October 1862, the *Daily Telegraph* wrote:

> From criminal at home he extended his enquiries to the convict in our Australian settlements . . . he did his work more through others, – his pen being merely auxiliary to his use of men. . . . There is no part of the British Empire which does not feel in the actual circumstances of the day the effect of Edward Gibbon Wakefield's labours as a practical statesman; and perhaps the same tangible results in administrative and constructive reform can scarcely be traced to the single hand of any one other man during his own lifetime.[48]

Epilogue

The marble bust of Edward Gibbon Wakefield, executed by Joseph Durham, ARA, exhibited at the Royal Academy in May 1876, was presented to the Colonial Office in London. Now in the collection of the Art Gallery of South Australia, Adelaide, it bears the inscription:

Edward Gibbon Wakefield
Born in London 20th March 1796
Died at Wellington (N.Z.) 16th May 1862
Author of 'The Art of Colonisation'
To Commemorate
His Statesman Like Qualities
For the Improvement
Of the Empire
His Friends and Admirers
Have Presented this Bust
To The Colonial Office

In the fourteenth-century Legh chapel in the church of St Oswald, Winnick, stands a fitting monument to the young woman who, having provided the impetus for Edward Gibbon Wakefield's historic achievement, left the scene so swiftly and so finally. This beautifully executed relief by the English sculptor, R.J. Wyatt, the only significant reminder of her life, depicts the nineteen-year-old Ellen, drawn away by the angel's hand, leaving behind her grief-stricken husband holding their year-old daughter, Ellen Jane. The inscription:

IN THE VAULT OF THIS CHAPEL
ARE DEPOSITED THE REMAINS OF
ELLEN
THE DEARLY BELOVED
AND MOST DEEPLY LAMENTED WIFE,
OF THOMAS LEGH ESQ.
OF LYME HALL, CHESHIRE,
AND DAUGHTER OF
WILLIAM TURNER ESQ.
OF SHRIGLEY PARK
IN THE SAME COUNTY;
BORN 12th FEBRUARY 1811,
DIED 17th JANUARY 1831.
LEAVING AN ONLY SURVIVING CHILD
ELLEN JANE LEGH,
BORN 20th FEBRUARY 1830.

ement of Edward Wakefield concerning the Abduction of
Turner, May 1826, qMS–2100, ATL, p. 12.
Trial of Edward Gibbon Wakefield, p. 206.
, p. 207.
ement of Edward Gibbon Wakefield concerning the Abduction of
Turner, May 1826, qMS–2100, ATL, p. 12.
Curwen, Kirbie Kendal (T. Wilson, 1900), p. 275.
Trial of Edward Gibbon Wakefield, p. 208.
tement of Edward Gibbon Wakefield concerning the Abduction of
ss Turner, May 1826, qMS–2100, ATL, p. 13.
d., p.14.
omfield, Edward Gibbon Wakefield, p. 244.
nutes of Evidence taken upon the Second Reading of the Bill
827), 1418.K.38(7)BL, p. 18.
d., p. 19.
e Trial of Edward Gibbon Wakefield, p. 29.
id.
inutes of Evidence taken upon the Second Reading of the Bill
827), 1418.K.38(7), BL, p. 19.
e Trial of Edward Gibbon Wakefield, p. 33.
id., pp. 210–11.
id., p. 212.
ames Fildes, In the Lakes, 31 August–14 September 1829, MISC
rchives, MCL.
id.
e Trial of Edward Gibbon Wakefield, p. 104.
id., p. 216.
Minutes of Evidence taken upon the Second Reading of the Bill
1827), 1418.K.38(7), BL, p. 22.
tatement of Edward Gibbon Wakefield concerning the Abduction of
Miss Turner, May 1826, qMS–2100, ATL, p. 15.
bid., p. 14.
bid., p. 16.
bid.

r title source: Une Nouvelle Manière d'Attrapper une Femme, Tracts
-36, British Library.
Westmorland Advertiser & Kendal Chronicle, 1 April 1826.
Imperial Magazine, Volume 8, 1826.
Ibid.
Mark Thomas, A History of Brougham Hall and High Head Castle
(Phillimore & Co. Ltd, 1992), p. 47.
Statement of Edward Gibbon Wakefield concerning the Abduction of
Miss Turner, May 1826, qMS–2100, ATL, p. 17.

Notes

ABBREVIATIONS

ATL   Alexander Turnbull Library, New Zealand
BL   British Library
BNL   British Newspaper Library
BPL   Blackburn Public Library
CL   Chetham's Library
CRO   Chester Record Office
ELD   Ewart Library, Dumfries
LANR   Lancashire Record Office
LRO   Liverpool Record Office
MCL   Manchester Central Library
NLW   National Library of Wales
PMC   The Priscilla Mitchell Collection
PRO   Public Record Office

PROLOGUE

1. Morning Chronicle, 27 March 1827, ELD.
2. Sunday Times, 7 April 1827.
3. Dumfries Weekly Journal, 27 March 1827, ELD.

ONE

Chapter title source: John Milton, Paradise Lost, Book III.
1. Minutes of Evidence taken upon the Second Reading of the Bill
    (1827), 1418.K.38(7), BL, p. 9.
2. The Trial of Edward Gibbon Wakefield (John Murray, 1827), p. 23.
3. Ibid., p. 54.
4. Ibid., p. 55.
5. Minutes of Evidence taken upon the Second Reading of the Bill
    (1827), 1418.K.38(7), BL, p. 6.
6. Ibid., p. 7.
7. The Trial of Edward Gibbon Wakefield, p. 27.
8. Minutes of Evidence taken upon the Second Reading of the Bill
    (1827), BL, p. 11.
9. The Trial of Edward Gibbon Wakefield, p. 28.

10. Ibid.
11. Minutes of Evidence taken upon the Second Reading of the Bill (1827), 1418.K.38(7), BL, p. 14.
12. Ibid., p.15.
13. Statement of Edward Gibbon Wakefield concerning the Abduction of Miss Turner, May 1826, qMS–2100, ATL, p. 6
14. *The Trial of Edward Gibbon Wakefield*, p. 92.
15. Statement of Edward Gibbon Wakefield concerning the Abduction of Miss Turner, May 1826, qMS–2100, ATL, p. 7.
16. Ibid.

TWO

Chapter title source: Proverbs 20:11.
1. Irma O'Connor, *Edward Gibbon Wakefield* (Selwyn & Blount, 1928), p. 20.
2. Letter from Catherine Bell to Edward Wakefield, 1801, PMC.
3. Paul Bloomfield, *Edward Gibbon Wakefield* (Longman, 1968), p. 16.
4. O'Connor, *Edward Gibbon Wakefield*, p. 22.
5. Dr R. Garnett, *Edward Gibbon Wakefield* (T. Fisher Unwin, 1898), p. 9.
6. Ibid., p. 7.
7. O'Connor, *Edward Gibbon Wakefield*, p. 23.
8. Priscilla Wakefield Diaries, 1799, PMC.
9. O'Connor, *Edward Gibbon Wakefield*, p. 22.
10. Priscilla Wakefield Diaries, 1796, PMC.
11. Ibid., 1798.
12. Ibid.
13. Ibid., 1799.
14. Ibid.
15. Letter from Edward Gibbon Wakefield, undated, PMC.
16. Priscilla Wakefield Diaries, 1799, PMC.
17. Ibid., 1802.
18. Ibid., 1803.
19. Ibid., 1803.
20. Ibid., 1806.
21. Ibid.
22. Ibid., 1807.
23. Ibid.
24. O'Connor, *Edward Gibbon Wakefield*, p. 26.
25. Priscilla Wakefield, *Juvenile Anecdotes – Founded on Facts* (Darton, Harvey & Darton,1825).
26. Priscilla Wakefield to Edward Wakefield, 6 October 1809, PMC.
27. Priscilla Wakefield to Edward Wakefield, 11 November 1809.
28. Priscilla Wakefield Diaries, 1810, PMC.
29. Ibid.

30. Ibid.
31. Ibid., 1812.
32. Edward Wakefield to Francis Place, 181[...] *Edward Gibbon Wakefield*, p. 28.
33. Edward Wakefield to Priscilla Wakefield, 17 [...]
34. Priscilla Wakefield Diaries, 1815, PMC.
35. Francis Place to James Mill, 20 July 1815; q[...] *Gibbon Wakefield*, p. 16.
36. Ibid., p. 17.
37. Priscilla Wakefield to Felix Wakefield, 17 Marc[...]
38. Priscilla Wakefield Diaries, 1815, PMC.
39. Francis Place to James Mill, quoted in G[...] *Wakefield*, pp. 18–19.
40. Priscilla Wakefield Diaries, 1816, PMC.
41. Edward Gibbon Wakefield to Frances Davi[...] Wakefield Family Papers, MS–0927, ATL.
42. Edward Gibbon Wakefield's First Elopement, [...] 4CS/13, CL.
43. Francis Place to James Mill, 9 August 1816[...] *Edward Gibbon Wakefield*, p. 19.

THREE

Chapter title source: *Love Laughs at Locksmiths*, Geor[...] Song.
1. Statement of Edward Gibbon Wakefield concern[...] Miss Turner, May 1826, qMS–2100, ATL, p. 7.
2. Ibid., p. 8.
3. *The Trial of Edward Gibbon Wakefield*, p. 194.
4. Statement of Edward Gibbon Wakefield concern[...] Miss Turner, May 1826, qMS–2100, ATL, pp. 9–[...]
5. O'Connor, *Edward Gibbon Wakefield*, p. 41.
6. Statement of Edward Gibbon Wakefield concern[...] Miss Turner, May 1826, qMS–2100, ATL, p. 11.
7. *The Trial of Edward Gibbon Wakefield*, p. 196.
8. Statement of Edward Gibbon Wakefield concern[...] Miss Turner, May 1826, qMS–2100, ATL, p. 111.
9. Minutes of Evidence taken upon the Second [...] (1827), 1418.K.38(7), BL, p. 16.
10. Statement of Edward Wakefield concerning [...] Miss Turner, May 1826, qMS–2100, ATL, p. 11.
11. Ibid.
12. Minutes of Evidence taken upon the Second [...] (1827), 1418.K.38(7), BL, p. 16.
13. *The Trial of Edward Gibbon Wakefield*, p. 203.
14. Ibid., pp. 203–5.

15. Sta[...]
    Mi[...]
16. The[...]
17. Ibi[...]
18. St[...]
    M[...]
19. J.P[...]
20. Th[...]
21. St[...]
    M[...]
22. It[...]
23. B[...]
24. M[...]
    ([...]
25. I[...]
26. T[...]
27. I[...]
28. M[...]

29. [...]
30. [...]
31. [...]
32. [...]

33. [...]
34. [...]
35. [...]
36. [...]

37. [...]

38. [...]
39. [...]
40. [...]

FOUR

Chapt[...]
1809[...]
1. [...]
2. [...]
3. [...]
4. [...]

5. [...]

6. *Gretna Hall*, Handbook, De 43 (728.5), ELD, p. 11.
7. Ibid., p. 11.
8. *Dumfries Weekly Journal*, 26 August 1805, ELD.

FIVE

Chapter title source: Alfred Lord Tennyson, 'The Northern Farmer'.
1. *Report on the Proceedings of the Trial of Edward Gibbon Wakefield, Edward Gibbon Wakefield's First Elopement* (J. Pratt, 1827),Trials 4C4/13, pp. 67–72, CL.
2. Ibid.
3. Ibid.
4. Ibid.
5. Eliza Pattle to Mrs Pattle, 14 June 1816, quoted in Bloomfield, *Edward Gibbon Wakefield*, p. 36.
6. *Report on the Proceedings of the Trial of Edward Gibbon Wakefield, Edward Gibbon Wakefield's First Elopement*, pp. 67–72.
7. Ibid.
8. Ibid.
9. Ibid.
10. Priscilla Wakefield Diaries, 1816, PMC.
11. O'Connor, *Edward Gibbon Wakefield*, p. 35.
12. *The Trial of Edward Gibbon Wakefield*, p. 229.
13. Ibid., p. 225.
14. Ibid., p. 229.
15. Statement of Edward Gibbon Wakefield concerning the Abduction of Miss Turner, 1826, qMS–2100, ATL, p. 3.
16. *The Trial of Edward Gibbon Wakefield*, p. 35.
17. Ibid., p.114.
18. Statement of Edward Gibbon Wakefield concerning the Abduction of Miss Turner, 1826, qMS–2100, ATL, p. 17.
19. *Leeds Mercury*, 1 April 1826.
20. Statement of Edward Gibbon Wakefield concerning the Abduction of Miss Turner, 1826, qMS–2100, ATL, p. 3.
21. O'Connor, *Edward Gibbon Wakefield*, p. 35.

SIX

Chapter title source: William Shakespeare, *Twelfth Night*, Act V, sc. i.
1. William Hill to Edward Wakefield, Genoa 1816, PMC.
2. Ibid.
3. Edward Gibbon Wakefield to Edward Wakefield, Genoa, 28 October 1816, PMC.
4. Francis Wilson to Francis Place, 16 December 1816, PMC.
5. Ibid.

6. Ibid.
7. Edward Gibbon Wakefield to Edward Wakefield, 23 November 1816, *Letters and Journals of Edward Gibbon Wakefield*, MS 0927–05, ATL.
8. Ibid.
9. Edward Gibbon Wakefield to Edward Wakefield, 11 January 1817, PMC.
10. Ibid.
11. Ibid., 16 November 1816.
12. Edward Gibbon Wakefield to Priscilla Wakefield, 20 February 1817, Wakefield Family Papers, MS–0927, ATL.
13. Ibid.
14. Flora Fraser, *The Unruly Queen* (Macmillan, 1996), p. 273.
15. Edward Gibbon Wakefield to Priscilla Wakefield, 20 February 1817, Wakefield Family Papers, MS–0927, ATL.
16. Ibid.
17. Edward Gibbon Wakefield, 3 April 1817, Wakefield Family Papers, MS–0927, ATL.
18. Ibid., 8 September 1817.
19. Ibid., 12 September 1817.
20. Edward Gibbon Wakefield to Edward Wakefield, 26 October 1817, PMC.
21. Ibid.
22. Correspondence of Edward Gibbon Wakefield, 4 November 1817, Wakefield Family Papers, MS–0222, ATL.
23. Priscilla Wakefield to Edward Gibbon Wakefield, 10 December 1817, PMC.
24. O'Connor, *Edward Gibbon Wakefield*, p. 34.
25. Correspondence of Edward Gibbon Wakefield, 17 December 1817, Wakefield Family Papers, MS–0222, ATL.
26. Ibid., 29 January 1818.
27. Ibid.
28. Edward Gibbon Wakefield to Edward Wakefield, 11 January 1817, PMC.
29. Ibid.
30. Ibid.
31. Ibid., 10 December 1817.
32. Ibid., 2 February 1818.
33. Ibid., 29 April 1818.
34. Eliza Wakefield's Diary, 1820, MSX 4857, ATL.
35. Bloomfield, *Edward Gibbon Wakefield*, pp. 41–2.
36. Ibid., p. 43.
37. Edward Gibbon Wakefield to Edward Wakefield, Dijon, 19 October 1819, PMC.
38. Eliza Wakefield's Diary, 1820, MSX 4857, ATL.
39. Ibid.
40. Ibid.
41. O'Connor, *Edward Gibbon Wakefield*, p. 35.

42. Edward Gibbon Wakefield to Catherine Torlesse, 1820, PMC.
43. Ibid., 23 January 1822, Wakefield Family Papers, MS–0927, ATL.
44. Ibid., undated.
45. Ibid., 26 August 1821.

SEVEN

Chapter title source: Sir John Suckling, 'A Poem with the Answer'.
1. *The Trial of Edward Gibbon Wakefield*, p. 36.
2. *Morning Chronicle*, 11 March 1826.
3. Statement of Edward Gibbon Wakefield concerning the Abduction of Miss Turner, 1826, qMS–2100, ATL, p. 1.
4. *The Trial of Edward Gibbon Wakefield*, p. 139.
5. *Weekly Dispatch*, March 1826.
6. Minutes of Evidence taken upon the Second Reading of the Bill (1827), 1418.K.38(7), BL, p. 31.
7. *Morning Chronicle*, 23 March 1826.
8. Ibid.
9. Canning to Lord Granville, 14 March 1826, FO 27 346, PRO.
10. *The Trial of Edward Gibbon Wakefield*, p. 40.
11. William Hopes to William Roscoe, 15 March 1826, LRO.
12. *The Trial of Edward Gibbon Wakefield*, p. 236.
13. Ibid., p. 18.
14. Minutes of Evidence taken upon the Second Reading of the Bill (1827), 1418.K.38(7), BL, pp. 37–8.
15. Statement of Edward Gibbon Wakefield concerning the Abduction of Miss Turner, qMS–2100, ATL, p. 19.
16. Minutes of Evidence taken upon the Second Reading of the Bill (1827), 1418.R.38(7), BL, p. 32.
17. Ibid.
18. Ibid., p. 37.
19. Ibid., p. 33.
20. Statement of Edward Gibbon Wakefield concerning the Abduction of Miss Turner, qMS–2100, ATL, p. 19.
21. Minutes of Evidence taken upon the Second Reading of the Bill (1827), 1418.K.38(7), BL, p. 33.
22. Ibid., p. 34.
23. Ibid.
24. Ibid., p. 35.
25. Ibid.
26. *Morning Chronicle*, 23 March 1826.
27. Minutes of Evidence taken upon the Second Reading of the Bill (1827), 1418.K.38(7), BL, p. 35.
28. Statement of Edward Gibbon Wakefield concerning the Abduction of Miss Turner, qMS–2100, ATL, p. 19.
29. Ibid., p. 20.

30. Minutes of Evidence taken upon the Second Reading of the Bill (1827), 1418.K.38 (7), BL, p. 38.
31. Ibid., p. 39.
32. Ibid., p. 40.

EIGHT

Chapter title source: *Une Nouvelle Manière d'Attrapper une Femme*, Tracts 1809–36, British Library.
1. Garnett, *Edward Gibbon Wakefield*, p. 30.
2. Minutes of Evidence taken upon the Second Reading of the Bill (1827), 1418.K.38(7), BL, p. 41.
3. *Macclesfield Courier*, 26 May 1827.
4. Ibid.
5. *John Bull*, 27 March 1826.
6. *Manchester Courier*, 18 March 1826.
7. Edward Wakefield to Frances Davies, 26 November 1823, PMC.
8. Mrs Bathurst to Mrs Turner, 29 March 1826, qMS–2100, ATL.
9. Betty Askwith, *Piety and Wit, A Biography of Harriet, Countess of Granville, 1785–1862* (William Collins, 1982).
10. Mrs Bathurst to William Wakefield,19 March 1826, Wakefield Family Papers, qMS-2100, ATL.
11. Ibid.
12. Ibid.
13. Ibid.
14. Ibid.
15. *The Times*, 21 March 1826.
16. Lord Granville to Baron de Damas, 19 March 1826, FO 27 349, PRO.
17. Ibid., 20 March 1826.
18. *The Times*, 21 March 1826.
19. Ibid.
20. Lord Granville to William Wakefield, 23 March 1826, FO 27 349, PRO.
21. Canning to Lord Granville, 23 March 1826, FO 27 346, PRO.
22. *John Bull*, 27 March 1826.
23. *Sun*, 22 March 1826.
24. *The Times*, 23 March 1826.
25. Ibid., 24 March 1826.
26. Ibid., 28 March 1826.
27. *Westmorland Gazette & Kendal Chronicle*, 25 March 1826.
28. The *Dundee Advertiser*, quoted in the *Manchester Guardian*, 28 March 1826.
29. *The Times*, 24 March 1826.
30. *Westmorland Gazette & Kendal Chronicle*, 15 April 1826.
31. Ibid.
32. Ibid.

33. *John Bull*, 27 March 1826, p. 101, MCL.
34. Mrs Bathurst to Mrs Turner, 29 March 1826, ATL.
35. Ibid.
36. Lord Granville to Canning, 31 March 1826, FO 27 349, PRO.
37. Garnett, *Edward Gibbon Wakefield*, p. 27.

NINE

Chapter title source: George Crabbe, 'The Newspaper', 1785.
1. *Manchester Mercury*, 4 April 1826.
2. *Macclesfield Courier*, 8 April 1826.
3. *Manchester Mercury*, 4 April 1826.
4. *Weekly Dispatch*, March 1826.
5. *The Times*, 1 April 1826.
6. *Westmorland Gazette & Kendal Chronicle*, 1 April 1826.
7. *Manchester Courier*, 1 April 1826.
8. *Morning Chronicle*, quoted in the *Westmorland Gazette & Kendal Chronicle*, 15 April 1826.
9. *Stockport Advertiser*, 7 April 1826.
10. *Morning Chronicle*, 4 April 1826.
11. Ibid.
12. *Westmorland Gazette & Kendal Chronicle*, 7 April 1826.
13. *Morning Chronicle*, 22 March 1826.
14. *Westmorland Gazette & Kendal Chronicle*, 7 April 1826.
15. Minutes of Evidence taken upon the Second Reading of the Bill (1827), 1418.K.38(7), BL, p. 30.
16. William Turner's Will, 19 September 1840, WS 1845, CRO.
17. *Macclesfield Courier*, 8 April 1826.
18. Nancy Mitford, *The Ladies of Alderley* (Hamish Hamilton, 1938).
19. Statement of Edward Gibbon Wakefield concerning the Abduction of Miss Turner, qMS–2100, ATL, p. 2.
20. Ibid., p. 3.
21. Ibid., p. 4.
22. *Manchester Guardian*, 24 February 1827.
23. *Macclesfield Courier*, 8 April 1826.
24. *Stockport Advertiser*, 7 April 1826.
25. *Macclesfield Courier*, 8 April 1826.
26. Statement of Edward Gibbon Wakefield concerning the Abduction of Miss Turner, qMS–2100, ATL, p. 4.
27. *Stockport Advertiser*, 21 April 1826.
28. *John Bull*, 17 April 1826.

TEN

Chapter title source: Bishop Joseph Butler, *Fifteen Sermons*, No. 7.
1. *Macclesfield Courier*, 15 April 1827.

2. Ibid., 19 May 1827.
3. Edward Wakefield to Frances Wakefield, 19 August 1823, PMC.
4. Frances Wakefield to Edward Wakefield, Archives, Queen Mary College, University of London, WFD/EGW/1.
5. Edward Wakefield to Frances Wakefield, 16 September 1823, PMC.
6. Ibid., 7 and 8 October 1823.
7. Ibid., 27 November 1823.
8. Garnett, *Edward Gibbon Wakefield*, p. 5.
9. *Macclesfield Courier*, 29 April 1826.
10. Ibid.
11. Statment of Edward Gibbon Wakefield concerning the Abduction of Miss Turner, qMS–2100, ATL, p. 1.
12. *Stockport Advertiser*, 26 May 1826.
13. *The Times*, 26 May 1826.
14. *Manchester Gazette*, 27 May 1826.
15. *The Times*, 26 May 1826.
16. *Manchester Gazette*, 27 May 1826.
17. *The Times*, 26 May 1826.
18. *Manchester Courier*, 27 May 1826.
19. *Stockport Advertiser*, 2 June 1826.
20. *The Times*, 27 May 1826.
21. *John Bull*, quoted in the *Macclesfield Courier*, 3 June 1826.

ELEVEN

Chapter title source: Richard Brinsley Sheridan, *The Rivals*.

1. Reverend G.N. Wright, *Lancaster, Its History, Legends and Manufacturers*, LANR.
2. Samuel Bamford, *Passages in the Life of a Radical* (Frank Cass, 1967), Vol. II.
3. J. Hall, *Lancaster Castle* (Whittaker & Sons, 1843).
4. Bamford, *Passages in the Life of a Radical*, Vol. II.
5. *Lancashire Gazette*, 21 September 1818.
6. Edward Gibbon Wakefield to Frances Wakefield, 26 May 1826, PMC.
7. James Weatherley, *Recollections of Manchester, and Manchester Characters . . . from 1800–1860*, manuscripts, MUN.A.6.30, CL.
8. *Macclesfield Courier*, 3 June 1826.
9. Edward Gibbon Wakefield to Frances Wakefield, 30 May 1830, PMC.
10. Weatherley, *Recollections of Manchester*.
11. Edward Gibbon Wakefield to Frances Wakefield, 5 June 1826, PMC.
12. *John Bull*, 14 June 1826.
13. *John Bull*, 20 August 1826.
14. *Chester Chronicle*, 14 July 1826.
15. Mark Thomas, *A History of Brougham Hall and High Head Castle* (Phillimore, 1992).
16. William Turner, *Riot* (Lancashire County Books, 1992).

17. *Macclesfield Courier*, 12 August 1826.
18. L.C. Waddington, *Practical and Pictorial Guide, 1913* (University of Lancaster).
19. *Macclesfield Courier*, 19 August 1826.
20. *Manchester Gazette*, 19 August 1826.
21. *John Bull*, 27 March 1826.
22. *Literary Magnet*, 3 OS2 10.
23. *Manchester Gazette*, 19 August 1826.
24. Bamford, *Passages in the Life of a Radical*, Vol. II.
25. *The Times*, 16 August 1826.
26. *Macclesfield Courier*, 26 August 1826.
27. Ibid.
28. Ibid., 19 August 1826.
29. Ibid.
30. Ibid.
31. *Wheeler's Manchester Chronicle*, 26 August 1826.
32. *The Times*, 23 August 1826.
33. *Wheeler's Manchester Chronicle*, 26 August 1826.
34. *The Times*, 23 August 1826.

TWELVE

Chapter title source: Terence, *Phormio*, 454.
1. *The Times*, 31 August 1826.
2. Ibid., 23 March 1827.
3. *Macclesfield Courier*, 17 February 1827.
4. Ibid., 12 August 1826.
5. L.C. Waddington, *Practical and Pictorial Guide 1913* (University of Lancaster).
6. *Westmorland Gazette & Kendal Chronicle*, 17 March 1827.
7. *Sun*, 24 March 1827.
8. *Westmorland Gazette & Kendal Chronicle*, 17 March 1827.
9. Ibid., 24 March 1827.
10. *The Times*, 23 March 1827.
11. *Westmorland Gazette & Kendal Chronicle*, 24 March 1827.
12. *Sun*, 24 March 1827.
13. *Westmorland Gazette & Kendal Chronicle*, 24 March 1826.
14. *Morning Chronicle*, 24 March 1827.

THIRTEEN

Chapter title source: *Kaleidoscope and Literary and Scientific Mirror*, 3 April 1827.
1. *Sun*, 24 March 1827.
2. Bloomfield, *Edward Gibbon Wakefield*, p. 60.
3. Ibid., p. 61.

4. *The Trial of Edward Gibbon Wakefield*, p. 13.
5. Ibid.
6. J.B. Priestley, *The Prince of Pleasure and His Regency* (Heinemann, 1969).
7. W. Beaumont, *History of the House of Lyme* (P. Pearse, 1876), p. 201.
8. *Sunday Times*, 7 April 1827.
9. *The Times*, 26 March 1827.
10. *Manchester Guardian*, 31 March 1827.
11. Ibid.
12. *The Trial of Edward Gibbon Wakefield*, p. 169.
13. Ibid., p. 175.
14. Ibid., p. 178.
15. Ibid.
16. *Blackwood's Magazine*, May 1827, p. 524.
17. *Dumfries Weekly Journal*, 27 March 1827, ELD.
18. *The Times*, 26 March 1827.
19. Priestley, *The Prince of Pleasure*.
20. *Blackwood's Magazine*, May 1827, p. 524.
21. Priestley, *The Prince of Pleasure*.
22. *Morning Chronicle*, 26 March 1827.
23. *Manchester Guardian*, 31 March 1827.
24. *The Trial of Edward Gibbon Wakefield*, p. 266.
25. *John Bull*, 22 May 1826.
26. *Weekly Dispatch*, 25 March 1827.
27. *Westmorland Gazette & Kendal Chronicle*, 31 March 1827.
28. *Kaleidoscope*, 3 April 1827.
29. *Manchester Guardian*, 7 April 1827.
30. *The Atlas*, quoted in the *Macclesfield Courier*, 7 April 1827.
31. *Stockport Advertiser*, 25 May 1827.
32. O'Connor, *Edward Gibbon Wakefield*, p. 47.
33. *The Trial of Edward Gibbon Wakefield*, p. 329.
34. *Sunday Times*, quoted in the *Macclesfield Courier*, 7 April 1827.
35. *The Trial of Edward Gibbon Wakefield*, pp. 310–11.
36. Ibid., p. 314.
37. Ibid., p. 311.
38. Deposition of Edward Gibbon Wakefield, Kings Bench, 14 May 1827, KB1/50/1, PRO.
39. *The Trial of Edward Gibbon Wakefield*, p. 336.
40. *Preston Chronicle*, 19 May 1827.
41. O'Connor, *Edward Gibbon Wakefield*, p. 45.

FOURTEEN

Chapter title source: Samuel Taylor Coleridge, 'The Rime of the Ancient Mariner'.

1. O'Connor, Edward Gibbon Wakefield, p. 51.

2. O'Connor ibid.; quoting Collier in EGW's *A View of the Art of Colonisation*, p. 49.
3. William Hepworth, *The London Prisons*, p. 194.
4. Samuel Leigh, *New Picture of London* (Leigh, 1827).
5. *Newgate Magazine*, Volume I, 1824–5.
6. *Gentleman's Magazine*, September 1827.
7. Edward Gibbon Wakefield to Catherine Torlesse, 23 January 1822, qMS–2098, ATL.
8. Ibid., December 1824.
9. *The Times*, 19 May 1827.
10. *Manchester Guardian*, 2 June 1827.
11. *Gentleman's Magazine*, June 1827.
12. *The Times*, 31 May 1827.
13. *Macclesfield Courier*, 26 May 1827.
14. *The Times*, 31 May 1827.
15. *John Bull*, 25 June 1827.
16. *The Times*, 26 June 1827.
17. *Macclesfield Courier*, 26 May 1827.

FIFTEEN

Chapter title source: William Shakespeare, *Julius Caesar*, Act I, sc. i.

1. *Manchester Faces and Places*, vol. II, No. 10, 10 July 1891.
2. *Manchester Scrapbook*, MCL.
3. *Manchester Faces and Places*, 10 July 1891.
4. Thomas Legh to Louisa Lloyd, 4 July 1815, NRA 30036 Aston Hall, Vol. 5 4204, NLW.
5. Ibid., 21 February 1815, 4203.
6. Ibid., 4 July 1815, 4204.
7. John Martin Robinson, *A Guide to the Country Houses of the North West* (Constable, 1991).
8. J. Aikin, *A Description of the County from 30–40 Miles round Manchester* (D. Charles, 1795).
9. *Macclesfield Courier*, 19 January 1828.
10. *Manchester Gazette*, 19 January 1828.
11. *Blackburn Mail*, 16 January 1828.
12. *Stockport Advertiser*, 28 February 1828.
13. *Manchester Scrapbook*.
14. Edward Gibbon Wakefield to Priscilla Wakefield, 27 February 1828, MS–0927, ATL.
15. Ibid.
16. Edward Gibbon Wakefield to Catherine Torlesse, undated, MS–0927, ATL.
17. Edward Gibbon Wakefield to Priscilla Wakefield, 27 February 1828, PMC.
18. Religious Tracts 41, 36 C7 1–38, BNL.

19. Bloomfield, *Edward Gibbon Wakefield*, p. 75.
20. Wakefield Family Papers, AW22/4, ATL.
21. O'Connor, *Edward Gibbon Wakefield*, p. 52.
22. A.J. Harrop, *The Amazing Career of Edward Gibbon Wakefield* (Allen & Unwin, 1928), p. 47.
23. Edward Gibbon Wakefield, *Punishment of Death in the Metropolis*, 2/3/PR1. Reproduced by kind permission of London Metropolitan Archives.
24. *The Condemned Sermon*, 1830, Popular Politics, 1837.
25. O'Connor, *Edward Gibbon Wakefield*, p. 82.
26. Robert Rintoul, editorial in the *Spectator*, 1830.
27. *Quarterly Review*, March/July 1832.
28. Garnett, *Edward Gibbon Wakefield*, pp. 57 and 58.
29. Edward Gibbon Wakefield, *Punishment of Death in the Metropolis*, 2/3/PR1, Reproduced by kind permission of London Metropolitan Archives.
30. Edward Gibbon Wakefield, *A Letter from Sydney*, edited by Robert Gouger (Joseph Cross, 1829).

SIXTEEN

Chapter title source: George Gordon, Lord Byron, *Don Juan*, Canto I, St. 7.

1. *John Bull*, 17 May 1830.
2. Priscilla Wakefield to William Wakefield, 6 May 1815, Wakefield Family Papers, MS–0927, ATL.
3. *Gentleman's Magazine*, October 1862.
4. Garnett, *Edward Gibbon Wakefield*, p. 83.
5. Ibid., Introduction.
6. Harrop, *Amazing Career of Edward Gibbon Wakefield*, p. 58.
7. Frances Torlesse, AW22/6, ATL.
8. Garnett, *Edward Gibbon Wakefield*, p. 81.
9. Edward Gibbon Wakefield, *Swing Unmasked; The Causes of Rural Incendiarism*, 1831.
10. *Manchester Courier*, 21 September 1830.
11. *Manchester Notes & Queries*, 27 November 1866.
12. Charles White, *The Arrest of Puerperal Fever* (Paul B. Hoeber Inc., 1923).
13. *Bell's Life in London*, 23 January 1831.

SEVENTEEN

Chapter title source: William Hazlitt, *The Spirit of the Age*.

1. William Durham, George C. Millar, *The Evolution of a Cotton Town* (THCL, 1951).
2. Handbill, 1841, P05, BPL.
3. *Squib*, 28 June 1841, P05, BPL.

NOTES

4. *Notice*, June 1841, P05, BPL.
5. Millar, *Evolution of a Cotton Town*.
6. Legh Muniments, p H No. 9, 25 February 1851. Reproduced courtesy of the Director & Librarian of John Rylands University Library.
7. Garnett, *Edward Gibbon Wakefield*, p. 47.
8. Keith Feiling, *A History of England* (Book Club Associates, 1972), p. 824.
9. Bloomfield, *Edward Gibbon Wakefield*, p. 124.
10. Garnett, *Edward Gibbon Wakefield*, p. 235.
11. Edward Gibbon Wakefield, *England and America*, 1833, 2V 8VO, MCL.
12. Ibid.
13. Nina Wakefield to Catherine Torlesse, undated, PMC.
14. Ibid., August 1835.
15. Nina Wakefield to Rosabel Attwood, 4 September 1834, PMC.
16. Edward Gibbon Wakefield to Mrs Attwood, 18 October 1834, PMC.
17. Edward Gibbon Wakefield to Catherine Torlesse, 5 November 1834, Wakefield Family Papers, MS–0927, ATL.
18. Edward Gibbon Wakefield to Catherine Torlesse, 17 January 1835, PMC.
19. Edward Gibbon Wakefield to Catherine Torlesse, 14 April 1835, Wakefield Family Papers, MS–2098, ATL.
20. Ibid.
21. O'Connor, *Edward Gibbon Wakefield*, p. 112.
22. Edward Gibbon Wakefield, *Address to the Electors of Birmingham*, 8 December 1836, PMC.
23. Garnett, *Edward Gibbon Wakefield*, p. 126.
24. *The Times*, 10 February 1838.
25. Garnett, *Edward Gibbon Wakefield*, p. 154.
26. Bloomfield, *Edward Gibbon Wakefield*, p. 189.
27. Garnett, *Edward Gibbon Wakefield*, p. 174.
28. Edward Jerningham Wakefield to Catherine Torlesse, 17 August 1846, MS–0203, ATL.
29. Ibid., 19 August 1846.
30. Ibid., 22 August 1846.
31. Garnett, *Edward Gibbon Wakefield*, p. 283.
32. Edward Wakefield to William Wakefield, 31 January 1848, Wakefield Family Papers, MS–0927, ATL.
33. Garnett, *Edward Gibbon Wakefield*, p. 279.
34. O'Connor, *Edward Gibbon Wakefield*, p. 219.
35. Garnett, *Edward Gibbon Wakefield*, p. 321.
36. Bloomfield, *Edward Gibbon Wakefield*, p. 316.
37. Edward Gibbon Wakefield to Lord Lyttelton, 8 October 1852, MS–2206, ATL.
38. Garnett, *Edward Gibbon Wakefield*, p. 344.
39. O'Connor, *Edward Gibbon Wakefield*, p. 233.

40. Edward Gibbon Wakefield to Robert Rintoul, 17 April 1853, MS–2207, ATL.
41. Garnett, *Edward Gibbon Wakefield*, p. 345.
42. Edward Gibbon Wakefield to Henrietta Rintoul, 19 April 1853, MS–2207, ATL.
43. Edward Jerningham to Catherine Torlesse, 8 May 1855, MS–0203, ATL.
44. Bloomfield, *Edward Gibbon Wakefield*, p. 335.
45. Garnett, *Edward Gibbon Wakefield*, p. 364.
46. Ibid., p. 368.
47. Hubert Church, *Volume of Poems 1912*, 'Embodied in a Fugue', Canto IX, ATL.
48. *Daily Telegraph*, October 1862.

Index